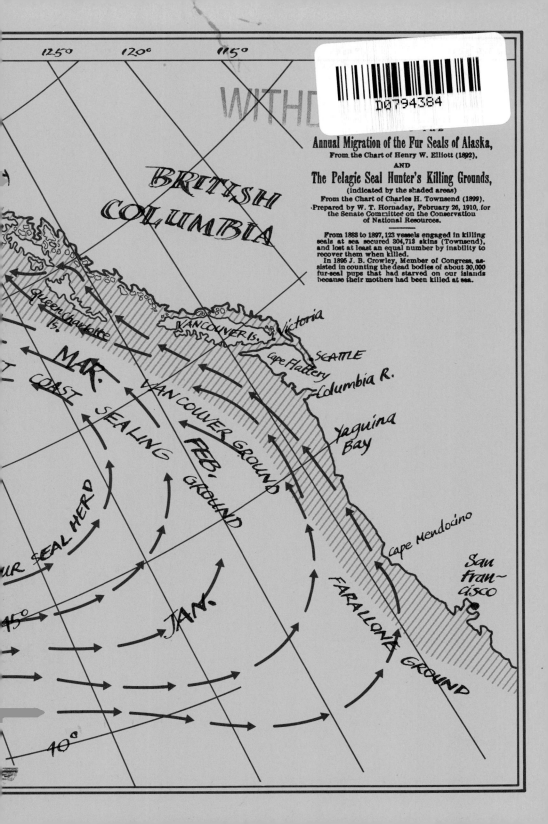

Annual Migration of the Fur Seals of Alaska,
From the Chart of Henry W. Elliott (1892),

AND

The Pelagic Seal Hunter's Killing Grounds,
(indicated by the shaded areas)
From the Chart of Charles H. Townsend (1899).
Prepared by W. T. Hornaday, February 26, 1910, for
the Senate Committee on the Conservation
of National Resources.

From 1883 to 1897, 123 vessels engaged in killing
seals at sea secured 304,713 skins (Townsend),
and lost at least an equal number by inability to
recover them when killed.
In 1895 J. B. Crowley, Member of Congress, assisted in counting the dead bodies of about 30,000
fur-seal pups that had starved on our islands
because their mothers had been killed at sea.

125° 120° 115°

BRITISH COLUMBIA

Queen Charlotte Is.

VANCOUVER IS.

Victoria

Cape Flattery

SEATTLE

Columbia R.

MAR.

COAST SEALING

VANCOUVER GROUND

FEB. GROUND

Yaquina Bay

FUR SEAL HERD

JAN.

Cape Mendocino

San Francisco

FARALLONE GROUND

45°

40°

THE
VAGABOND
FLEET

Markland entering Clayoquot Sound, 1906

THE
VAGABOND
FLEET

*A Chronicle
of the North Pacific
Sealing Schooner
Trade*

Peter Murray
COLOUR PLATES BY CMDR. MAURICE CHADWICK

SONO NIS PRESS
VICTORIA, B.C., CANADA

Canadian Cataloguing in Publication Data

Murray, Peter, 1928-
  The vagabond fleet

  Bibliography: p.
  Includes index.
  ISBN 1-55039-000-7

  1. Sealing — North Pacific Ocean — History.
2. Bering Sea controversy — History. 3.
Schooners — North Pacific Ocean — History.
I. Title.

SH363.N67M87 1988   639'.29'091643   C88-091388-6

Publication financially assisted by the
Canada Council Block Grant Program
and the Government of British Columbia
through the British Columbia Heritage
Trust and British Columbia Lotteries.

Designed and printed by
MORRISS PRINTING COMPANY LTD.
Victoria, B.C., Canada

To my wife, Pat

Contents

Preface

This is not an anti-sealing book. The events took place a century ago, when conservation was not a word applied to wildlife. The killing of animals for their fur was unquestioned. It would be wrong to impose today's values on that era.

While not critical of sealing as such, the book *does* condemn the cruel and wasteful practices of the Canadian hunters who harpooned or shot the fur seals in the ocean as they headed toward their breeding grounds on the Pribilof Islands. From the time it bought Alaska from Russia in 1867 until the mid-1980s, the United States continued to harvest the seals on these Bering Sea outposts. There were some excesses and mistakes in the early years, but on the whole the Americans managed this natural resource on a humane, rational basis.

Most Canadians are unaware that their country was at the centre of an international dispute almost a century before the controversy over the killing of harp seal pups in the Gulf of St. Lawrence. The earlier confrontation took place on the opposite shore of the continent and involved a different species of seal, but there was one striking similarity between the two events. Canada was widely regarded as the villain in both. Now that the killing of seals for fur has virtually been abandoned everywhere, it is something for the nation to ponder.

But mostly I have written about the men — native Indians and whites — and the schooners they sailed into the treacherous North Pacific to hunt the fur seal. Lawyers, financiers and politicians also play a prominent role in the story. Pelagic, or open ocean, sealing was a contentious but profitable business which set off a prolonged controversy involving five nations. Out of the diplomatic turmoil, in 1911, came the first international agreement regulating a maritime resource.

The number of seals on the islands has been steadily declining in recent decades for a number of reasons. And the market for animal fur has almost disappeared, partly the result of emotionalism but also because of a more enlightened attitude toward preserving the world's wildlife. (It is worth noting, however, that at the time of writing the Province of British Columbia is considering killing harbour seals in the mistaken belief that they eat too many salmon.)

9

They were mostly a rag-tag lot, these ships and men, although it was not always so. In the beginning there were a handful of proud, honest seamen who owned the sealing schooners themselves and kept them trim and swift. As the fortunes of the business fell, however, the vessels ended up in the hands of mortgage holders and speculators, kept afloat "with paint and putty." The best seamen drifted off into other work. Crews for the schooners, never the cream of the waterfront, came more and more from the ranks of scroungers and hangers-on rounded up in harbour saloons.

As sealer Victor Jacobson put it, "One could not altogether blame the Americans for getting mad with the sealers. They caused a lot of trouble at the different settlements where they landed. It was not the Indians so much as the white hunters. They were, for the most part, a lot of dare-devils, hoodlums, just into the thing for the excitement and the fun." Some settlements were set afire and there was random, drunken shooting when men went ashore.

It is not surprising that most of the men were hard-bitten. The work was not pleasant. When hunting was good the men skinned the seals in their canoes or small boats to make room for more. Otherwise the seals would be brought back to the schooner in the evening for skinning and salting down. The sealers in time became immune to the stench and handling of greasy carcasses, often those of nursing females who had left their pups ashore while they hunted food. But the effect on less hardened observers was devastating.

"The snow white milk running down the blood-stained deck was a sickening sight," wrote Victoria journalist Robert McManus after a voyage on the schooner *Otto*. Hunter Niels Bonde said he had seen live pups cut out of their mothers crawling around the decks for a week before being skinned for their fur.

Some men were unaffected by the work; others had to steel themselves. One hunter was quoted as saying the sleeping seals looked so innocent coiled up in kelp beds that it seemed a sin to kill them. "But you see I was not there to look for sin, it was seals I was after."

The fur seal has been the cause of more years of bitter conflict and contention between nations, between corporations and between individuals, than any other wild animal species that ever lived on this earth or in its waters... the history of the fur seal species, and of the contentions regarding its slaughter and its salvage, fill a larger number of bound volumes than the strongest man could pick up and carry away... the blundering and the chicanery that first and last has developed in connection with this picturesque animal literally staggers the imagination.

—WILLIAM T. HORNADAY, *Thirty Years War for Wild Life*

CHAPTER ONE

Clayoquot

*Whatever other people may have to say about the morality of the
calling, it is greatly to be preferred to life spent in cheating your
neighbour in trade, or in other sharp practices which are so
prevalent in these days.*

—Sealer HAROLD J. SNOW

Along the Pacific coast of North America, Indians had been pursuing the
fur seal for centuries. In the beginning they hunted mostly for food. The
earliest record comes from fur seal bones uncovered by archaeologists at
Ozette, on the northern coast of Washington. They are at least 2,000 years old.
The seals were taken as they lingered in late winter at feeding grounds over
Umatilla Reef, just three miles offshore. The reef is the closest point to land
where the seals feed on their annual migration north.

The best time for hunting was a calm day following a spell of bad weather.
Most seals sleep soundly then. They cannot rest in rough water, and are edgy
and restless in rain and breezes which signal the approach of a storm.

The Quileutes of Ozette and the Makahs of Neah Bay, a branch of the
Nuu-chah-nulth (Nootka) tribes living on the west coast of Vancouver Island
across Juan de Fuca Strait, went out in three-man, 25-foot cedar canoes. The
canoes, exquisitely designed for the open sea, were flat-bottomed for
stability, with flared gunwales to prevent shipping too much water. A high,
vertical stern and equally high out-reaching bow topped with the traditional
"dog's head," gave them a rakish, seaworthy appearance. They sometimes
carried a small sail for use in favourable winds. Their paddles had long
tapered blades that entered the water silently so as not to waken the sleeping
seals as the canoe approached.

Some natives used bow and arrow and others a net, but the most common
weapon was a harpoon, or spear. Twelve to 15 feet long, the spears were an
inch or so in diameter. The handle and two fastened-on prongs, one 30
inches long and the other 15, were usually made from crabapple wood.
Although retrievable, a pair of extra spears was taken along.

The spearheads — mussel shells, deer and elk horn points or sharpened
stone in the early days; old files or pieces of steel after the white men came —

were fastened on the end of the prongs with sinew or twine, all sealed together by a thick coating of spruce gum. Each spearhead was attached to a 12-fathom cod-line coiled to allow running, with the end tied to a canoe thwart.

Gliding toward the sleeping seal, the bowman rested the harpoon in a notch between the "ears" of the dog's head in the bow of the canoe until almost within spearing distance — about 30 feet. After raising the spear with the left hand he grasped the handle with the right, drew the line taut along the length of the spear, and hurled the shaft with both hands. The spear was aimed to hit the water four feet short of the seal and skip into it, in order to avoid missing over the top of the dozing animal.

The larger prong was always uppermost — if it missed then the shorter one usually connected. The barb was designed to turn crossways upon entering the body of the animal. Sometimes it would go right through and "toggle" on the other side. As soon as the seal was struck the spear shaft detached itself from the line and floated on the water, where it could be recovered.

Then the battle began, the seal being played like a salmon. After the whites brought metals to the coast, the first 10 feet or so of the line was sheathed in copper wire so the seal could not bite it through. The hunters often suffered hand burns and lacerations when the line was pulled through their palms. Occasionally the spearpoint would snag a flipper, which was like hooking a big fish on the back or tail. In that event the struggle could cover miles and take hours.

After the desperate animal had been exhausted by repeated dives, it was pulled to the side of the canoe and gaffed under a flipper. Gaffs were usually 10 to 12 feet long with up to three hooks. The squirming seal was difficult to subdue and struggled for up to 10 minutes before it could be finished off with a club and pulled aboard. In later years the Indians used guns for the *coup de grace.*

A vivid description of this hunting technique was given by a white observer who watched as the Indians paddled to within 40 feet of a sleeping seal off Cape Flattery: "The hunter stood braced, spear in hand, and with true aim hurled it with all his force... in an instant the scene of repose was changed into one of intense excitement and pain. With a jump the seal instantly disappeared below the surface... soon it came up to breathe and renew its desperate struggle for liberty. It stood in the water facing us, with its body half exposed as if taking in the situation, and with a kind of low piteous growl, as though it realized its end was near, it renewed the contest. It fought madly, diving, jumping, and swimming with great speed, first in one direction, then in another, sometimes on one side of the canoe and then on the other, the Indian all the time holding on to the spear rope, trying to draw the seal near the canoe, so as to strike it on the head with the killing club. In its frantic efforts to escape it bit at the line several times, but soon abandoned the idea of gaining its freedom in such a manner and again resorted to jumping and diving...the loss of blood soon caused it to grow weak, and after a fight, which lasted perhaps five minutes, it ceased to struggle altogether and was hauled to the side of the canoe and dispatched with the club."[1]

The pioneer coastal trader John Meares observed "seals without number" while travelling in 1788 between the Columbia River and Vancouver Island. But the white men did not become established on the coast until the mid-19th century. Even then their main interest was the sea otter, whose skins had become scarce as the result of intense hunting but were still available in small numbers from the Indians.

Gradually the natives began trading fur seal pelts with their other skins to the Hudson's Bay Company for store-goods. The Quileutes and Makahs initially sold their skins in Astoria, but later found it more convenient to take them to Victoria.

On the northern coast the Haida were among the first to take advantage of this new trade, about 1846. They had previously hunted the fur seal only for its meat, considered a delicacy. The hind flippers, boiled, were especially favoured. The Haidas went out from Masset into Dixon Entrance and Hecate Strait in large canoes with four paddlers and a hunter in the bow. Their season came a few weeks later, in March, as the seals moved north. The Haidas were the first natives to hunt with rifles and shotguns, spearing the seals as soon they had been shot to prevent them sinking. From 1875 on the Haidas were selling up to 1,000 skins a year to the new H.B.C. trading post at Masset which had been established primarily to handle fur seal pelts.

The Tsimshian hunted around Zayas Island in Dixon Entrance. At first they sold the skins to the H.B.C. at Fort Simpson, but later switched to the missionary-trader William Duncan at Metlakatla, who paid them better prices. The Kitkatla band of the Tsimshians were the most noted for their seal-hunting ability. Their favourite area was around Bonilla Island in Hecate Strait. The Hailzuk band also found fur seals in Milbanke Sound. To the south, the Kwakiutl hunted fur seal in the winter months off the northern tip of Vancouver Island around Hope Island and Nawitti.

But it was the Nuu-chah-nulths who were the greatest seal hunters. The main centre of activity was Clayoquot Sound, where once 4,000 Indians lived on the many inlets and islands. It was the most populous Nuu-chah-nulth grouping on the coast, but disease reduced their numbers to about 600 by the 1870s. The Clayoquots hunted on the La Perouse banks off the entrance to Barkley Sound, a shallow area with a sandy bottom rich in sea life reaching 40 miles offshore.

The Pacheenahts of Port San Juan were also active sealers. "At one time, seals were a major source of meat for the people of this area," Chief Charlie Jones recalled in 1981. "Seals were to the Indians what cows are to the white man. In the old days, we would go out in 40-foot long canoes and hunt seals off Cape Flattery. My father used to take the seal pelts to Victoria to trade with the Hudson's Bay Company. My father would leave our village at two o'clock in the morning, April through May, to go seal hunting. We would paddle as far as 20 miles out into the ocean, so that we could catch the seals as they followed the tide drift looking for food." Jones himself accompanied his father aboard the schooner *Saucy Lass* on a sealing voyage to the Bering in 1900. He paddled and steered the canoe while his father held the spears in the bow.[2]

The first whites to work up a trading business with the Nuu-chah-nulths for furs and oil were a small group of west coast traders headed by William Spring. Spring was born in Russia in 1831 to a Scottish engineer and a Russian woman. Soon after arriving in Victoria in 1853 at the age of 22, he formed a partnership with C. B. Young and opened a store for miners at Bella Coola. They jointly owned a schooner skippered by Hugh McKay, a Scotsman who had arrived in Victoria in 1848. McKay was a cooper by trade and had set up shop in Sooke harbour. He and Spring teamed up in 1855, operating a saltery and making barrels for the fishing industry.

Their first vessel was a long-boat purchased from the sunken sailing ship *Lord Western*. They fitted the little vessel with a schooner rig and named her the *Ino*. She ran a freight and mail route to Olympia in Washington Territory before being sold. In 1856 the partners bought the *Morning Star*, a schooner which carried trade goods around southern Vancouver Island until wrecked on Discovery Island in 1859. She was replaced by the schooner *Surprise*, and in 1864 another schooner, the *Alert*, was added to their growing fleet.

In 1864 Spring joined Peter Francis' trading station at San Juan, along with 24-year-old James Christiansen from Denmark, who had jumped ship from the *King Oscar* in Victoria. Christiansen hired on as mate under Francis in the *Alert*, later becoming skipper. Spring and Francis bought dried fur seal skins from the Indians at San Juan and transported them to Victoria, where they were re-shipped to London for dyeing. (Christiansen later found a way to keep skins fresh during sealing voyages by stowing them below decks in coarse salt). McKay came into the firm six years later. Part of their business was buying oil and pelts, including fur seal, from the Indians for re-sale to the Hudson's Bay Company. Spring and McKay opened a trading post in Kyuquot and also cured salmon for the growing trade with Hawaii.

In 1867 it was observed that fur seals were more plentiful than usual. It is not certain whether the Indians or Christiansen first suggested that a

Favorite *Becalmed in Dawn Mist*

Father A. J. Brabant

Chief Charlie Jones

Indian seal hunting and skinning, La Push, Washington

schooner carry their canoes out to the feeding grounds. In either case, the Indians were receptive to the idea. On their own in the past they had lost many men to sudden storms which blew up when they were 20 miles or more offshore and unable to get back home.

Christiansen proposed to Spring that they take the Indians out in the *Surprise.* During a lull in trading in early 1868, Spring gave him the go-ahead. While Francis continued trading with the *Alert,* Christiansen went to Clayoquot to pick up the Indian hunters. He secured four large canoes and 12 men for that first expedition. An agreement was made that the schooner would keep one of every three skins.

About 30 miles offshore, the canoes were lowered and the Clayoquots began hunting. There was some fog but the sea was calm. The catch was poor. Two of the canoes became lost in the fog that first day but the hunt went on for two more days until the wind came up. When the schooner returned to port it was found that the other two canoes had reached shore safely. Christiansen salted down only nine skins as his one-third share. The *Surprise* made another two trips in the next few weeks, also with poor results.[3]

When word got back to Victoria of Christiansen's pioneering effort, the waterfront old-timers scoffed. And the fur buyers in Victoria, most of whom had come originally from San Francisco, were angry at Christiansen for taking the Indian catch away from them.

Others with a grievance against Christiansen were the Pacheenaht Indians of San Juan, who thought that since the owners of the *Surprise* were based near their village, they should have made the first trip. So in 1869 when Christiansen went out again after fur seal, he took a crew of San Juan natives. This time he took 10 two-man canoes, smaller than those used by the Clayoquots and easier to launch and stow on the schooner deck. It was a successful move, because the total catch this time was 900 skins, sold to the H.B.C. for $10 each.

Meanwhile, Peter Francis also went sealing in 1869 off Barkley Sound in the other company schooner, the *Alert.* He took on 12 canoes and hunters at Ucluelet, where he now made his home. His catch was also about 900 that season.

As word of this new success spread in Victoria, others took steps to enter the pelagic sealing business. One of the earliest was Joseph Boscowitz, a Victoria fur-dealer who also owned a trading post across Juan de Fuca Strait at Neah Bay in Washington Territory for a time. Boscowitz, gruff and controversial, was accused of using liquor in his trade dealings with the Indians.

The same charge was levelled against James Douglas Warren, another tough-minded independent trader and fur dealer. Born in Prince Edward Island in 1837, Warren arrived in Victoria in 1858 and began trading on the west coast with the 29-ton sloop *Thornton* out of Clayoquot Sound, where Boscowitz ran another trading post. Built in 1861 at Dungeness, Washington

Territory, with a sturdy oak frame, the *Thornton* was a broad, flat-bottomed craft.

In April of 1867 Warren appeared before William Duncan, a magistrate as well as missionary at Metlakatla, on a charge of selling liquor to Indians on the Nass River. He was accused of selling two kegs of rum, one of them watered down, and some bottles of gin. Warren told Duncan he had not wanted to deal in liquor but had been told by others he could not trade among the Indians without it. After his conviction Warren asked for time to prove it was his first offence, which Duncan granted. Warren was fined $400 and jailed for two months, but managed to avoid confiscation of the *Thornton* by taking her into Russian waters.[4]

A year later Warren and the *Thornton* were involved in one of the most sensational confrontations between whites and Indians along the B.C. coast. On June 13, 1868, Warren and his five-man crew were attacked by a group of armed natives while the sloop was becalmed in Queen Charlotte Sound. The raiders were beaten off with a rapid-fire Henry repeating rifle. Fifteen Indians were killed and a number of others wounded.[5] Warren, who had suffered a chest injury, rather than being hailed as a hero was arrested June 22 and accused of shooting an Indian. The charge was dismissed by a Victoria court on September 4 but the impression was left that the Indian attack on Warren might not have been unprovoked.

Rather than compete, Warren and Boscowitz formed a partnership. In early 1871 Boscowitz purchased the schooner *Anna Beck* in San Francisco to join the *Thornton*, now converted to a schooner rig, in sealing. At 40 tons and able to carry 20 canoes, the *Anna Beck* was the largest vessel in the growing Vancouver Island fleet, which numbered seven that year. She was placed under Captain Sam Williams, who picked up canoes and hunters at Ahousaht. Spring had purchased the veteran schooner *Carolena*, formerly owned by Duncan at Metlakatla, and had her rebuilt. He also put the sloop *Reserve* under Captain Neils Moos and chartered the little schooner *Wanderer* under Captain John Flett Sabiston of Nanaimo, who had arrived in Victoria in 1848 and gone to work for the H.B.C. on the *Beaver.* Both the *Reserve* and *Wanderer* sailed out of Dodger Cove in Barkley Sound with Ohiaht Indians. The *Surprise* and *Alert* were also out that year. Catches were generally poor but prices were up because the end of the Franco-Prussian War had resulted in boom times and increased demand for furs in Europe and the United States.

In 1868 Spring's group had built the French-design, 80-ton schooner *Favorite* at the Muir boatyard near Sooke. This stoutly-made vessel, built of Douglas fir from the Sooke hills, was destined to become one of the longest-serving and most successful in the sealing fleet. She was intended originally to catch cod in the Sea of Okhotsk in the Western Pacific for delivery to Hawaii, but this venture proved uneconomic. The *Favorite* was then used to carry freight between Victoria and Honolulu, San Francisco and Acapulco. On her voyages to Hawaii, the *Favorite* took fish, shingles, liquor, and iron, bringing back sugar, molasses and fruit. Spreading 3,700 square feet of sail, she made good time on these voyages. She also took coal and lumber to Mexico and returned with California redwood to Victoria.

In 1873 she began her eventful sealing career. On her first trip she picked up some Nuu-chah-nulths at Kyuquot and then went to Cumshewa in the Queen Charlotte Islands, where a few Haidas were taken aboard to hunt in that area. After that the Haidas seldom went out in the schooners. They preferred to make offshore forays, complaining that increased hunting had made the seals more shy and driven them farther out to sea. The Haidas also lost favour with the schooner owners when they refused to lower their canoes to hunt on Sundays no matter how many seals were about. They paid more attention to the teachings of the missionaries than most of the other coastal tribes.

Eleven schooners in all went out in 1873, including four from Neah Bay. By this time Spring had added trading posts at Pachena Bay, Dodger Cove, Ucluelet, Hesquiaht, Friendly Cove, and Nuchatlaht. His store at Kyuquot had been abandoned. Warren and Boscowitz operated stores at Village Island and Ecoole on Seddall Island in Barkley Sound, as well as Clayoquot and Ahousaht. Each took in about 1,000 fur seal skins in 1873, including the catch of the Indians still operating in canoes independently of the schooners. Spring sold the *Carolena* to the Pilotage and chartered the 40-ton *Juanita*, built in Seattle.

The spring of 1875 was stormy and in May some 70 Nuu-chah-nulth canoes hunting seals from a number of villages were caught in a sudden storm with offshore winds of unusual force which drove them to the southwest. A few Hesquiahts managed to reach the Washington coast, but more than 100 men were drowned. From that time onward the natives were more fearful of going out on their own and it became easier for the schooners to recruit hunters.

They got help from the missionaries, who preferred the natives to be at sea rather than in the Fraser River canneries, where the whites plied them with liquor and prostituted the women. Not long after establishing a mission at Hesquiaht, Father A. J. Brabant urged the Indians, who had been living on fish and potatoes, to go out sealing. He also persuaded them to extract dogfish oil to sell to the trading schooners. The young natives wanted the money to buy trade goods, especially English-style clothing. So the traders, who often had close ties with the schooner owners, also encouraged the Indians to sign on for sealing voyages.

To Brabant's dismay the Indians continued the "osemitch" ceremonies to ensure the success of their hunt. "When the young men are out sealing," he wrote, "the doors of the houses must remain closed and the room be kept as dark as possible. Dogs, chickens and even children are turned outside. I heard a young man say he missed and attributed his ill luck to the fact that at that very time a band of dogs had a row in his house, as he was afterwards informed by the women."[6]

When the canoes were caught by storms the men prayed to a queen known as "Wakioux" who dwelt in, above or beyond the seas. "They ascribe to her the heaving or swelling of the waves," Brabant recorded. "They shout out to her asking her to cause the waves to calm down." At other times in bad weather they threw food on the waves and blew a whistle which was used in the ceremonial Wolf dances.

The *osemitch* involved a rigorous routine of fasting for four days and diving into the sea four times each night. Bathing in fresh water was also required. "Everyone goes in turn, apart from the tribe, and the company of his friends, to pray. As a rule he goes to the woods, strips naked alongside of a stream or a clear pool of water, and then rubs his body with a kind of grass, or brushwood or roots. In many cases he leaves marks on his body and draws blood ... he constantly repeats in short shout-like accents, a formula of prayer expressing the object he prays for ... often small cedar sticks are put up to represent a man with a spear in his hands aimed at a bunch of fern roots, or the like, representing a fur seal."

Brabant also recorded the following bizarre incident: "I know an Indian who went sealing the other day. Before he left he opened the coffin of an old woman, cut or plucked out one or both of her eyes and put them in his pocket. When he arrived at the sealing ground, he rubbed his face with them in the region of his eyes. This was done to clear them and discover the seals as they slept on the waves."

Another aspect of sealing expeditions was the enforcement of sexual abstinence: "The old people preach strict continence to the young men and none who do not live apart from their wives can expect to be successful in the pursuit of whales and fur seals. As a preparation the time limit is ten months for whales and five calendar months for fur seals. This mode of living is only to be given up when the hunting season is at an end."

The seal hunters also gathered a particular millipede which they squeezed to procure a sharp-smelling juice rubbed on their necks and faces to mask their human scent.[7]

Meanwhile, there was increasing sealing activity on the American side of Juan de Fuca Strait. One of the first whites to take it up was Captain James Dalgardno, who had arrived in Port Townsend in 1855 from Edinburgh and later took charge of a pilot boat. When he acquired his own schooner, the *Anna Dalgardno*, built in San Francisco, he took her outside Cape Flattery with a small white crew to hunt fur seals. Another pilot boat, the *Lottie*, based in Port Townsend, sealed off the entrance to Juan de Fuca when her regular business was slow. In 1869 the *Lottie* took 180 skins with spears borrowed from the Makahs at Neah Bay. In later years the *Lottie* dropped the pilotage business altogether and became a sealing charter boat based in Neah Bay.

Among the first American schooners to take the Indians and their canoes off Cape Flattery was the *Mary Parker* of Port Townsend. She made sealing voyages in 1878 and 1879 with 40 Makahs aboard. The schooner *Champion* was built at Port Townsend by Captain E. H. McAlmond, who sealed with her until 1886, when she was sold to Chief Peter of Neah Bay. The Indians owned three other small schooners at this time.[8]

An adventurous American seaman from southern California had also begun moving northward on the track of the fur seal. Captain Martin Morse Kimberly, born to a New England lighthouse keeper in 1826, brought his 80-foot schooner *Cygnet* around Cape Horn from Guildford, Conn., to Santa Barbara in 1851. The *Cygnet* had been built in 1833 as a partial square-rigger and later changed to the regular fore-and-aft schooner rigging. In 1856 Kimberly moved to San Nicholas Island in the Channel group offshore from Santa Barbara, taking with him sheep, cattle and horses. The southernmost of the Channel Islands, San Nicholas, was unoccupied when Kimberly arrived but had been a base for smugglers. He employed the *Cygnet* for otter-hunting and whaling in the area.

When the sea otter became scarce off California, Kimberly made a two-year voyage in 1872 to the Sea of Japan, hunting otter and fur seal after first looking for whalebone on ships trapped and abandoned in the ice of Bering Strait. He delivered 200 otter skins worth up to $90 each in Hakodate, Japan, where he spent the winter. On this trip Kimberly took only six white crewmen, two small boats and four Kentucky muzzle-loading rifles.[9]

On May 3, 1874, the *Cygnet* sailed out of San Francisco, bound for the North Pacific. After picking up some Indian hunters at Neah Bay and Clayoquot, Kimberly reached Unimak Island in the Aleutians July 18. On August 29 a party of 11 men headed by H. H. McIntyre of the Alaska Commercial Company boarded the schooner off Otter Island and accused Kimberly of raiding the rookery. The decks were littered with carcasses, but Kimberly insisted his Indian hunters had shot seals in the water only for food. He surrendered 35 inferior quality skins, however, and headed back to Unimak Pass. On October 17 he arrived at Neah Bay, where he sold 135 fur seal pelts to Boscowitz and paid off the Indian hunters. Kimberly then headed across the Strait to sell 20 otter skins in Victoria.

After laying over two months in Port Townsend, Kimberly resumed sealing on January 2, 1875. He spent the next four months cruising off the entrance to Juan de Fuca Strait, ducking in for shelter during storms to Neah Bay or Barkley Sound. On May 26 he headed north once again toward the Aleutians. After shooting deer for food on an islet off Kodiak Island, Kimberly met the schooner *Dashing Wave* and purchased five sacks of salt. On

July 11 he took 47 seals at latitude 56° north and longitude 169° west on the main route of the fur seals to the Pribilofs. Between July 14 and 28 the *Cygnet* took between 50 and 70 seals a day off St. George Island. On August 13 she passed back through Unimak Pass and after getting a few more seals in the Gulf of Alaska, returned to Neah Bay. On landing two Indian hunters there, he sailed to Victoria to dispose of his season's catch, 569 sealskins. Kimberly arrived at Santa Barbara near the end of November and hunted otter. He went north again in the spring of 1876 but nothing more is known of his activities except that he made another voyage to the Asian coast. The *Cygnet* vanished with all hands during a storm somewhere in the North Pacific in 1878.

Another sea-faring adventurer was Harold J. Snow, an Englishman living in Japan. Snow was involved in a number of raids on Russian-owned rookeries in the Eastern Pacific. He was a rarity among the seal hunters in that he was a writer and scholar. His memoirs are among the very few set down by a sealer.[10]. Snow was a member of the Royal Geographical Society and his charts were used by the British Admiralty. He belonged to the fashionable, international-flavored Yokohama Club, where it is believed he met Rudyard Kipling and entranced the poet with stories of his own exploits and those of other notorious poachers. It is known that Kipling never sailed on a sealing schooner himself and wrote his famed *Rhyme of the Three Sealers* in Japan after visiting the Yokohama Club.

Snow was not apologetic about his work. He regarded the rookery plunderers as brave men who risked their capital and their lives to reap the resources of nature. The rookery owners, on the other hand, he likened to "that pirate of the gulls, the skua, amongst the kittiwakes, who, instead of seeking his own food, watches until another bird captures a fish, and then swoops down upon him, compels him to give it up, and swallows it himself." Above all, it was an exciting way of life: "Whatever other people may have to say about the morality of the calling, it is greatly to be preferred to a life spent in cheating your neighbor in trade, or in other sharp practices which are so prevalent in these days."

In addition to thousands of seals, Snow took more than 900 sea otter on his various voyages between 1872 and 1895. His first sealing venture was aboard the 118-ton schooner *Swallow*, built in Nagasaki. His next vessel, the *Otome*, was placed under the U.S. flag in 1878 because war between Britain and Russia seemed imminent. (In future years the sealing schooners would frequently switch to flags of convenience.) On that voyage he met the *Cygnet* not long before she was lost. A total of 14,000 seal pelts were taken along the Asian coast in 1878 by 11 schooners. The *Diana* was fired upon by natives on Copper Island when she attempted to land, and a number of Japanese crewmen were killed. The Russians seized 500 skins and rejected a claim for damages. The captain protested that he was merely seeking to buy skins from the natives.

Snow took 1,200 seals in three days on the Srednoy Rocks rookery in the Kurils in 1881, despite being bitten through his leather boot by an angry bull. Another 500 skins were ruined when the seals became over-heated while being chased on the rookery and shed their fur. In 1882 there were 13 schooners sailing out of Japan, almost all of which had switched from hunting otter to fur seal. That year the group made a deal in advance to divide their catch. Each received 16 otter pelts and 1,050 sealskins at the end of the season.

During a raid on Bering Island on the *Otome* in 1883, Snow was forced to flee before he could recover the skins of 600 clubbed seals. After a chase his schooner was caught by a Russian steamer. Snow was arrested, the *Otome* was confiscated, and he was imprisoned briefly in Vladivostok. His claim for $50,000 damages was later dropped. In 1884 Snow bought the schooner *Nemo* from the Russians and went over to the Pribilofs.

To illustrate the perils of his trade, Snow listed 52 schooners which had engaged in otter hunting and sealing in the Kurils between 1875 and 1900. Most were from San Francisco, with no more than 12 operating in a single season. Of the 52 a total of 13 were lost with all hands, 17 wrecked with the loss of 12 lives, and 5 seized by the Russians.

One of the dangers faced by a poacher was the increasing number of guards on the rookeries. In 1888 Snow's raiders were fired upon by Copper Island natives. Three of his men were killed and a number wounded. Britain was not persuaded to protest to the Russians on his behalf. After 1889, when the Japanese government banned its citizens from shipping on vessels other than those of their own flag, Snow took out a Chinese crew.

Another poacher was Captain Adolphe F. Carlson, notorious for his exploits as skipper of the *Adele*, which came to be known in the fleet as the "Flying Dutchman." In 1880, as master of the *Alexander*, owned by San Francisco fur dealer Herman Liebes, Carlson landed on unguarded Otter Island in the Pribilofs and took 300 skins. During the same voyage he also killed 1,200 seals on Copper Island, but escaped with only 100 skins when fired upon by Russian guards and island natives. Protection had been stiffened earlier that year after 600 men from 30 Japanese schooners went ashore and fired shotgun blasts in an attempt to drive off the guards. But as soon as the Japanese began taking seals the Russians opened fire with rifles and many raiders were killed.

The 50-ton *Adele* was built in Shanghai as a pilot boat. Owned and registered in Yokohama for a time, she also sealed under the Russian flag and later switched her registry to Hamburg in order to use German colours. In 1880, under Captain Albert C. Folger, she raided the Robben Reef rookeries with 11 other schooners, which took 3,800 skins in all. In 1884 Captain Gustave Hansen was in command of the *Adele*, with a crew of 18 Japanese, when she raided St. Paul Island and was captured by Lieutenant John E. Lutz of the U.S. Revenue Service. Lutz had been dropped off by the cutter *Thomas Corwin* to guard the rookery.

By 1876 the Victoria sealing fleet had grown to nine vessels — five belonging to Spring and his partners, the *Thornton* and *Anna Beck* of the Boscowitz-Warren partnership, the new *W. P. Sayward*, operated by Captain Andrew Laing, a former storekeeper for Spring on Diana Island in Barkley Sound, and the 81-ton *Black Diamond*. The latter vessel, destined to have a number of owners over the years, began her days carrying coal from Nanaimo as far north as Sitka. She was bought by Spring as a replacement for the *Alert*, which sank with 700 sealskins on the Great Bear Reef in Barkley Sound. Spring then sold the *Black Diamond* to Joe Quadros and Captain William Munsie, who took her out sealing that summer.

The competition was keen during this period between the Spring group and Boscowitz-Warren. In 1881 Warren added steam to the *Thornton* and *Anna Beck*, as well as the newly-acquired *Dolphin* and *Grace*, to enable them to get in and out of port without paying towing charges and to ease the passage through the tide rips of Unimak Pass. Spring decided not to follow suit because he felt it was uneconomic. His view proved to be correct and few of the sealing schooners over the next three decades had auxiliary steam engines.

After the third of the original schooners owned by Spring and his partners, the *Reserve*, was wrecked in 1878 in Barkley Sound, the firm began to split up. Hugh McKay sold his share in the *Favorite* to Spring and bought the 50-ton *Onward* in San Francisco. Captain Owen Thomas was placed in command. The following year Spring bought the *Mary Ellen* in San Francisco on his own.

The Indian shore hunters enjoyed a bonanza in 1880. More than 900 sealskins were brought in to Hesquiaht alone. The natives earned $30,000 in three months, some making as much as $120 a day.

By 1881 the Victoria fleet numbered 11 vessels, while the American fleet included the *Anastasia Cashman, Teaser* and *Ariel*. Catches were good. The *Ariel* got 131 skins in a single day and the *Juanita*, now owned by McKay, took 500 in two and a half days. McKay bought his second vessel in San Francisco, the 68-ton *Alfred Adams*, which had been built in Massachusetts and sailed around the Horn. When McKay died the next year, Spring purchased both the *Onward* and the *Alfred Adams*. To raise capital for his expanding fleet in 1880, Spring took on a partner, Victoria fur dealer and financier Theodore Lubbe, who acquired a half interest in William Spring & Co.

In 1882 a dozen new ships were added to the Canadian and American fleets. By now they were beginning to equip for longer voyages, following the migrating seals up the coast into the Gulf of Alaska and the sealing areas of Portlock Bank and the Fairweather Grounds. Portlock Bank, northeast of

Kodiak Island, is 50 miles across. The waters are less than 50 fathoms deep, so seals can reach the bottom to catch halibut, cod, flounder and sole. Vast numbers of capelin, sandlance and pollack drift in the upper waters. Sea birds and porpoises also converge on the bank. The Fairweather sealing grounds, where some of the largest catches were made, is also a shallow area, some 70 miles off Cape St. Elias.

The Victoria-based schooners alone hired more than 400 Indians for the coast hunt. At least two schooners went into the Bering Sea that year. The *Triumph* under Captain William Douglass and the 39-ton *San Diego*, owned and skippered by Captain James Carthcut, cruised as far north as 60° latitude, 150 miles above the Pribilofs. Carthcut's crew included brothers Dan McLean as navigator and Alex McLean, boat-puller.

Carthcut had also gone into the Bering in the *San Diego* in 1881. He was mainly after walrus on that trip, but shot 194 seals from the deck of the schooner. His seal catch was 326 in 1882 and 916 in 1883. These catches were sold in Victoria to Lubbe, representing the Martin Bates Fur Company of New York. Lubbe also bought 5,000 pounds of walrus ivory from Carthcut in 1881.

The competition between fur buyers was intense. "Joseph Boscowitz and I were at war continually," said Lubbe, who insisted on taking the whole catch of a schooner so that the skins could not be picked over and the prime ones sold elsewhere. Boscowitz thrived under the competition and lived in style. In April of 1869 a handsome rockaway carriage seating six arrived by steamer from San Francisco for him. Five years later Boscowitz purchased $100,000 in city waterworks debentures. He was constantly embroiled in controversy and litigation. In 1875 he sued a former partner, Francis Armstrong, who Boscowitz had outfitted for a trading post upcoast and allegedly owed $3,000 in unpaid bills.

A letter writer signing himself "watch-dog" wrote to the Victoria *Standard* in 1876 accusing Boscowitz of bribing members of the Legislative Assembly. Boscowitz retorted that he had turned down an M.L.A. who had tried to borrow $100. "The writer who uses the name of 'watch-dog' may prove to be a cur," he snarled. Before leaving Victoria for an extended stay in Britain, Boscowitz was treated to a "sumptuous" dinner by his friends in August, 1877. Three weeks earlier all the furniture of his Pandora Street mansion had been sold at auction. Auctioneer W. R. Clarke described the items as "some of the most choice and expensive articles ever imported into this province."

At the end of 1882 the Victoria *Colonist* noted the growing importance of the sealing industry. More than $200,000 was spent during the year on wages and supplies. American vessels also paid large sums in the city for outfitting. There were now 14 Victoria schooners, including seven Spring vessels and the Boscowitz-Warren fleet numbering four. In the U.S. there were 12 schooners sailing out of Neah Bay, Port Townsend, and Astoria, as well as a number from San Francisco. Bad weather during the 1882 season held catches down to an average of 500 skins per vessel. To make matters worse, the price dropped by $1 to $6 a skin.

An estimated 50 Nuu-chah-nulth offshore sealers were drowned during the late spring storms, their canoes swamped as they attempted to reach the American shore. The human loss seemed of little concern to the industry, however. As the Seattle *Post-Intelligencer* put it, "Fortunately for all concerned, these disasters occurred near the close of the sealing season."

By 1884 the practice of first sealing up the coast and then proceeding into the Bering in June as the seals neared the Pribilofs was well established. There were 34 schooners in all hunting fur seal that year. At least one of their number, the *Allie I. Alger* of Seattle, took 800 skins in a raid on a St. George Island rookery. Fifteen men killed 1,000 seals in one night's work, but left 200 skins behind. William Spring sent the *Mary Ellen* into the Bering for the first time. Skippered by Dan McLean, she had four sealing boats and a crew of white hunters, the first to sail out of Victoria. McLean first lowered his boats February 5 in latitude 38° north off San Francisco and took a total of 1,954 seals by September. William Spring died that year and the business was taken over by his 25-year-old son, Charles, who had worked for the H.B.C. since the age of 17. He proceeded to buy out Lubbe's share of the company.

William Spring had intended sending out two schooners, one with white hunters, the other with Indians, to compare results. His plan had been thwarted in 1884 but his son carried out the project the following year. The *Mary Ellen* went again under Dan McLean with white hunters and his brother Alex took the *Favorite* with Indian hunters. The results of the test were inconclusive, with catches and costs approximately the same.

The methods of white hunters in 3-man, double-ended boats fitted with both a sprit sail and a jib, differed only slightly from those of the Indians in canoes. The boats averaged 16 feet in length, with a 4½-foot beam, and were fitted for three pairs of oars. Some carried food for five days in case they became separated from the schooner, and five gallons of water. They also took flares and rockets. Each hunter had three guns and 200 shells, powder, shot and wads. Most used double-barrelled No. 10 shotguns because the seals too often sank when hit by rifle bullets.

The "steerer" was in the stern facing forward, usually standing as he pushed rather than pulled on the oars. When the seal was sighted it was his job to set the boat in the best position for the kill. Amidships sat the "puller" with a second set of oars facing the steerer. He would know by the steerer's signals for silence when the seal was near. The hunter was poised in the bow with a shotgun or rifle. Despite precautions, the seals sometimes awoke when approached and quickly dived. If still within range, they would be shot at when they resurfaced. Hunters fired with rifles from 60 to 100 yards. If the seal was not killed outright, they kept firing, sometimes as many as a dozen shots. The wounded animals tended to move to windward, giving an advantage in pursuit to 3-men boats and canoes. Sometimes the hunters would deliberately wound a seal so that it could be recovered as it flopped around on the surface instead of sinking quickly as they tended to do when killed instantly.

Hunters divided seals into "travellers," who raced through the water, sometimes leaping or "breaching" like dolphins through the waves; "moochers," slower movers who only occasionally raised their heads for a look around; and the "sleepers," who lay on their backs, some with flippers on chests, others with flippers lowered into the water for balance.

One sealer described the sleeping seal this way: "Lying on his back, with his hind flippers doubled up over his belly, the forward flippers crossed over the breast, and the head thrown back so that the mouth and nostrils are out of the water, he looks to the uninitiated like a log of driftwood, but the practised eye of the hunter detects the familiar form immediately." With their acute sense of smell seals could detect a hunter at 300 or 400 yards and so were approached from the leeward in calm or light wind seas. In choppy water the Indians advanced broadside to the wind, bringing the canoe closer in the troughs of the waves. As they drew near the seal, the hunters watched its breathing motions. They tried to shoot only when the seal's lungs were full of air so it would stay afloat after being shot.

The seals were usually taken back to the schooner unskinned, but if the catch was large, they were skinned in the boats. Some blubber was left on so that layers of salt separating the pelts during long periods in the hold of the schooner would not burn the fur.

Victor Jacobson had entered the business as an independent in 1884 and continued to operate as a loner long after the others had organized in a bid to save their dying industry. Jacobson had gone to sea at the age of 12 in his native Finland. In 1879 he jumped ship in Victoria from the iron-hulled windjammer *City of Quebec* which had just brought a load of tinplate around Cape Horn for the new coast salmon canneries. Deserting was regarded as a serious offence and anyone who captured a runaway seaman could collect a $100 reward. Jacobson and a shipmate were separated while being chased by a constable and he eventually found shelter on a Saanich farm where he was given work. After saving up $100 he took a job with Spring as a carpenter and built stores and trading posts at Nootka and Ucluelet. Jacobson went back to sea in 1882 as a mate on both the *Mary Ellen* and *Favorite*.

The next year for $400 he bought a little schooner abandoned and half full of mud and water in Victoria harbor. She was the *Mountain Chief*, just 23 tons and 38 feet in length, built of yellow cedar by a Nass Indian chief. That first season in a vessel of his own Jacobson took on 20 Indians at Village Island in Barkley Sound and got 700 skins in just six weeks. He paid the Indians $2 per skin, which he sold for $8 in Victoria. Delighted that the Indians were willing to accept hardtack and molasses as their diet, Jacobson cleared $1,000 on the voyage. He sailed the *Mountain Chief* until 1888, even taking her into the Bering in 1887, but had increasing difficulty each season recruiting native hunters. They did not want to sail on such a small vessel with meagre rations. The Indians preferred the larger schooners which had less crowding in the fo'c's'le where they were quartered, and handled the big seas more easily and safely. Jacobson was forced to take a number of Clayoquot women to act as paddlers for their husbands.

Other sealers also began to have problems recruiting Indian hunters. The natives were reluctant to make the long Bering voyage which kept them away from home for months. Others, becoming aware of their increasing importance to the industry, held out for a bigger share of the profits. When Captain Alex McLean arrived in Kyuquot in January of 1885 offering to pay only $2.50 for a large sealskin, the men of the village decided not to go out. They demanded $5. The situation had not changed by March 8 when Captain John Riley went to Ucluelet on the *Kate* to seek a crew. But on April 3 word reached Kyuquot that the schooner owners had agreed to pay $4 per skin and when Riley returned May 8 he had no trouble getting hunters.

On June 4 the *Favorite* under Alex McLean arrived en route to the Bering. He had taken on 17 Hesquiahts and three Clayoquots and 10 canoes. McLean on that voyage took one of the largest sealskins ever caught at sea in the Bering — 12 feet long and five feet across. The big bull fought fiercely. After being hooked by two spears and peppered with shotgun pellets, the seal was finally killed when an Indian broke a musket over its head at the gunwale.

Their first sealing voyage turned into an unexpected adventure for two Hesquiahts that year. The pair became separated in their canoe from McLean's schooner and landed on one of the Aleutian Islands. A friendly Aleut directed them with signs to a trading post. The white storekeeper provided some provisions and sent them to a nearby bay where American fishermen were at work. Eventually they were placed on the steamer *Dorah* and taken to San Francisco. The Indians were treated kindly by the captain and crew and on their arrival in the big, bewildering city the first officer took them to the British Consul, who paid their passage to Victoria. "They are now back," Father Brabant wrote, "and pose as heroes," regaling the villagers with their tale.

CHAPTER TWO

St. Paul

*The magnetism, the electric vitality, the heat and fury of these
stallions of the sea impregnate the very atmosphere.*

—WATSON COLT ALLIS

It is one of nature's most awesome annual shows. Starting in May, when
snow patches still dot the ground, hundreds of thousands of fur seals gather
on the lonely beaches of the Pribilof Islands. Since leaving these Bering Sea
outposts the previous autumn, they have cruised for seven months in the
North Pacific without touching land. Some, mostly the females, have travelled
up to 7,000 miles in a vast migratory loop.

The adults return to the volcanic islands to participate in an unusual
breeding rite. Within 36 hours of arriving at a rookery, usually the site of her
birth, the cow delivers a single pup weighing about 10 pounds. With its
round, liquid, darkly lustrous eyes already open, the pup struggles to free
itself of the birth sac. It does so with no help from the mother. Her only sign
of affection is to join in a mutual sniffing and calling to establish recognition.

Mother and pup are together for the next six days on the crowded
rookery. After the first 24 hours, she makes no attempt to protect it from the
crush of seething bodies. The pup must fend for itself, even if it has the
misfortune to fall into a crevice. The mother's only indulgence is to make
herself available for suckling.[1]

A week after giving birth the cow comes into heat and seeks out the bull
who controls the little territory she has selected, along with about 40 other
females. Weighing more than 500 pounds, with a short, bushy mane, he is
about six times her size, the largest disparity between the sexes among
mammals. They copulate quickly while the bull keeps a wary eye out for
intruders in his space.

The competition between bulls for territory is fierce, resulting at times in
the death of one of the combatants. The battles were vividly described by the
pioneer fur seal naturalist, Henry Wood Elliott: "Their hoarse roaring and
shrill, piping whistle never ceases, while their fat bodies writhe and swell
with exertion and rage; furious lights gleam in their eyes, their hair flies in the

air; their blood streams down."[2] Contrary to the opinion held in Elliott's day, the bull does not attempt to prevent cows leaving his area — it is the territory he is defending, not his "harem." With his demanding guard duties and mating activity, the bull cannot leave his space. He does not eat during his time ashore but lives on accumulated fat, losing 200 pounds in two months of sleepless activity.

After mating, the cow returns to her pup for another 48 hours or so. Then she will leave it to swim away in search of food. She eats mostly at night when the species that comprise her diet rise toward the surface. On this first trip she will be away about five days before returning with a supply of rich, life-sustaining milk for her pup. It will consume about half a gallon in an almost continuous two-day feeding before the mother sets off to sea again. In her search for food — primarily capelin, squid, anchovy, sandlance, pollack and herring — she may travel up to 250 miles from the islands.

The mother does not seek out her pup on her return but simply goes to the spot where she gave birth. The pup in the meantime has joined the other newborns wandering around the rookery. Like fat little Newfoundland puppies, they play and swim close to shore and search for their mothers daily. Aided by calls, they will be united when the pup nears her selected spot at the birth site. If the pup becomes desperately hungry before the mother's return, it will try "sneaking" milk from another cow on the rookery. But mothers will nurse only their own offspring, and as soon as the little stranger is discovered it will be chased away. If the mother fails to return, the pup will die of starvation. Despite the gregariousness of the seals on the rookery, they have no social bonds. The fate of a single animal has no effect on the behaviour of the others.[3]

The clamour of the rookery is overwhelming, night and day. The sound from a distance of up to six miles was described by Elliott as a "deep booming, as of a cataract." The bulls have a variety of bellows, snorts and whistles; the shriller cries of the females and pups are often likened to the bleating of sheep.[4]

One man who watched over the annual rites of the Pribilofs for 40 years said he was overcome with wonder each time at the incredible number of animals, their movements and the noise. The rookery, he said, resembled "a silvery-brown larva-like mass, seething, dissolving, re-forming in fantastic rhythm." At the centre of this maelstrom were the bulls: "The magnetism, the electric vitality, the heat and fury of these stallions of the sea impregnate the very atmosphere." [5]

Although clumsy on land, the bulls can move swiftly. Running on all four flippers, they can catch a fleeing man within 50 yards. Their lumbering, shambling gait is best described by Lewis Carroll's verb "galumphing." To see them move is to understand why the Russians first called the fur seals sea bears.

The intelligence of fur seals is a matter of disagreement among scientists. One says they are are "highly intelligent animals that can learn as quickly as cats or chimpanzees."[6] Another says fur seals follow perfectly the ways of their ancestors, but if forced to do anything different are "robotic, indifferent and untrainable."[7] Their life-cycle follows a deep instinctual pattern of repetition, an inflexibility that has been a severe liability. In two centuries of slaughter they never found or even sought a way to avoid their greatest predator: man.

Chinese and Japanese scholars had described them a century before, but the northern fur seal *Callorhinus ursinus* first entered the annals of science in 1751. Georg Wilhelm Steller, naturalist with the Vitus Bering expedition, discovered and classified the animal on what became known as Bering Island in the Kommandorski (Commander) group 100 miles off Russia's Kamchatka Peninsula. The seals were already being killed for their pelts in local native commerce, but at that time the Russians were covetous only of the lustrous pelt of the sea otter, worth 25 times the price of a fur seal skin.

Seal skins were considered useful only as elegant insulation on the walls of homes of the Russian nobility. It was not until the end of the 18th century that their value as garments and robes was appreciated. That came when the Chinese discovered a method of shaving the underside of the skins to cut off the roots of the stiff guard hairs so they could be removed without damaging the fine under-fur. Sealskins are heavier and more durable than otter, but soft and pliable. They began to be used for hats, carriage wraps, coats and "buggy robes." Catherine the Great had a large wardrobe of sealskin garments. In 1843 the Russians began shipping skins to London and New York.

For some years the Russians had observed the seals swimming north each spring through the passes between the Aleutian Islands. They had been hunted there, mainly for food, by the Aleuts in their skin-covered kayaks or "bidarkas." In the early summer of 1786, Gerassim Pribilof, an employee of a Russian fur company in the Aleutians, headed his sloop *St. George* north in the wake of the migrating seals. Three weeks and 200 miles later, on June 25, Pribilof heard the roar of the seals and knew he was near their breeding place. He moved slowly through the fog and landed on the island he named St. George after his little vessel.

His crew of Aleuts and Russians set to work clubbing the seals and stowing their pelts aboard the *St. George*. When Pribilof headed back to Unalaska with his cargo, 20 men stayed behind to winter on the island, gathering more furs for transport the following year. On the first clear day in July, when Pribilof had not yet returned, they saw the outline of another island 40 miles to the northeast. The by now anxious men set off in a bidarka, arriving July 11, the Russian holy day of St. Peter and St. Paul. This second island was immediately given the double name, but in a short time became known simply as St. Paul. Since then the Pribilofs, which also include three smaller islands — Otter and Walrus Islands and Sea Lion Rock — have been known variously as the "Seal Islands," the "Golden Islands" (because of the wealth they have yielded), and the "Mist Islands." The latter name is somewhat of a euphemism, since the fogs enveloping the islands most of the year have been more accurately described as "thick as mush."

At 33 square miles, St. Paul proved to be slightly larger than St. George. Its less precipitous shoreline provided a more hospitable home for the seals and the sandy beaches were dense with animals. It was said that from Hutchinson Hill, looking toward St. Paul's Northeast Point, could be seen the greatest number of wild animals from any one spot in the world. The total number on the islands in 1867, when the United States obtained the Pribilofs from Russia as part of the "Alaska Purchase," became a matter of controversy, but was close to 2,000,000.

There are 16 major rookeries on St. Paul and six on St. George. The large rookeries have up to 2,000 separate territories, each presided over by a mature bull or "beachmaster." Most are close to the water, but one rookery on St. George is on a grassy hill 200 feet above the beach.

The filth and stench of the rookeries contrasts with the surrounding landscape. After the snow departs in May the wild grasses spring up quickly and a bright green ground willow spreads out among the rocks. No trees grow in the thin volcanic soil of the undulating tundra, but colourful mosses abound. Wild peas, yellow arctic poppy, monkshead, saxifrage, harebell and forget-me-nots are soon in bloom and the lupins reach waist-high. Bird life is abundant. There are 100 species in all, of which 20 breed in the Pribilofs. Most numerous are gulls, puffins, murres, ducks, geese, sandpipers, cormorants, kittiwakes and least auklets. On rare days when the sun burns through the fog it throws a rainbow light on the jade-green ocean. At other times, when sun and fog are at a standoff, the Pribilof light is soft and diffuse, giving the islands a hazy, ethereal appearance.

Within two years Gerassim Pribilof's hunters took 40,000 fur seal and 2,000 otter, as well as 6,000 blue fox skins, more than 15 tons of walrus ivory, and nine tons of whalebone. The indiscriminate killing went on for a number of years, with pups and females included in the slaughter. In 1803 the Russians shipped 280,000 fur seal skins from their Sitka headquarters. Another 500,000 were stored in warehouses, partly to maintain prices but also because they had been poorly dried and cured and were worth little. The large number of southern fur seals still being killed kept prices low. It is estimated that between 1804 and 1812 one million damaged Pribilof pelts were destroyed in huge bonfires, or thrown into the sea.

At the beginning of the 19th century, competing Russian sealing firms were consolidated into the Russian-American Company and granted a 20-year lease by Emperor Paul. Controls were imposed to protect the dwindling seal population. Hunting was banned entirely from 1804 to 1808, but it was

William Spring

Andrew Laing

J. D. Warren

White hunters, Aleutians, *circa* 1906

Hunting Boats Returning to Dora Sieward in Fog

Captain M. M. Kimberly

Cygnet of Santa Barbara

Revenue Cutter *Thomas Corwin* leaving San Francisco

Fisheries Inspector Thomas
Mowat

Top right:

Admiral M. Culme-Seymour

William Munsie

not until 1834 that the consequences of random killing practices were fully realized. In that year the catch on St. Paul was limited to 5,000. The following year, when drifting ice floes after an unusually severe winter prevented most of the seals from reaching the islands, there was no killing. From that time until 1867, the Russians zealously protected the herd. Whaling ships and other sea hunters were banned from the adjoining waters. The killing of females was forbidden and only those males deemed surplus to the breeding process were taken. Although an estimated 2,500,000 seals were killed between 1786 and 1867, the population had been restored to approximately its original figure by the time the Americans took over.

When the Boston sealing fleet had expanded operations to the North Pacific early in the 19th century its inroads on the Russian trade caused Emperor Alexander I to issue a ukase in 1821 banning any foreign vessel within 100 miles of the coast between the Bering Strait and 51° north latitude. The Americans and British protested that this unprecedented Russian claim interfered with their rights at sea. (The vigorous objections raised by Secretary of State John Quincy Adams were invoked against the U. S. many years later when the seals became the subject of a prolonged diplomatic dispute with Britain). In the face of the united opposition, Alexander relented. In separate treaties with the two nations in 1824 and 1825, the southern boundary of Russian America was fixed at 54°40′ north latitude and the claim of jurisdiction over the high seas abandoned. The government likely backed off because it had not been in favour of the measure in the first place. As the Alaska Commercial Company pressured the United States government in later years, so did the Russian American Company put the squeeze on St. Petersburg to protect its monopoly.

Between 1803 and 1812 a number of the Boston men made unusual contracts with Alexander Baranof, the Russian Fur Company overseer and ruler of the fledgling Russian colony. In exchange for a share of their catch, he agreed to supply the American vessels with Aleut hunters and bidarkas which were taken to the Farallon Islands outside the Golden Gate and the Channel Islands off Santa Barbara, where they killed thousands of fur seals. The Aleuts with their spears and bidarkas set out from the mother ship each day and returned with their catch for a small share of the eventual profit. In the winter of 1810/11 Captain Jonathan Winship took 30,000 seals in five months. [8] This was the earliest form of what was to become known as commercial pelagic sealing, hunting the fur seals on the high seas rather than at their rookeries.

In addition to the Pribilofs and the Commanders, the northern fur seal breeds on Robben Reef in the Sea of Okhotsk and a few islets in the Kuril chain. There is some intermingling of the Asian and Pribilof herds — it has been estimated that a third of the young males from the Pribilofs winter in the Sea of Japan — but each generally follows its own migratory route. It is only

33

170 miles from Attu at the end of the Aleutian chain to Copper Island in the Russian Commander group.

Starting in September, the Pribilof seals move down through the Aleutian passes into the warmer Pacific waters. The mature males remain in the Gulf of Alaska, however, and are the first to arrive back at the Pribilofs in the spring. During the winter the islands are surrounded by ice driven south by Arctic storms. Meanwhile, the pregnant females, travelling singly or in pairs, have made their way to the southern California coast and begin moving slowly north, arriving on the rookeries in July to give birth. The younger males and females do not arrive until August, when some breeding takes place. The pups born the previous season do not return to the islands until their second year, spending much of the time in large feeding grounds in the North Pacific. They are on their own after the females depart. Less than 50 percent of the pups survive the depredations of winter storms, killer whales and disease.

Although the older females are bred in early July and give birth almost exactly a year later, the actual gestation period is only nine months. The cows are bi-uteral, with each uterus functioning in alternate years. The embryonic cell lies dormant for about three months until the pup is weaned. The average cow bears a total of six pups in a lifetime of about 15 years.[10]

The tumultuous annual breeding has been described as "a celebration of life," but for one group of seals it is a time of organized, ritual death. These are the three to five year old bachelor seals, or "holluschickie" as the Russians called them. Arriving about the same time as the big bulls, the young males are forced to the rear of the rookery. Congregated here, sheathed in the finest fur and considered surplus to the need of the herd, they are the obvious choice for harvesting.

Until about 1835 the Russians took young pups of both sexes. The steady decline of the herd led to the realization that a different approach must be taken. From that time the pups and females were spared and killing was restricted to the bachelors. Even this harvest was strictly regulated, with one-fifth of the young males preserved each season to sustain future breeding stock.

When the Pribilofs were first discovered they were uninhabited. The Russians had to transport Aleuts each year from Unalaska to conduct the harvest. Over the years about 250 people took up permanent residence on the islands, with the largest group on St. Paul.

Each day during June and July in the early hours of dawn, when the grass was cool and wet with dew, a dozen or so men would round up a number of the young bachelor seals and guide them with shouts and prodding poles over well-worn pathways from the rookeries to the killing field. The Aleut name for this site is *ungisxalgeq*— the place without hope. When the weather was warm, the seals were allowed to halt periodically and cool off or bathe in a marshy pool before resuming their death march, which usually took about two hours. They frequently stopped and waved their flippers about to release excess body heat.

A few animals were rejected for one reason or another and allowed to make their way back to the rookery. The others, in groups of 100 or so, were quickly dispatched with one or two blows to the head with a six-foot hickory club. Then the bodies were laid out in rows of 10 and skilled skinners went to work with razor-sharp knives no larger than ordinary kitchen utensils. The most accomplished workers removed the fur in 90 seconds of flashing movement; the average was about three minutes. An experienced team of Aleuts killed and skinned 1,000 seals an hour. The skins were then stretched over rocks heated by a driftwood fire for 24 hours until dried.

Using these methods, the Russians killed from 5,000 to 10,000 seals annually between 1840 and 1855. Then, as the herd expanded, the take was raised to about 30,000 in each of the 10 years before the Pribilofs were turned over to the United States.

Despite a century of control over the territory that was to become known as Alaska, Russia never felt completely secure in North America. The great distance from St. Petersburg made the colony difficult to administer. Shipping costs were astronomical. In an attempt to become more self-sufficient, the Russian-American Company traded for food in Hawaii and started ranching in California, but these projects were soon abandoned as uneconomic.

There was considerable friction between the Russians and Americans. After the sea otter had been hunted almost to extinction, and the rookeries of the southern hemisphere fur seal *Arctocephalus* cleaned out, the far-ranging Boston traders had turned their attention to the northern fur seal. The Russians were alarmed, too, by the growing encroachment of British traders in the area.

American entrepreneurs were also beginning to cast covetous eyes on Alaska and its riches. In 1859 Senator William M. Gwin of California, representing a group of San Francisco businessmen, proposed in a series of interviews with Russian officials to purchase the interests of the Russian-American Company. His negotiations, although sanctioned and assisted by the State Department, eventually collapsed.

A new attempt was made in 1865 by Lewis Goldstone, an American fur dealer based in Victoria. In a bid to take over the soon-to-expire Hudson's Bay Company fur trade sub-lease in Russian territory, Goldstone set up the California Fur Company in San Francisco. Two principals of the new firm were financier Louis Sloss and General John F. Miller, customs collector for the port of San Francisco. Both men were to play leading roles in the coming financial manipulations to gain control of Alaska trade.

Another California Senator, Cornelius Cole, was legal adviser to Goldstone's firm. Cole sought the support of the U.S. Minister to Russia, Cassius M.

Clay, for Goldstone's bid to procure the lease, but had no more success than Senator Gwin before him, even though he was a friend from school days of Secretary of State William H. Seward. By this time, however, the Russians were beginning to consider selling out not just the H.B.C. lease, but their entire Alaska holdings.

The U.S. had always been concerned about Russia's presence on the North American continent. That fear had been a factor in the proclamation of the Monroe Doctrine in 1823. For their part, the Russians were aware the Alaska colony would be indefensible in time of war. As long as the profits continued, however, there was no interest in pulling out.

Eventually, as the sea otter population was reduced by slaughter to the point that profits were declining, Russia decided to expand in another area closer to home, the Amur River valley of China. The last lease of the Russian-American Fur Company had expired in 1861 and was not renewed. Its affairs were taken over by the government, which took only a desultory interest.

In December of 1866 Emperor Alexander II and his advisers decided the time had come to relinquish the colony. The United States was the logical country to approach. Relations were good at that time between the two nations. The Russians had conspicuously supported the North during the American Civil War, while many Britons had been openly sympathetic to the Confederacy.

The Russian minister in Washington, Baron Edouard de Stoeckl, who made the initial overtures, had a most willing listener in Seward. The feisty little secretary of state, an unexpected loser in the 1860 presidential nominations to an obscure Illinois politician named Abraham Lincoln, was an ardent expansionist. Seward had long coveted Canada and had urged U.S. capitalists to buy up the rights of the Hudson's Bay Company. He also backed a proposal made at the end of the Civil War that Britain cede her colonies of British Columbia and Vancouver Island to the U.S. in payment of damage claims arising from the war. But Canada was in a nationalistic mood herself by 1867 and there was little support for the idea there.

So Seward had to be content with buying Alaska. He offered $5,000,000 to de Stoeckl, but that figure was eventually raised in negotiations to $7,200,000. The Russian treasury actually received only $7,000,000 — de Stoeckl used $200,000 to buy the votes of Congressmen who had condemned the deal as "Seward's Folly." The Russian envoy had a personal incentive to complete the transaction — he had been promised a $20,000 bonus by the Emperor when the treaty was ratified. In May, 1867, he received his reward.

There was another Russian who benefitted in a direct way from the Purchase: Prince Dimitri Petrovich Maksutof. Since 1863 Maksutof had been the government's chief manager in Sitka of the Russian-American Company. By June of 1867 adventurers and profiteers were on the Prince's doorstep trying to make a deal. The competition was intense and many merchants from Victoria and San Francisco made exploratory trips to Sitka in 1867 and 1868 disguised as fishing or hunting expeditions.

Among the first contingent were two American citizens operating out of Victoria, Leopold Boscowitz and Captain William Kohl. Boscowitz operated a fur-buying store with his brother Joseph at Wharf and Bastion Streets, one of the city's first business establishments. They also owned a tobacconist's shop nearby. Leopold later moved to San Francisco and played a leading role in the formation of the Alaska Commercial Company. The brothers were born in Bavaria and emigrated to the eastern U.S. with their parents before going off on their own to San Francisco and then Victoria.

Kohl, of Pennsylvania Dutch origin, was involved in a number of enterprises, some of a dubious nature. A builder and owner of ships, he also promoted coal fields developed by California capital in Bellingham, Washington Territory. The mines were "inexhaustible," Kohl told potential Victoria investors in 1866.

Both men knew Prince Maksutof from earlier business dealings, and when Boscowitz arrived in Sitka in the fall of 1867 he approached the Prince about buying furs stored in the Russian-American Company's warehouse. Maksutof offered to let him have them all, but the cautious Boscowitz took only 16,000 at the bargain price of 40 cents apiece. After selling these for up to $3 each in Victoria, he later came back for more, but was too late.

Boscowitz and Kohl teamed with Captain Gustav Niebaum during their first visit to Sitka after the Purchase. Niebaum was a Finnish-born employee of the Russian-American Company. Although a Russian subject, he elected to take advantage of a Treaty clause allowing him to take out U.S. citizenship at the time of the Purchase. Niebaum promptly bought the 162-ton brig *Constantine* from Maksutof for $4,000 and was setting off for the Pribilofs to pick up some fur seal pelts when approached by Kohl and Boscowitz. They joined forces and later sailed for San Francisco with 30,000 pelts, which were sold to a fur dealer associate of Boscowitz, August Wassermann, who was also taken into the firm. (Wassermann was said to have begun his commercial career by importing cats from the East to combat a plague of rats in San Francisco.)

Another vessel involved in these early transactions was the *Fideliter*, a 105-ton "jobbing steamship" which not long after arriving on the coast from England had been sunk in a collision with the sternwheeler *Alexandria* off Victoria's Clover Point. After being raised and refitted she was purchased by Kohl. Because of his American citizenship, Kohl registered the vessel in the name of John Dutnell of Victoria. In June of 1867, claiming to be acting for Dutnell but actually for himself, he made a sham sale to Joseph Lugebil, a Russian citizen in Sitka. The object of these transactions was to switch the *Fideliter* to American registry after the Transfer was effected. A number of lawsuits ensued and in 1869 she was confiscated briefly by the U.S. government on grounds of fraud. Customs Collector W. S. Dodge of Sitka was alleged to have connived with Kohl in the scheme. Everyone wanted a piece of the action in that heady period.

Meanwhile, a new man had arrived on the scene who would score the biggest coup of all. Hayward M. Hutchinson was a young Baltimore business-man who made his first money in the Civil War. With his brother Elias, he was awarded a contract to supply tin and iron kettles to the Union army. During the war he became friendly with General Lovell H. Rousseau, who was later designated by Washington to formally accept Alaska from the Russians at Sitka. Hutchinson was looking for new business opportunities after the war and Rousseau persuaded him to go west as his private secretary. A partner, Abraham Hirsch, also went along.

When Rousseau left San Francisco September 27 on the warship *Ossipee* for Sitka, Hutchinson stayed behind, seeking capital for the deals he intended to make in the north. One of the first men he approached was Louis Sloss, who had come west in a covered wagon in 1849 from Missouri and made his fortune in wool, hides and mining stocks. Sloss was a stocky, genial man; Hutchinson tall and urbane. The two hit it off and Sloss took Hutchinson to meet some of his wealthy San Francisco associates, including his brother-in-law and life-long partner, Louis Gerstle. Sloss had first became interested in the possibilities of Alaska as a member of the ill-fated Goldstone venture. He knew huge profits were possible because Russian property transferred to U.S. jurisdiction by the treaty could be imported duty-free.

The fur industry in California at that time was controlled almost exclusively by Jews who had learned their trade in Eastern Europe before emigrating to the United States. A grandson of Louis Sloss has written that "there was a sort of informal freemasonry among the German Jews of the time throughout the U.S." and Hirsch was undoubtedly useful to Hutchinson in his dealings with this group. He probably carried a letter of introduction to Sloss.[10]

General Rousseau and Prince Maksutof signed the transfer papers at a ceremony in Sitka on October 18, 1867. Princess Maria wept as the Russian flag was hauled down for the last time. The feelings of her husband are not recorded. Perhaps he was too engrossed in dispensing the company assets to worry about the loss of his position. Despite the money he was making on the side in these transactions, it was not a task the Prince enjoyed. A former naval officer, he found the constant haggling distasteful.

Hutchinson and Hirsch did not reach Sitka until December. They sought out Maksutof immediately and Hutchinson's charming manner captivated the Russian aristocrat. Although he had already made a tentative sale of the company's assets to San Francisco financier J. Mora Moss, Maksutof was persuaded to change his mind. "You have treated me like gentlemen," he told Hutchinson and Hirsch. "You are the only men who have not tried to beat me out and cut my prices."

They agreed to pay $350,000 for the principal company assets. Maksutof also made other, separate agreements with the pair. He told them of some 70,000 fur seal pelts in the St. Paul Island warehouse that were not included in the company property list, offering them at $1 each.

There was also the sidewheel steamer *Politkofsky*, the last vessel constructed in the Russian shipyard at Sitka, to be disposed of. A former gunboat built of cedar planking fastened with hand-made copper spikes and outfitted with an expensive copper boiler and engines made in Baltimore, she went first to Hutchinson-Hirsch for $4,000 and a year later to Hutchinson-Kohl for $8,000. Snub-nosed and boxy, the *Politkofsky*, or "Polly" as she came to be known, was not a handsome craft. On her way south in April under the command of Captain Kohl, the *British Colonist* of Victoria commented caustically that she "is one of the most magnificent specimens of home-made marine architecture we have yet beheld. She looks as if she had been thrown together after dark by an Indian ship carpenter, with stone tools." The newspaper added that the boiler alone was worth more than the purchase price, which proved to be the case when it was removed in San Francisco and sold. The *Polly* later worked as a towboat on Puget Sound before ending her days at St. Michael in Norton Sound during the 1898 gold rush.[11]

With Hutchinson firmly in the driver's seat, the various individuals and partnerships which had been wooing Prince Maksutof began to coalesce. Hirsch dropped out — or was ousted by Hutchinson — early in 1868. Hutchinson, backed by Sloss and Gerstle, and another associate of theirs, Simon Greenewald, then merged with William Kohl, and the firm of Hutchinson-Kohl & Co. was created in February. Kohl's main contribution was the *Fideliter*. When Niebaum arrived in San Francisco March 2 with the *Constantine* and another load of fur seal pelts, he was also invited into the firm. The *Constantine*, bought for $4,000, was now sold for $35,000. In addition, goods which had been purchased through Maksutof for $155,000, including such items as 10,600 gallons of seal oil, were shipped to San Francisco by Hutchinson-Kohl and sold for $241,181.

The *Constantine*'s voyage south from Sitka had not been without incident. She was holed on a rock off Discovery Island near Victoria but stayed afloat. Although an inspection showed damage was slight, Hutchinson-Kohl claimed that furs and other freight valued at $10,000 had been lost. An owner of one of the lots of furs aboard, David Shirpser of Victoria, not believing the shipowners' story, snooped around Leopold Boscowitz' backyard. There he found a number of casks of furs stamped with his name hidden under a shed. Shirpser went to court and got an order for the arrest of Hutchinson, who posted $10,000 in bonds to gain his release. Eventually the case was settled out of court.

Shirpser had moved to Victoria from San Francisco in 1860 and with his brother Herman, established Cheap John Clothiers and Auctioneers on Johnson Street. He left Victoria for Sitka in May of 1867 and set up a grocery business and auction house. He later expanded his business to include a general store on Kodiak Island and 14 trading posts and a number of small trading vessels. Shirpser became one of the most vocal critics of the Alaska Commercial Company monopoly.[12]

The *Fideliter* was also involved in a scrape with the law. After the steamer made a trading voyage along the coast in 1868 the U.S. Customs Service obtained evidence that Captain M. C. Erskine was trading liquor to the Aleuts and Indians for furs. The vessel was confiscated the following year, but later released.

By now the firm that was to dominate Alaskan trade for the first 20 years under American rule was beginning to take shape. Its principal architects were Hutchinson and Sloss. On September 17, 1868, the Alaska Commercial Company was officially formed when incorporation papers were filed with the county clerk in San Francisco. It was capitalized at $2,000,000. For $1,729,000 the new firm took over all the Hutchinson-Kohl assets, which by now included furs worth $870,000, some 45 trading stations scattered about Alaska valued at $200,000, buildings assessed at $80,000, and three steamships worth $195,000.

Sloss became the first president. He and Hutchinson decided the objectives of the A.C.C. would be to develop mercantile trade in the area and obtain a lease from the government to control the valuable Pribilof Island fur seal business. They appeared to be in a commanding position to achieve both goals, but soon discovered that other powerful interests had similar designs on the Pribilofs.

On March 28, 1868, Captain Ebenezer Morgan of the Boston whaler *Peru*, based in Honolulu, sailed out of Sitka on a "whaling and sealing voyage" to the Pribilofs. When the *Peru* dropped anchor off St. Paul, Morgan claimed possession of the island. He did so, according to legend, by showing the Russian agent still in charge of the island a masonic membership certificate. It also turned out that the vessel was loaded with building materials to establish a base on the island.

Three weeks later Gustave Niebaum arrived on the *Fideliter* at St. Paul and found men working for Morgan staking claims on the rookeries. Niebaum managed to drive them off, but two weeks later Morgan was back. He raised the American flag and prepared to kill seals. The best solution seemed to be to join forces to block other sealers hovering around the Pribilofs. In June three schooners outfitted by San Francisco banker John Parrott arrived and were persuaded by Niebaum and Morgan to confine their activities to St. George Island, where they proceeded to take 80,000 skins. The profits on these enabled Parrott to buy into the A.C.C. and become a director. Morgan's employer, the firm Williams, Havens and Co. of New London, Connecticut, with world-wide shipping interests, did even better, acquiring 30 percent of the A.C.C. stock.

While all the wheeling and dealing was going on in Sitka, the sealers were having a bonanza on the Pribilofs. Thomas Morgan, son of Ebenezer and himself an employee of the A.C.C., later estimated that 240,000 skins were taken in 1868 alone, 65,000 of them on St. George. Many were smuggled to foreign ports, including Honolulu in the Sandwich Islands. Some 85,000 walrus were also slaughtered between 1869 and 1874, wiping out the Pribilof herd. Even the Aleuts, who had long suffered under the harsh treatment of the Russians, were alarmed by this new orgy of reckless slaughter by the Americans. They bravely tried to curb the killing of females.[13]

When word of the carnage filtered back to Washington, Congress temporarily banned all killings. The order did not reach the islands until the fall, however, too late to end the butchery. The Congressional order gave responsibility for management of the seal herd to the Treasury Department. In March of 1869 the Pribilofs were declared a special government reservation on which it was unlawful for anyone to land without permission of the Secretary of the Treasury.

In 1869 the two firms of Hutchinson-Kohl and Williams, Havens & Co. were the only ones allowed to take furs. Although the Treasury officers sent to the islands said they could take only the minimum number of seals needed to supply the natives with food, the total number of skins reported was 85,901, far in excess of any food requirements since the total Aleut population at that time was only 371. The man who helped the firms get around the limit by permitting the Aleuts to sell skins to them was H. H. McIntyre, the top Treasury agent on the islands, who was soon to be rewarded by the grateful A.C.C.

Meanwhile, the man who did the most to help the A.C.C. gain its monopoly, Maksutof, returned to Russia, a forgotten figure. Two years later, however, the company called on his services again. In 1871 the Russian government granted a lease to the A.C.C. to harvest its Commander Islands fur seals. When St. Petersburg stipulated that a Russian citizen be appointed a director to represent the government, the A.C.C. executed yet another crafty move. The old firm of Hutchinson-Kohl & Co. was resurrected and its name changed to "Hutchinson, Kohl, Maksutof and Company." As soon as this firm obtained the Russian lease, it designated the A.C.C. as its operating agent. The company's vessels flew the Russian flag but were registered in the United States. So for 20 years, until the lease ended in 1891, the Bering and Copper Island operations were directed from A.C.C. headquarters at 310 Sansome Street, San Francisco. A company employee on the Pribilofs, Captain Daniel Webster, was sent to the Commanders to teach the natives the Aleut methods of taking and curing skins, which were shipped to San Francisco by way of

Petropavlosk. Through careful management the harvest was increased from 30,000 skins annually at the beginning of the contract to 50,000 by 1891.

The Prince gave up his salaried sinecure within two years, investing his Alaska profits in a Volga River canal project. When that venture failed, he declared bankruptcy in 1879. Not long afterward when A.C.C. vice-president Gustave Niebaum, now a wealthy man, was visiting St. Petersburg he was importuned by Maksutof. Niebaum gave him a paltry $250.

CHAPTER THREE

Sitka

*The fur seals are not more entitled to the protection of the law
than the Indian, the buffalo, or beaver.*

— Furrier THEODORE LUBBE

The Alaska Commercial Company skilfully manipulated Congress into
giving it the inside track to domination of the Pribilof fur trade. And as far as
the Congressmen and Senators who approved Seward's Purchase were
concerned, there was nothing else in Alaska but the fur seals. The seals had
made money for the Russians and now would do the same for the Americans.

After a protracted debate, Congress passed its third version of the Fur
Seal Bill on July 1, 1870. The government's minimum terms were a $50,000
annual rental and $2 per skin. Bids were called and when 14 were opened
in Washington on July 20 the lowest had been submitted by the A.C.C.
The highest bid of $55,000 rent and $2.62½ per skin was submitted by Louis
Goldstone, acting for a San Francisco group that included the American-
Russian Commercial Company.

As the result of some behind-the-scenes manoeuvring, believed to have
been directed by the ubiquitous Senator Cole, Goldstone suddenly withdrew
his bid. The A.C.C. was allowed to match his offer of $2.62½ per pelt and was
awarded the contract after agreeing to furnish food, fuel and schools for the
Aleuts. After the posting of a $500,000 bond, the lease was signed August 3 by
Treasury Secretary George S. Boutwell despite his earlier opposition to a
private monopoly. At one point Boutwell had proposed that the government
manage the fur seal harvest itself, but his plan was attacked by the Eastern
press and found little support in Congress.

The official rationale was that the A.C.C. was the only bidder with
sufficient expertise and capital to carry out the lease. General Miller, the San
Francisco Customs Agent who had played such a key role in the wheeling and
dealing leading up to the lease, pointed out that it would have been difficult
for any other firm to carry out its terms because all the buildings and
equipment on the islands belonged to the A.C.C. as a result of the Hutchinson
coup. When the lease was assigned, the A.C.C. claimed inflated capital
holdings of $9,000,000 on the Pribilofs and 50 trading posts scattered around

the territory. Miller, a former Indiana lawyer who had fought alongside Ulysses Grant in the Civil War and maintained good connections in Washington, got his reward later that year when he took his place at the head of the A.C.C. board of directors, replacing Sloss, who had resigned.

Resentment against the A.C.C. monopoly was quick to surface, and continued throughout the term of the lease. The *Alta California* expressed astonishment at the proposal to turn over the entire territory to a single firm. It claimed that not only politicians, but newspaper editors and reporters had been bribed to support the Bill enacting the lease. The A.C.C. was described as a "knot of jobbing speculators" to whom the poor Aleuts would be "handed over, body and soul, to the tender mercies of a single grasping firm."

These views were echoed by the *Evening Bulletin*, which declared that under the Bill "the natives would be fed on dried salmon as of old, and for religion they would be taught that 'the earth is Hutchinson, Kohl and Company's and the fullness thereof.'" The *Bulletin* referred to conditions in the land south of Alaska: "The experience in British Columbia and Vancouver Island is that these fur-trading monopolies are opposed to increase of population, civilization of the inhabitants, and development of the country. Their policy is to maintain a few hunters, with their families, whom they rule with a rod of iron, and keep in a condition of abject servitude, and to leave all the country outside their own scattered forts and villages a barren waste and silent wilderness."

In 1875 General O. O. Howard, after an inspection of Alaska military establishments, attached to his report, in a routine way as a matter of information, a pamphlet accusing the A.C.C. of criminal neglect and abuse of its privileged franchise. Entitled "A History of the Wrongs of Alaska," the document had its origins in a number of resolutions approved in 1874 by a group known as the Anti-Monopoly Association of the Pacific, based in San Francisco and closely tied to Louis Goldstone and his associates. More than 750 merchants and residents had signed a petition to the government. The Association said it had been published because its appeals to the government had failed and it was now addressing the public directly. Granting of the lease was claimed to be an "open violation of the Constitution and a flagrant breach of policy" which had been achieved through the "most shameless lobbying and corruptness of administration." The A.C.C. was using its power to crush rivals in the fur trade and other businesses. It placed obstacles in the way of immigration, exploration and even the federal government's coastal surveys. By forcing other businesses out, it had gained control over not only the Pribilofs, but the whole territory of Alaska. In short, it had been invested with the same power as the old Russian American Company.

The pamphlet said it was hard to prove that government agents had been bribed by the A.C.C., "but their favoritism was so undisguised and rewards they received for their services so openly distributed, there can be no doubt in this matter." The company was also accused of "tyrannical" treatment of the Aleuts, who were held in "a state of bondage and slavery" like a colony of convicts. Twenty-nine leading Aleuts had asked Congress for help in 1872, but the plea was ignored after the A.C.C. claimed their petition was fabricated.[1]

Goldstone later formally repudiated the pamphlet, as did San Francisco newspaperman Robert Desty, who had written a number of articles highly critical of the A.C.C. Desty admitted he had been broke and was paid to write the articles by the company's opponents. Much of his material, he said, had come from the *Alaska Herald*, a strident periodical published by Agapius Honcharenko, a Russian Orthodox priest who was bitterly opposed to the A.C.C.

A subsequent Congressional investigation into the award and carrying out of the contract concluded however that "none but experienced, judicious, and cautious parties should have been intrusted with the privilege" of the lease and the A.C.C. was "composed of capitalists of conceded strength and high character." The committee said the lessees had "faithfully complied with their part of the contract."[2] However, as one historian has commented on the manoeuvres involved in the A.C.C. coup, "the stakes were big, and the game was played ruthlessly in the field, more suavely in the national capital."[3] A prominent Alaska figure of the period, William H. Dall, said there was evidence that in order to crush the small businesses seeking to share in the bonanza, the A.C.C. had employed "force, fraud and corruption."

Under the terms of the lease, the company was to be allowed a maximum of 100,000 skins a year, 75,000 from St. Paul and 25,000 from St. George. It was barred from taking any female seals or pups less than one year old. Killing was restricted to the period from June 1 to October 31.

The A.C.C. was also required to supply the Aleuts annually with 2,500 dried salmon, salt and barrels to preserve seal meat, and 60 cords of firewood. The latter was subsequently changed to 20 tons of coal from Nanaimo. A school was to be maintained on both islands for not less than eight months a year.

There was time to harvest only 3,473 seals in the first year, and the company was quick to draw attention to its losses. But on the proceeds from 101,425 seals taken in 1871 it was able to declare a dividend of $200,000 in January of 1872 on 20,000 shares held by 16 stockholders. The lucky 16 did even better in succeeding years. In 1875 they received a 37.5 percent dividend on their total $2,000,000 investment; in 1878, 45 percent; and in 1880 a comforting 100 percent, or $2,000,000.

General Miller was not the only government official rewarded by the A.C.C. for services rendered. Treasury Agent Dr. H. H. McIntyre had played a hand in getting the lease for the company and persuaded the government to allow a higher take of seals than the Russians had thought prudent. Based on the estimated rookery population in 1867, the Russians limited their kill that year to 76,000. Despite the huge number taken in 1868 which further reduced the herd, McIntyre recommended that the annual take be 100,000. As one historian has noted, "he was the first of many subsequent government officials connected with sealing, suspected of more devotion to Hutchinson than to the interests of the American citizens."[4] Any doubt was removed when he accepted the position in 1870 of superintendent of the A.C.C. operations on the Pribilofs, a job he held for the duration of the lease.

Over the next 20 years a number of Treasury Agents were posted to the Pribilofs, most for just one or two years. It was not a choice assignment, a bleak outpost for those who had hoped for something better from a political appointment. One such was newspaperman Harrison Gray Otis, who after his term on the Islands, with $1,000 saved from his $10 a day wage and $5,000 from the sale of his Santa Barbara newspaper — which he had left in the charge of his wife — bought a quarter share in the Los Angeles *Times*, the genesis of one of the most powerful newspaper and real estate empires in the United States.

On his arrival at St. Paul in 1879 Otis did not wait long before showing he was a force to be reckoned with. The very next day he seized the schooner *Loleta* for having illicit furs aboard and sent her to Unalaska. But his three-year tenure on the Islands is remembered most for his battle to get the Aleuts off "quass," their potent homebrew. In Russia quass was the national peasant drink, a sour concoction made from fermented rye without sugar. The Aleuts had their own version made from flour, dried apples and sugar, to which they added berries which seemed to possess toxic qualities for some of its imbibers. Otis had this to say about the drink in a report to his Washington superiors: "Raw quass takes rank as the most villainous compound that ever traversed the human gullet, making the drinker not only drunk but sick also and unfits him for work, even after the stupor has passed off." A stubborn martinet, Otis twice cut off the natives' supply of sugar, and each time they quit their jobs in protest. They gave in when he threatened to bring in Unalaska labourers to take over their high-paying jobs as seal clubbers and skinners.

Henry Wood Elliott was a man of a different stamp. Frail health had forced Elliott to leave high school in his native Lakewood, Ohio. A self-taught artist and naturalist, he first saw Alaska in 1865 on an expedition sent out by Western Union to map the ill-fated Collins Overland Telegraph line. Elliott then spent two years at the Smithsonian before Spencer Baird of that Institution managed to have him appointed a special Treasury agent with an assignment to gather the first scientific data since Steller on *Callorhinus ursinus*. After arriving on the Islands April 8, 1872, at the age of 26, Elliott devoted the rest of his life to the fur seals. He made a meagre living in various small businesses in Cleveland in later years but never gave up his interest in the seals. His methods as a self-proclaimed expert were often erratic and always controversial.

A gangling, purposeful, mildly eccentric young man, he began making the first detailed maps of St. Paul and St. George. With notebook, sketchpad and survey instruments, Elliott tramped the beaches of both islands and traversed their gently rolling terrain.

Although both were associated with the Smithsonian, Elliott was unawed by William Dall's reputation as an expert on all things Alaskan. A month after arriving on the islands he wrote Baird: "This exhibition of seal life is really a wonderful sight and it has thus far been touched by Dall and (Treasury Agent Charles) Bryant in the most superficial manner, especially Dall. That which Captain Bryant has written is full of error from beginning to end."[5]

A year later the brash young Elliott wrote Treasury Secretary Boutwell: "I have to inform you that the report of Mr. Bryant, the Agent placed by you in charge of these Islands, is a perfect burlesque; his description of the Islands is a caricature, and every single paragraph that he has given to you and to the scientific world relative to the fur seal is either totally wrong or simply ridiculous." Elliott was already giving evidence of a later historian's description of him as "dogmatic, logical, intemperate, courageous, tactless, idealistic and fundamentally quixotic."[6] Or as another observed, "Mr. Elliott is specially happy in his epithets."[7]

He sent back more than 200 field sketches to the Smithsonian after his first season on the Pribilofs and completed a number of watercolours. The camera had not yet replaced the artist's depiction of natural phenomenon. His paintings, although realistic, have a haunting, romanticized appeal. Elliott was not lacking confidence in this field either. He told Baird he was confident his first watercolours would give him "an enviable name among Artists and win the hearty approbation and interest of men who loom up in the intellectual world." Indeed, later naturalists concluded that Elliott was a better artist than scientist. Said one: "While truth poured straight from his paintbrush it often strayed from his pen, diverted by his strong convictions."[8]

Elliott counted and delineated the rookeries, then set out to establish a census. He carefully measured the fur seal carcasses, the space they appeared to occupy on the beaches, the dimensions of the rookeries — and began to multiply. The figures he came up with were astounding and, as proved many years later, quite wrong. Elliott declared, with the confidence of youth, that there were 4,700,000 seals on the Pribilofs in 1873, "the lowest reasonable computation." When Elliott returned to St. Paul in 1874 he revised his estimate up to 6,000,000.

Despite a busy work-load, Elliott found time to court 14-year-old Alexandra Melovidov, the daughter of a former official in Sitka and an Aleut woman. Her father was a "Creole," offspring of the marriages between Russians and

Indians during the long colonial period. Elliott and Alexandra were married in July, just three months after his arrival.

After spending the winter and following season on St. Paul, the Elliotts returned to Washington in the fall of 1873 with the first of their 10 children. They were not happy in the capital, where Alexandra, a strikingly handsome woman, was spurned by Washington social circles as a "native wife."

Elliott was naive about many things. Like others before him, he was smitten by the easy charm of the A.C.C.'s Hayward Hutchinson. The company could do no wrong. It has been suggested that his marriage, frowned upon by the government agents, brought him closer to the A.C.C. staff on the island.[9] It is also true, however, that his views on the limited future of Alaska coincided with company policy.

On the eve of leaving the Pribilofs after five years in 1875, Agent Bryant believed he detected a decline in the size of the herd. He recommended to Washington that the quota for the following year be reduced to 75,000. That came as a surprise to the Treasury Department, since only two years previously Bryant had urged that the quota be raised to 130,000. Bryant was a retired whaler with a taste for liquor who had been farming in Massachusetts for a decade when he was sent to the Pribilofs by the government in 1869 with H. H. McIntyre. Like McIntyre, he had been considered a good friend of the A.C.C. Elliott reacted furiously when Bryant urged the cutback and persuaded the government it was unnecessary.

Another recommendation, more defensible, was accepted from Elliott that year. Although the quota had been set at 75,000 seals from St. Paul and 25,000 from St. George, Elliott found the actual population ratio on the two islands was 18 to 1, so the harvest was adjusted accordingly.

As well as submitting his report to the Treasury Department on his return to Washington, Elliott published a book on the Pribilofs and an article in *Harper's*, both of which played down the value of Alaska apart from the fur seals. There would be no need, Elliott wrote, for any form of territorial government or federal expenditure on such frills as post offices or light-houses. Education of the "better class of the natives" should be left to the Russian Orthodox Church. Fishing or mining would never be profitable. The climate would always "unfit the territory for the proper support of any considerable population." In other words, leave Alaska to be run by the dictates of the A.C.C.

Dall and the Senior Treasury agent for Alaska, William Gouverneur Morris, both foresaw the great economic potential of the district and wrote angry rebuttals. Morris accused Elliott of being "the enemy and natural foe of Alaska (who) decries and belittles the country on every occasion." Dall pointed out that Elliott had seen less than two percent of Alaska and "his actual residence has been confined to two little barren islands."

Mary Ellen *Close-Reefed in Northerly Gale*

Victor Jacobson

Charles Spring

James Christiansen

Killing ground, St. Paul Island

Nevertheless, Elliott's misguided advice had more influence on Congress than the others "because he spoke unequivocally with a most unscientific lack of caution, and because he said what the Congress preferred to believe."[10] And so Elliott at numerous congressional hearings became the most listened-to witness opposing requests for civil government in Alaska.

Despite his marriage to a native girl, Elliott seemed unconcerned about the welfare of the Aleuts. He considered them an inferior race and said so publicly. "The character of the natives of St. Paul Island," he told a Congressional Committee in 1888, "would be very properly summed up as one of docility and apathy. They are amiable, they are respectful, but they are indolent."

Wrong-headed and dogmatic as he was on so many matters, Elliott never swerved in his single-minded devotion to the fur seals. Their cause was uppermost in his mind at all times. As a leading modern expert on the seals has pointed out: "Conservation of marine resources is at times advanced by the efforts of odd-ball individuals, visionaries ahead of their time."[11]

During the 20-year term of its lease the A.C.C. harvested an average of 93,000 seals a year, close to its limit of 100,000, despite a steady decline in the size of the herd. When it chose to take fewer it was only in the interests of keeping up the price by not flooding the market. The company ignored the inroads of the small number of pelagic sealers, provided they stayed off the rookeries. But as the fleet expanded and the increased number of pelagic skins resulted in a price decline in the mid-1880s, the company suddenly became aware of the threat to its profits. It had spent $100,000 on an advertising campaign to popularize fur seal garments and did not appreciate others cashing in on its investment, and what it began to claim as its property, even when in the sea.

The pelagic sealers averaged only 7,193 skins a year from Alaskan waters during the first decade of the A.C.C. lease. After 1880, however, this figure climbed rapidly as more schooners joined the fleet. The Victoria-based sealers alone accounted for 12,500 skins in 1879 and 30,955 in 1886. In all, 50,000 skins worth $350,000 were brought into the city in the latter year, including the catch of American schooners. The average value of $7 a skin represented the landed price only. After they had been shipped to London to be treated and dyed by C. M. Lampson & Company, they were worth between $20 and $35.

It is also likely that the actual pelagic catch in the 1880s was greater than the official reports showed. A later study found, for instance, that the logbook of the *Mary Ellen* showed bigger catches than those registered by the Customs House in Victoria. The study suggested that some might have been sold in San Francisco. There was no accurate record of catches by U.S. vessels before 1890.[12] Theodore Lubbe estimated that 10 percent of the skins he bought in Victoria in 1885 had been obtained illegally in rookery raids.

In any case, the 50,000 reported skins taken by pelagic sealers in 1886 represented only a small proportion of the loss to the herd. Based on an estimate that six out of every seven seals shot by the hunters sank before they could be recovered, that meant a total loss of 350,000 seals, not counting unborn pups of females bound for the rookeries. The arithmetic gets worse. Since most of the seals caught in the Bering were nursing mothers seeking food, with a hungry pup on the shore and carrying the embryo of next year's pup in her uterus, the numbers become astronomical. It was little wonder the herd was declining at a rapid rate.

The sealers themselves, of course, would have no part of these statistics. They denied their losses amounted to six out of seven and insisted that half their catch was males. Schooner owner William Munsie claimed, in fact, that his hunters took only bachelor seals and lost only one in 50.

But there were a few responsible officials in Victoria who knew these claims were false and were aware of the impending disaster. Thomas Mowat, the Dominion Inspector of Fisheries for B.C., in his report to Ottawa for 1886, said: "This enormous catch, with the increase which will take place when the vessels fitting up every year are ready, will, I am afraid, soon deplete our fur-seal fishery, and it is a great pity that such a valuable industry could not in some way be protected."

American officials expressed greater outrage at the depredations of the pelagic sealers. Treasury Agent George R. Tingle in his report for 1886 said: "The logs of marauding schooners have fallen into my hands, and they have convinced me that they do not secure more than one seal out of every ten that they mortally wound and kill, for the reason that the seals sink very quickly in the water. If we did not allow these cheeky, persistent, insolent, British Columbia seamen to go there and defy the United States and its authorities, it would very soon be stopped." Tingle did not mention the cheeky American seamen sailing on U.S.-owned vessels.

There had been earlier warnings. In 1872 the Chief Collector of the San Francisco Customs Office, T. G. Phelps, told his superiors that a number of vessels were being prepared in ports around the world to enter pelagic sealing. Treasury Secretary Boutwell told him the U.S. did not have jurisdiction to curb their activities outside the 3-mile limit, a position the government would soon abandon. The legislation passed in 1868 had declared that "no persons shall kill any fur seal or other fur-bearing animals within the limits of Alaska Territory or in the waters thereof." The word "waters" implied a claim of jurisdiction beyond the normal three-mile limit, but this was never spelled out. Boutwell later claimed his reply to Phelps referred only to waters south of the Aleutians.

Elliott learned of the potential hazard posed by the schooners while aboard the Revenue cutter *Reliance* in 1874. He wrote of the danger in his book, but the chapter was allegedly dropped at the urging of a Smithsonian colleague who said the information would tip off the sealers, who did not yet realize that all the seals they caught off the coast were bound for the Pribilofs, and might follow them to the rookeries there.

As the number of schooners outfitted in Victoria and San Francisco grew from 16 in 1879 to 34 by 1883, the A.C.C. launched a campaign in Washington to have these vessels barred from Alaska waters.

In 1881 the federal government responded by declaring that all fisheries, including the fur seal, were the exclusive property of the United States between the coast of Alaska and the international dateline at the western end of the Aleutian Islands in mid-Pacific. Legal notices to this effect were placed in newspapers along the U.S. west coast. The government ignored the fact that a similar claim by the Russians in 1825 had been rejected by both the U.S. and Britain. The Americans attempted to make it clear they were asserting Bering sovereignty now for the sole purpose of protecting the seals. And so the Revenue vessels interfered with the sealing schooners only when they ventured north of the Aleutian chain, which became in the words of one observer, a "curious meridional boundary."

The edict was not fully enforced until the fateful summer of 1886. The events of that year marked the real beginning of the dispute over pelagic sealing, which would last for 25 years.

A number of schooners had been stopped and warned in 1885 but not apprehended. In June, 1886, Captain Charles A. Abbey of the Revenue cutter *Corwin* boarded the San Francisco schooner *Sierra* in the Bering 30 miles north of Unimak Pass. There were no seals aboard because her voyage had just begun, but Abbey seized all the guns and sealing clubs aboard and the *Sierra* was forced to return to port.

The *Corwin* had a colourful career before her involvement in the Bering seizures. The New York *Times* said she had "seen more active service and received harder knocks than any U.S. vessel afloat." Under Captain Michael A. Healy she had made seven cruises into the Arctic Ocean, including one 1,200 miles beyond Bering Strait to rescue a number of whaling ships caught in the ice. As a Revenue cutter she had a crew of 40, with four breech-loading, 3-inch rifles and two Gatling guns. Her low, rakish lines were designed for speed. Topsail-schooner rigged, she was said to be capable of 12 knots under sail alone in good winds and 13-14 knots with steam and sail.

A month after the *Sierra* incident, another American schooner, the *San Diego*, was stopped and boarded by the *Corwin* near Unalaska. When sealskins were found aboard, Captain Charles E. Raynor claimed they had been taken outside the Bering Sea. But a sharp-eyed *Corwin* officer uncovered 14 skins with fresh blood. Abbey promptly seized the schooner and turned her over to the deputy marshal of Unalaska.

On August 1 the *Corwin* intercepted a small boat from the schooner *Thornton* of Victoria with eight newly killed seals. The three hunters had breech-loading rifles and were about 60 miles southeast of St. George Island. Owned by the Warren-Boscowitz partnership, the *Thornton* was under the command of Captain Hans Guttormsen. Warren himself was in the Bering aboard his larger, faster *Dolphin*, which carried extra supplies for the *Thornton*. Both had auxiliary steam engines, but the *Thornton* was so underpowered she needed a tow from the 73-ton *Dolphin* to get through Unimak Pass against the tide, even though "under a full head of steam" and all available sails set. The 25-year-old former sloop was in a dilapidated condition. Her mainmast was broken off seven feet below the crosstrees and the fore-rigging had been carried away.

When Abbey and his officers boarded the *Thornton* they found 15 men aboard — 12 whites, two Indians and a Chinese cook. There were 20 freshly-killed seals on the deck and 403 skins below. When Guttormsen was asked what he was doing, he gave the obvious answer: "Catching seals." He was convinced he was violating no law. Eight other white hunters were out in small boats shooting seals with rifles and shotguns. When the boats returned they were also found to have dead seals aboard. The *Thornton* was placed under arrest. An officer and two crewmen from the *Corwin* were placed aboard and she was taken in tow by the cutter toward Unalaska.

At 6 p.m. that same day the *Corwin* encountered the *Carolena*, the former Metlakatla mission schooner now owned by William Munsie, who had purchased her from the Pilotage. The *Carolena* was under the command of Captain James Ogilvie and carried an 11-man, all-white crew. She was drifting with sails down and canoes out hunting. Dead seals were found on the forward deck and a total of 685 sealskins stowed below. The catch, comprising mostly females but including 12 pup pelts, was seized, along with five shotguns, four rifles, a musket and ammunition. Another three men from the cutter went aboard the *Carolena* and she was added to the tow.

At 5 a.m. the next morning it was the turn of the 35-ton schooner *Onward* of Victoria to become a captive of the *Corwin*. Owned jointly by Charles Spring and Alex Mclean, the California-built *Onward* was under the command of Daniel Monroe when she was seized 70 miles north of Unalaska Island. There were 16 Indians and four whites to man the eight canoes and one small boat. She had 400 skins aboard at the time of the seizure. The boarding party also found spears and 12 shotguns, six of which were owned by the Indians. Earlier the *Onward* had landed 600 skins from the coast catch at Kyuquot and entered the Bering July 12 with no skins aboard. On July 28 she had transferred 508 skins to the larger *Favorite* which under McLean already had 1,290 of its own skins. The 400 new seals had been taken by

Onward in four days. Twenty-five of these had been taken by one canoe the previous day, and had not yet been skinned. Three crewmen from the *Corwin* were placed aboard the *Onward* and she was ordered to follow to Unalaska. The little flotilla took 28 hours to reach its destination, where the skins were unloaded and stored in an A.C.C. warehouse.

At 2 a.m. on August 2, four hours before picking up the *Onward*, the *Corwin*, with the first two schooners in tow, had encountered the *Favorite*. The big schooner with its large crew seemed too much of a challenge for the short-handed cutter, and Captain Abbey merely warned her to leave the Bering. McLean had already caught 1,700 seals and was in no mood to give up such good hunting. He headed south toward the Four Mountains Islands and after sailing about 70 miles put out 20 canoes again, taking another 675 skins before heading home with a doctored logbook.

Meanwhile, the crews of the three seized schooners were kept aboard their vessels for a week in the harbour at Unalaska. Then the Indians aboard the *Thornton* and *Onward*, plus a few whites from each, were ordered to transfer food to the seized U.S. schooner *San Diego*, an aged, 38-ton vessel which then made an uncomfortable 12-day voyage to Sitka. The three seized Victoria schooners were left at Unalaska. One of the men crowded aboard the *San Diego* was John Margotich, mate of the *Onward* and interpreter for the Indians, who later operated a store at Ucluelet. Captain Ogilvie and mate James Blake of the *Carolena* were taken to Sitka on the *Corwin*, while the rest of her crew along with all the other whites — except the six captains and mates — were dispatched on the A.C.C. steamer *St. Paul* to San Francisco.

On their arrival in Sitka the Indians were "freed." In fact, they were now stranded 1,000 miles from home. The 18 *Onward* Indians had been paid $324 by Captain Monroe as an advance on their share of the catch, but he told Spring in a letter September 3 that they had spent this money on clothes and gambling. Margotich tried to help the Indians by throwing a few dollars out of a courthouse window for food. Monroe gave them an extra $5 and they scrounged around the town as best they could.

The six officers, meanwhile, were given the option of sleeping on the *San Diego* or taking over a jury room in the courthouse until their trial was complete. They chose the jury room and were held a total of 15 days with the captain and mate of the *San Diego*, but were allowed to walk about the town. Although they later claimed they had been mistreated, the men were regarded as something other than prisoners.

Harry Norman, also known as Tug Wilson, was mate on the *Thornton*. Despite his rank, which paid only a little more than that of ordinary seaman, Norman also functioned as fireman and engineer aboard the schooner, in addition to being boat-puller and boat-steerer when hunting. After coming ashore from the *San Diego* he wandered around the streets of Sitka looking for a place to sleep. After selling his watch to buy a meal he had enough left to take a hotel room for the night. The next day he checked into the courthouse jury room.

One man did not live to face trial. Captain Ogilvie of the *Carolena* left the jury room on the day before his scheduled court appearance and did not return. An older man, he had told Captain Raynor in Unalaska that he was suffering from a painful, advanced case of syphillis and had been treated by a doctor aboard the *Corwin* with potash, which might have affected the brain. Six weeks later, after all the other Canadians had left Sitka, his body was found by two Indian boys in alder brush about 100 yards behind the old Russian cemetery. His throat was cut and a razor was clutched in his right hand. "When I saw him first he was laying on his face," said Raynor, "and the doctor turned him over and the razor fell out of his hand."

First word of the seizures did not reach Victoria until August 19, by way of San Francisco where the *St. Paul* arrived with the 20 white crew members from two of the three seized schooners. A report was sent August 24 by Rear-Admiral Sir Michael Culme-Seymour at Esquimalt to the Admiralty in London. On September 9 the Foreign Office asked the U.S. for particulars.

Victoria's newspapers were slow to react. On August 26 the *Colonist* predicted "international complications" as the result of the "extravagance of the assumption upon which the seizures were made." The editorial accused the U.S. of taking rash action that was "bitterly unjust (and) manifestly illegal." The first *Times* editorial on September 1 was tepid in comparison. It seemed more concerned with seizures of fishing boats on the Atlantic coast. Even the *Colonist* conceded the next day that the U.S. had made a "possibly praiseworthy attempt to preserve the seal." It suggested the seizures might have been an American reprisal for the confiscation of some U.S. vessels in the Atlantic fisheries dispute.

The same connection was made by the *New York Times*, which urged Washington to ignore protests by Canadian sealing "poachers." The seizures "may suggest to John Bull that it makes a difference whose ox is gored ... the fishermen of Portland (Maine) and Gloucester complain that there is a sudden increase of stringency in the enforcement of customs regulations on the Canadian coast, but their complaints are not listened to by the Dominion authorities."

The Brooklyn *Eagle* was more critical of U.S. actions. It said that under the policy invoked, the schooners could have been seized as far as 500 miles from the mainland. The *Eagle* wondered whether the rules had been enforced only for the benefit of the A.C.C. The Portland *Oregonian* said the government had suddenly become more aggressive, changing its policy from one of defence to offence. The seizures were "manifestly illegal," the newspaper said.

Not unexpectedly, Victoria's shipping community expressed its outrage in strong terms, especially after the crewmen arrived home from San Francisco with embellished tales. J. A. Bechtel, half owner of the *Carolena*, marched into the office of the U.S. Consul in the city, Colonel Robert J. Stevens, to protest. He had in tow Thomas McLardy, the *Carolena* cook. The men had been shabbily treated, McLardy told Stevens, and arrived destitute in San Francisco. The acting British consul there had been unsympathetic to their plight. The consul told them they had been "caught at some illegal business outside his jurisdiction." Some hot words were exchanged, to no avail. The men slept on the wharf. Four men borrowed money from Welch, Rithet and Co., a Victoria-based firm, to pay their passage home. The others were advanced funds by J. D. Warren, and Munsie eventually paid the fares of the *Carolena* crewmen.

Lubbe also told Stevens he had written in the spring to Victoria Member of Parliament Edgar Crow Baker in Ottawa asking about the upcoming season. Baker had shown the letter to Prime Minister John A. Macdonald, who told him to assure Lubbe there was nothing to fear. Lubbe complained to Stevens that it was wrong of the U.S. to attempt to save the seals, which were "no more entitled to the protection of the law than the Indian, the buffalo, or beaver."

Stevens reported to the State Department that he had been unable to track down reports of illegal activities by the Victoria sealers. There were many rumours in the city, "where detrimental and slanderous reports are so remarkably rife."

Alexander R. Milne, the Chief Customs Collector and Registrar of Shipping, who identified closely with the schooner owners, expressed outrage at the "harsh and inhuman treatment" inflicted on the sealers. Without knowing anything except the first exaggerated reports, Milne said the men had been imprisoned in an "Alaska dungeon fit only for a savage Aleut."

Meanwhile, the trial of the captains and mates began at Sitka September 1. They appeared before Layfayette Dawson, sitting as an Admiralty Court judge. Dawson did not take long to bring in a guilty verdict. In his address the judge declared: "The purchase of Alaska was unquestionably made with a view to the revenues to be derived from the taking of fur seal in the waters of Bering Sea ... the industry and consequent revenues would be hopeless without the residuary power of the United States to protect and regulate the taking of fur-bearing animals in that part of the domain. The effort of the United States to seize and drive out the illicit piratical craft that have been navigating those waters for years, indiscriminately slaughtering fur-bearing animals ... is a legitimate exercise of the powers of sovereignty under the law of nations, with which no nation can lawfully interfere."

The two surviving captains were each fined $500 and jailed 30 days, while the three mates received similar prison terms and $300 fines. They were convicted on the grounds they had been "found engaged in killing fur seal within the limits of Alaska Territory and in the waters thereof in violation of section 1956 of the Revised Statutes of the United States." On October 4 Dawson ordered the three schooners confiscated on the same grounds. "All the waters within the boundary set forth in this treaty to the western end of the Aleutian Archipelago and chain of islands are to be considered as comprised within the waters of Alaska," Dawson said, "and all the penalties prescribed by law against the killing of fur-bearing animals must therefore attach against any violation of law within the limits before described."

Governor Alfred P. Swineford, a sharp-tongued critic of the A.C.C., intervened with Dawson on behalf of the Canadians and persuaded the Judge they should be released 15 days before the end of their sentences so they could catch the steamer *Anaconda* home on its last voyage of the year. Swineford said the men were "without means, and, had they been detained until the expiration of their sentences, they would have become objects of charity among strangers until the sailing of the next monthly steamer." Their fines were also remitted on their release. Warren advanced the money for their passage home but recovered it later. Raynor, the American captain, served the full 30 days.

Swineford, a newspaper publisher, was also noted for his sympathy toward the natives of Alaska, an uncommon attitude among the white merchants of Sitka. He urged Captain Abbey to see that the Indians were returned safely to British Columbia. Abbey complied by taking the 20 natives aboard the *Corwin* and dropping them off at Nanaimo on his way to Port Townsend. Charles Spring transported them from Nanaimo to Victoria, from where they made their way back to their west coast villages. Spring paid the Indians the balance of $1,816 owing for the seized skins they had caught, but they lost their canoes aboard the *Onward.*

Later that fall the A.C.C. sent an agent to Victoria to buy up the skins of the unseized schooners in an effort to "regulate" the market. The company offered $6.25 a skin. A number of schooners had scurried home quickly from the Bering on learning of the *Corwin*'s activities. One of them was the *Black Diamond,* now owned by Morris Gutman and skippered by Henry Paxton. She had been warned to stay out of the Bering by the Collector of Customs at Unalaska when Paxton called in for water in July. He carried on anyway and did not leave the Bering until the first week of August, but later put in a claim for damages for prospective lost catches because of "molestation." Warren brought the *Dolphin* home with 2,000 skins after he saw the *Corwin* with three seized schooners and scooted off.

In November the *Penelope* arrived from Shanghai under Captain Edgar Pratt Miner with a Japanese crew. She was a racy vessel, black-hulled with a gold band along the gunwales. Miner, who was from Santa Barbara and had been implicated in the desertion of a Navy paymaster from the *Ossipee,* sold 33 sea otter pelts to Lubbe for $4,000. Consul Stevens reported the skins were "dry" and had probably been bought in Shanghai to conceal the purpose of voyage, which was to slip back into the U.S.

From the wording of his courtroom statements, it was apparent that Judge Dawson relied heavily on the arguments presented in a pamphlet, "The Dominion of Bering Sea." The author was Noah Lemuel Jeffries, a former brigadier-general for the Union forces in the Civil War, now attorney and active lobbyist for the A.C.C. in Washington. In a letter to former Secretary of State Thomas F. Bayard in 1893, the pre-eminent U.S. expert on international law, John Bassett Moore, said of Jeffries that he "was the prolific source of most of the articles that appeared in the press — a fat, sleek, oil-faced man, not unsuggestive of a seal."[13]

It was later learned that Jeffries had also played a key role in the events leading to the unprecedented actions of Captain Abbey and the *Corwin* during the 1886 season. The Treasury Secretary had sent the usual instructions to the Revenue cutters that year, not intending them to be interpreted as authorizing seizures in the Bering. President Grover Cleveland and the other cabinet members directly concerned — Secretary of State Bayard and Attorney-General A. H. Garland — had never discussed the matter. The seizures were brought about through Jeffries' lower-level manoeuvring in the capital.

The Sitka legal proceedings were prepared without the instructions of the Attorney-General's Department. Judge Dawson relied upon Jeffries' brief outlining Russian actions in the 1820s, and presented the questions of international law on that basis. The brief had been sent by Jeffries to the District Attorney in Sitka, who passed it on to Dawson. When the Attorney-General belatedly learned what happened, he sent a telegram ordering dismissal of the case and the release of the men and the seized schooners. Because his telegram was not confirmed by a following letter in the usual manner, however, it was regarded by Dawson and Sitka Marshal Barton Atkins as spurious and not acted upon.

To John W. Foster, a future Secretary of State and key player for the U.S. in the international fight over the seals, this train of events "revealed the fact that a great government might be betrayed into a line of policy through the machinations of a private corporation, influenced by pecuniary motives, which put in peril its relations with a powerful neighbor and subjected it to the condemnation of an international tribunal for conduct taken unadvisedly and unwisely."[14]

The truth of his words was confirmed in the diplomatic storm that followed.

CHAPTER FOUR

Washington

Who is the poacher — the man who kills on the nest or the man who kills in the open field?

— STANLEY HILL, M.P.

The century-old dispute between Britain and the United States over the eastern Canada fisheries had come to a head in 1886. After the American Revolution in 1776 Britain agreed to allow New England fishermen to continue using the Gulf of St. Lawrence and offshore banks of Nova Scotia and Newfoundland. But following the War of 1812 Britain insisted on restrictions to curtail the growing American presence in Canadian waters. Friction had mounted during the 19th century as a number of vessels were seized.

In April of 1886 the American schooner *David J. Adams* was apprehended when it went into Digby, N.S., to buy bait for an offshore fishing voyage. An angry Congress retaliated by blocking Canadian fishermen from entering the harbour at Gloucester, Mass., where they had found they could outfit more cheaply than at home. Britain was anxious to avoid a showdown with the U.S. on the issue and the Colonial Secretary, Lord Granville, ordered a stop to the seizures. But Canada impounded more boats, on what often appeared to the Americans to be trivial grounds.

When Secretary of State Bayard protested to Britain, the Governor-General, Lord Lansdowne, reassured Prime Minister Macdonald: "Mr. Bayard apparently misapprehends our Constitution. The Imperial Parliament has delegated to that of Canada the power of legislation on matters affecting her rights and interests." Canada was flexing her little muscles.

But the responsible voices in Washington had no more desire for hostilities than London. When Secretary of the Navy William C. Whitney blustered in cabinet about making a show of force in Canadian waters, Bayard cooled him off. A calm, logical politician, Bayard had served in the Senate from 1869 to 1885. He sought the Democratic presidential nomination unsuccessfully three times before the election of party colleague Grover Cleveland in 1884 catapulted him into the position of Secretary of State.

Unlike his Republican successor, James Blaine, who would later heat up the fur seal dispute, Bayard was not a jingoist. He always sought rational solutions to American foreign policy problems, particularly those involving Britain.[1]

Bayard's job was made more difficult when the Canadian Fisheries Minister, George E. Foster, brought in restrictive new measures against U.S. vessels in the Atlantic. The seizures were resumed there and hostility mounted in the U.S. Feeling against Britain was also exacerbated by her refusal to grant home rule to Ireland, a popular cause in the U.S.

Seizure of the three sealing schooners in the Bering Sea came, then, at a volatile time. Lansdowne told Macdonald the American seizures were "far more open to criticism than anything we have done." There was a significant difference for Canada, however, between the two fishing disputes. On the Atlantic coast territorial waters were involved and Canada could act as a quasi-sovereign state. But in the Bering she must rely on the British because the seizures were outside her jurisdiction. Canada could not even control the schooners based in Victoria. They were registered under the British Merchant Shipping Acts and subject to their regulations.

In London the Foreign Secretary, Lord Iddesleigh, expressed concern at the breach of international law in seizing vessels more than 60 miles from shore. He instructed the British envoy to the U.S., Lionel Sackville-West, to protest.

Sackville-West was not highly regarded in Washington. Bayard considered him a "mere postage stamp" and in March of 1886 asked the U.S. envoy in London, Edward J. Phelps, whether he could prevail upon Westminster to appoint someone more suitable. Phelps replied that West had too many friends in high places to be removed.

It is not surprising that the judicious, hard-working Bayard did not take to the British aristocrat. West simply did not fit into the American experience. The fifth son of the fifth Earl de la Warr, he had no prospect of inheriting the family fortune and so at the age of 20 had entered the Foreign Office. He held a number of minor posts in British embassies around Europe before his appointment in 1852 as attaché at Stuttgart, where he met and fell in love with Pepita, a Spanish gypsy dancer. Unfortunately, Pepita happened to be already married. The marriage was soon ended, however, with the assistance of her mother seeking a better match, and Pepita lived with West until her death in 1871. They had two sons and three daughters, including Victoria, the mother of author Vita Sackville-West, who has written an engaging account of her grandfather's unusual liaison and lifestyle.[2]

West was a shy, taciturn man. When appointed First Secretary to the Embassy in Paris, he kept his family in the background. Pepita was not part of the Embassy social life but her existence was known and accepted by the tolerant British. Vita summed it up: "He was a peace-loving and indeed a lazy man who liked to have everything arranged for him and did not want to be bothered. Considering the very unconventional private life he had led, running parallel to the most conventional of professions, he had succeeded with remarkable skill in achieving his desire. He had managed to keep Pepita as his mistress and Queen Victoria as his employer concurrently for nearly twenty years."

When the widowed West was appointed minister to Washington in 1885, Victoria, a lovely young girl of 18, accompanied her father to act as hostess, even though her command of English was shaky at best. But her beauty, innocence and expressive gestures soon had Washington society at her feet. It was said that a smitten President Chester Arthur, also a widower, had proposed marriage, as did a number of other, younger men. All were politely turned down. In light of her father's role in the Bering Sea dispute, it is noteworthy that on winter outings Victoria wore a tight-fitting sealskin jacket and a little sealskin cap.

In October West passed on to Bayard the official British protest, which rejected the U.S. claim that "exceptional title" to the Bering Sea had been conveyed to her by Russia through the Purchase. Britain pointed out that the Russian "pretension" to control of the Bering had not been recognized by either the U.S. or Britain. Despite its generally hostile attitude toward Britain, the U.S. press tended to agree. The San Francisco *Chronicle* pointed out that the historic policy of the U.S. had been to reject the claim of closed seas — in the Baltic, the Black Sea or the Bay of Fundy. It suggested the 1868 Act banning the taking of fur-bearing animals in the waters of Alaska was probably unconstitutional. While headlining front-page stories on "The British Seal Pirates," and insisting that Canada must make concessions in the Atlantic fishery, the *New York Times* conceded that the U.S. could not justify a claim for such wide jurisdiction over the Bering. The *Times* called for "judicious diplomacy" to resolve the dispute.

There were dissenters to national policy in each country. Britain's largest fur dealers, C. M. Lampson & Co., which processed and dyed all the Bering sealskins, both for the A.C.C. and the pelagic hunters, sent a letter to Lord Iddesleigh pointing out that 10,000 people were employed by the industry in London. The company said if Britain blocked U.S. efforts to protect the fur seals, they would soon be exterminated like those in the South Atlantic: "We therefore earnestly trust the British government will see its way to give its friendly support to the United States in the exercise of their right to protect and preserve an article of commerce equally affecting the interests of both countries." Lampson was supported by the London *Times*: "If sealskin is to continue to protect the lungs of mothers in climes where the hardiest races of men are bred, extended protection should be afforded to the Pribilof Island fisheries."

In Victoria the first shots were fired in a propaganda war that would echo for years over which was the most wasteful and cruelest method of sealing. In a letter to Fisheries Minister Foster, schooner owner William Munsie denied that pelagic sealers lost more wounded animals than they recovered and said he doubted if the loss was as great "as that caused by the rejection of skins after being clubbed by the A.C.C. on the islands." British MP Stanley Hill asked the Royal Colonial Institute rhetorically: "Who is the poacher — the man who kills on the nest or the man who kills in the open field?" The Seattle *Post-Intelligencer* said, "considered merely as a manly sport, pelagic sealing is entitled to rank as high as the pursuit of any game in the world."

Edinburgh lawyer Andrew Wishart said "the seal hunter in his canoe with gun (seems) a much less destructive agency than the men with the clubs who drive the animals by thousands to their killing ground." The latter were "engaged in a work that requires no spark of courage, exhibits no element of skill, suggests no sentiment of romance." Wishart added: "But it is unnecessary to say that no man more than an Englishman abhors the slaughter of any wild animal during its pregnancy."[3]

Bayard told President Cleveland he was unable to find satisfactory grounds to justify the seizures. He recommended the prosecutions be dropped and the vessels discharged. Aware that Cleveland favoured the popular hard line against Britain — he was going to be seeking another term in 1888 — Bayard stressed that the Bering was "part of the high seas of the world, and equally open to the navigation of all nations." He told the President the dispute should be settled by international agreement, adding that Britain had a strong financial interest in preserving the seals.

Attorney-General A. H. Garland sent instructions to Judge Dawson and U.S. Attorney M. D. Ball in Sitka to release the three seized schooners to their owners. Bayard advised Sackville-West a week later that the action was taken "without conclusion at this time of any questions which may be found to be involved in these cases of seizure."

In a letter to Phelps in London, Bayard complained about British indifference "to the insolent provocation and irritating pretensions of the Canadian officials." Neither side seemed to know how to deal with the recalcitrant child. Bayard said the U.S. was reluctant to "bully" Canada. Lord Salisbury, the Prime Minister, confided to Phelps that Britain's role was that of a broker between the U.S. and Canada and she had great difficulty managing her Canadian clients.

As the diplomatic feud over the Bering seizures smouldered during the fall of 1886 while Bayard assessed the U.S. position, there was another problem to be faced. What about next year? On November 27 Lansdowne advised the Colonial Office that some sealing schooners were already fitting out for the start of the southern coast season around December 10. Assurances were sought that they would not be seized.

The Colonial Office suggested that Canada use legal avenues rather than diplomatic ones by appealing the Sitka verdicts. When Lansdowne repeated his request for assurances of protection in April of 1887, London replied tartly that his inquiry would "tempt the United States Government to ask in return whether they may depend upon being similarly unmolested in Atlantic waters."[4]

Feelings were running high in Victoria. The sealers were angered on learning that the U.S. schooner seized with the three Canadian vessels, the *San Diego*, had been cleared. While her case was being appealed to the U.S. Supreme Court on grounds the sealskins on board had not been caught in the Bering, Treasury Secretary Daniel Manning intervened with his discretionary power to overturn the conviction. There were reports, relayed to Ottawa by B.C. Lieutenant-Governor Clement Cornwall, that the sealers were arming to resist arrest. When Salisbury was informed, he ordered the Navy to disarm any schooners preparing for battle, even though such talk was all bluff.[5]

Previously, the owners of the *San Diego* and the 75-ton *Sierra*, which had been forced to give up her guns and 1,000 rounds of ammunition and was warned out of the Bering by the *Corwin*, had sent a strongly-worded protest to President Cleveland. The L. N. Handy Company of San Francisco accused the government of "preying upon the commerce of its own citizens." The *Sierra's* owners launched a suit in Admiralty Court in Boston for $22,500 damages for lost earnings. The Victoria sealers took up a collection to help pay the American schooner's legal costs.

On April 20 the Treasury Department issued an order cancelling clearances for American vessels on pelagic sealing voyages into the Bering. Sackville-West advised Salisbury that after the A.C.C. pressed the government for more protection against the schooners, a U.S. Navy vessel, the *Thetis*, had left New York to sail around Cape Horn and up the west coast to the Aleutians. With a reinforced hull to protect against ice, the *Thetis* had been built as a steam barkentine whaler in Scotland before being acquired by the Navy. After long service on patrols in Alaskan waters she was sold, ironically ending her days as a sealing vessel in Newfoundland in 1950.[6]

In May the Canadian minister of finance, Charles Tupper, went to Washington to meet Bayard. The two men agreed to attempt a settlement on all outstanding issues between the U.S. and Canada by setting up a Joint High Commission. Salisbury approved the plan in early July.

On July 20 word reached Victoria of new seizures in the Bering, all made by Captain L. G. Shepard of the cutter *Richard Rush*. The first schooner to be apprehended, on June 30, was the *Challenge* of Port Townsend, which was anchored off Akutan Island with 151 skins of females and unborn pups. Over the next two weeks four Victoria schooners were seized and taken to Unalaska —the *Anna Beck, W. P. Sayward, Dolphin* and *Grace*, as well as the

Lillie L. of San Francisco. All were more than 40 miles from land, with the *Grace* being 96 miles north of Unalaska.

The *Sayward* had been seized by the cutter *Bear*, which had escorted the schooner to Unalaska and then ordered her to Sitka. When the crew refused to go because they said there was no pay for them after being seized, Captain Healy of the *Bear* pointed to the hulks of the *Carolena, Thornton* and *Onward* on the beach. "Do you see those three rotten British hulks there?" he asked Captain Van Pelt. "Take her (the *Sayward*) down to Sitka, or else I will haul her over there, and let her rot, and I will put your crew on the beach, and take you down in one of the cutters as a prisoner to Sitka." Van Pelt and the crew complied.

The *Alfred Adams* was added to the list on August 10 and two weeks later the *Ada* was apprehended by the *Bear*. In addition the *Triumph* was warned out of the Bering by the *Rush*. In each case the skins were taken off at Unalaska and the schooners escorted to Sitka, where the captains and mates were held for trial on charges of hunting seal in the Bering Sea. The crewmen were "set free," which meant they had to make their own way home. When 50 Indians on the *Grace* and *Dolphin* attempted to stay aboard the schooners, they were ejected by Marshal Barton Atkins and spent a night on the beach in the rain before Governor Swineford ordered them returned to their vessels. Seventeen Indians and three whites from the *W. P. Sayward* set out from Sitka in canoes and a small boat, headed south for Victoria. They took 19 days to paddle to Port Simpson, where the canoes were sold for food. The men were stuck in Port Simpson a month before being taken on the steamer *Barbara Boscowitz* and allowed to work their passage to Victoria.

The Indian hunters from the *Dolphin* were detained in Sitka for 2½ months. They also sold their canoes for food. Some were able to pay their passage home on the steamer *Idaho* and were dropped off at Nanaimo to hike the trail over the mountains to Alberni. Two Kyuquot natives from the *Henrietta* stayed in Sitka over the winter and joined another schooner in the spring on her way north to the Bering. The Indians who reached Victoria later complained that they were not paid for their skins seized by the Americans. Each was out an estimated $300 for the season.

The captains and mates were released on bond but then had to ask for the bond money to be returned because they had no food. This was done and they were returned to the custody of the Marshal. Andrew Laing, mate and part owner of the *Sayward*, had enough funds to take a passenger ship from Sitka to Victoria while free on bail and make a report to Admiral Culme-Seymour at Esquimalt. Before returning north for his trial, Laing said the U.S. authorities had been courteous and the owners were confident they would be compensated.

However, when mate M. L. McKeil of the *Anna Beck* was released he asked Judge Dawson how he and the others were expected to get home.

Dawson replied curtly that there was plenty of timber and they could make a raft. Warren eventually paid McKeil's fare on the steamer, but collected the amount later. McKeil's wages lasted only to the time of the seizure.

The *Colonist* was in a war-like mood by now and said a number of Royal Navy gunships idle at Esquimalt should have been in the Bering protecting the schooners. There was too much diplomatic dithering, the paper said. It did praise the Dominion government, however, for agreeing to provide legal counsel at the forthcoming trials in Sitka. Victoria lawyer M. W. T. Drake was sent up to defend the accused schooner officers and seek release of the vessels.

A letter from Captain William Petit of the *Grace* added new information on the seizures. He said that while the *Sayward* was en route to Sitka the *Onward* came alongside during the night and took off all her guns and ammunition while the two prize crewmen from the *Rush* were asleep. Petit also reported that the *San Diego*, seized in 1886, was now hauled up on the beach at Sitka after 12 months at anchor in the harbour.

Warren denied telling Captain Shepard of the *Rush* that he sent his fleet to the Bering with the intention of being seized and suing for compensation because that was better than having schooners tied up in Victoria. He had not expected further seizures, Warren said.

Salisbury protested to Bayard that Britain had assumed from his note of February 3 that while negotiations were going on no more British vessels would be seized. Bayard replied through Sackville-West that after re-examining his note about releasing the three vessels seized in 1886 he could "discover no ground whatever" for the British to make such an assumption.

Once again Victoria was outraged. The *Colonist* headlined its story: "Another Piratical Act By The American Revenue Cutters." Captain Louis Olsen of the *Anna Beck* was quoted as telling the Sitka *Alaskan* it was "common talk" in Victoria before he sailed that the schooners would not be harassed. Olsen said no warning had been given by Customs Collector Milne when he issued clearance papers for sealing voyages to the Bering.

Olsen also offered an ingenuous defence: "I don't understand why my vessel was seized, as personally I was not engaged in catching seals. I purchase the seals from the Indians for the owners of the schooner, and I have no control whatever on the natives after they leave the vessel in their own canoes. I am not responsible if they catch seals after they have left the schooner's side; they can come and go when they please." That would have been news to the Indians. In the negotiations that followed, Britain wisely never attempted to pursue Olsen's line of argument.

The Victoria *Times*, a firm supporter of the Liberal party, seemed more interested in attacking Macdonald's Tory government than the Americans. It blamed Ottawa's "apathy and indifference" for not pressing the Canadian case in London and Washington.

Pathfinder *Boiling Home, Close-Reefed in Nor'uester*

Unidentified schooners near Victoria, 1883

Revenue Cutter *Richard Rush* at anchor

At Bayard's urging, President Cleveland partially defused the crisis by ordering the release of the schooners' officers. The men protested that after spending six weeks in detention for a crime they did not commit, they wanted a trial. The vessels themselves remained under confiscation. Sixteen had been apprehended during the summer. Five British schooners were confiscated and a sixth ordered out of the Bering. Of the 10 American ships boarded, only the officers of the *Challenge* were tried. Her skipper, Captain H. B. Jones of Seattle, was acquitted on the grounds there was no proof the seals he had aboard had been caught in the Bering. Some of the others ignored orders to go to Sitka and ran to San Francisco.

Early in September the schooners which had eluded the cutters began arriving in Victoria. The *Pathfinder*, under Captain William O'Leary, was first with 2,377 Bering skins and 437 from the earlier coast catch. Six hunters got 247 during a day's work in the Bering and one hunter, Joe Dupont, got 57 himself. The *Pathfinder*'s total catch was worth $20,000, a good profit for owner William Munsie.

Penelope was next with 1,500 skins from the Bering to add to her earlier coast catch of 1,324. On September 6 the *Mary Ellen*, with brothers Dan and Alex McLean aboard, came in with 2,457 skins for the season. When the *Black Diamond* arrived she blamed rough weather in her area of the Bering for a poor catch of 965. The canoes were lowered on only 12 days. "There would have been a much bigger catch had the Indians not proved such cowards, being afraid to venture out," the *Colonist* reported.

J. D. Warren arrived home on September 17. He had been master on the *Dolphin* and had stayed aboard her with mate John Reilly after the seizure. Warren said fog was to blame — when it lifted suddenly his two schooners were close to the *Rush* and unable to escape.

Also aboard the S.S. *Ancon* from Sitka with Warren was lawyer M. W. T. Drake, who said Alaskans generally disapproved of the seizures. Drake also confirmed that the schooners *Carolena*, *Thornton* and *Onward*, ordered released in January, were still in custody at Unalaska, a year after they had been seized.

It was October 12 before Bayard advised Sackville-West that because of "some misconception and mistake" in Sitka the release order had not been carried out. Renewed instructions had been sent, Bayard said. But Dawson wasn't easily cowed. He proceeded to order the sale of the seized guns and ammunition, which in the original telegram had been ordered released. In Bayard's second order they had not been mentioned.

By now it was almost too late to do anything about the three schooners. Warren said it would be too costly to refit them for the voyage to Victoria. The *Thornton* and *Onward* were lying on the beach near Unalaska, while the *Carolena* rode at anchor in the harbor, stripped of all her outfit and running gear. She was later hauled up on the shore alongside the others.

Warren was sent to Ottawa that fall—with Joe Boscowitz paying his fare—to draw up legal declarations of claims for damages to be presented to the U.S. for the seizures of the past two seasons. The claims included $36,817 for the *Thornton*, $23,867 for the *Onward* and $24,313 for the *Carolena*, which included the estimated lost catch in 1886 in addition to the seized skins. As well as these claims for the vessels, Captains Daniel Monroe and Hans Guttormsen claimed $8,000 each in personal damages, and mates John Margotich, Harry Norman and James Blake $5,000 each, the same amount as that claimed by the estate of Captain James Ogilvie.

When London learned the extent of the claims, it was aghast. "Consider the amount filed undesirable to present," Sir Henry Holland of the Colonial Office advised Lansdowne by telegram. "Claims obviously excessive." They were subsequently reduced.

The case against the *W. P. Sayward* opened in Sitka before Judge Dawson on September 17. She was the only schooner released on bond and was regarded as a test case. Captain George E. Ferey and mate Andrew Laing were accused of altering the ship's logbook to show that no seals had been taken in the Bering. Two Indians out in a canoe when the schooner was boarded were alleged to have disposed of their seals before returning. On October 11 Dawson ordered the confiscation of the *Sayward* and all the other seized vessels, but "out of generosity" released her officers. The judge neglected to say he had been ordered to do so by Washington.

This marked a change of policy by the U.S. government between 1886 and 1887. In the first year the vessels were released and the officers fined and jailed; in 1887 only the vessels were held, so as to allow appeals to higher courts. Six American vessels were confiscated in 1887, but three were released on bond.

In these cases Dawson openly acknowledged his reliance once again on A.C.C. lawyer Jeffries. In preparing his elaborate judgement he admitted being "largely indebted" to Jeffries for the collection and citation of authorities: "And for the want of books at my command upon this question, I am compelled to rely for historical facts upon his carefully prepared brief."

Two of the seized U.S. schooners, the *Ellen* and the *San Jose*, had been ordered to Sitka but went instead directly to San Francisco. The Treasury Department subsequently ordered their release on the grounds that federal officers in San Francisco had no jurisdiction over offences in Alaska, a ruling that would encourage other vessels to try the same tactic in future years.

One of the seized Victoria schooners directed to Sitka also made a run home. Captain W. H. Dyer of the *Alfred Adams* claimed his Indian crew mutinied and compelled the vessel to go to Victoria under the direction of a white crewman. Dyer and his mate, meanwhile, were detained in Sitka for six weeks before being released.

Bayard's conciliatory attitude was not widely approved in the U.S., even within the Cleveland administration. George Jenks, the acting Attorney-General, insisted the U.S. could assert jurisdiction over vast stretches of the Bering. He was among the first to claim the U.S. had the right of protection over the fur seals because it was their "usual custom" to return each year to the same home on American territory.

The most belligerent American official was Edward J. Phelps, a Vermont lawyer appointed U.S. minister to Britain by Bayard in 1885. Unlike many U.S. envoys to London over the years, Phelps never became an Anglophile. Rather, he retained "a Yankee suspicion of things British." Puffed with self-esteem, Phelps was not well-regarded by his colleagues. A friend told Bayard he was a "shoppy little Yankee attorney, quite dizzy over an elevation for which he was unprepared and intoxicated with swelling and swelldom." Complaining of British vacillation whenever Canada was involved, Phelps had advised hanging on to the seized schooners in an effort to force the British Foreign Office to come to terms. He told Washington it was putting too much emphasis on the principle of the closed sea, *mare clausum*.

Meanwhile, as British protests mounted against the new seizures, Sackville-West was busily relaying messages between Salisbury and Bayard. Salisbury's main interest was foreign affairs, and he continued to run that office as Prime Minister even though Iddesleigh was nominally Foreign Secretary.

On August 19, while the seizures were still going on in the Bering, Bayard invited Britain, France, Germany, Japan, Russia and Norway and Sweden to join in cooperative measures to preserve the fur seal herd. Russia and Japan immediately indicated approval — they both also owned rookeries — but Britain was cautious because the U.S., during prosecution of the seized schooners in 1887, had revived the claim that the Bering was an inland sea and therefore a *mare clausum*.

Bayard referred to the common interest of all nations in preventing extermination of an animal which contributed so greatly to the "commercial wealth and general use of mankind." The U.S. favoured a ban on pelagic sealing north of the 50th parallel between 160° and 170° west longitude from April 15 to November 1, he said. Bayard also suggested that vessels breaking the ban should be turned over to their own governments for prosecution. The reason for this proposal, he confided to Phelps, was that "I do not want to be obliged to define our claim of jurisdiction."

The U.S. asked Britain not to grant clearance papers in Victoria for vessels proposing to hunt seals during 1888 in the Bering. In exchange for such an agreement, Bayard would recommend that secret instructions be given to the Revenue cutters not to molest British vessels outside the 3-mile limit in the Bering while negotiations were pending. The Colonial Office took him at his word, but told Lansdowne the assurances should be kept "strictly confidential" so as not to encourage the sealers to go out. But the Governor-General said the Canadian Government could not prevent the sealers from hunting as usual during 1888.

Bayard came close to reaching an agreement with Britain, but it was turned down by Ottawa, smarting after the U.S. Senate rejected a draft treaty ending the Atlantic fishery dispute. The Secretary of State was now unable to hold back the tougher-minded members of the administration and Congress gearing up for the November election. Cleveland's Democrats went down to defeat. Benjamin Harrison and the Republicans were swept into office, ushering in a new, more difficult era in relations between the U.S., Britain and Canada.

Harrison was a quiet, sensible, thorough man, qualities offset, however, by the most powerful member of his cabinet, the mercurial James G. Blaine. Blaine had hoped for the nomination and presidency himself, but had to settle for the post of Secretary of State. The American tradition at that time was to appoint a powerful political figure to the post rather than the most experienced man in foreign affairs. Blaine and Harrison were never personally close and had an uneasy working alliance. Harrison regarded the brilliant but irascible Blaine as a rival.

Unlike his predecessor Bayard, Blaine was no friend of the British. Like many other Americans of his generation, he never forgot their lack of support for the North during the Civil War. Blaine had only disdain for Canada and was convinced the colony would eventually seek annexation to the U.S. His attitude toward Britain and Canada has been described as "always suspicious, sometimes hostile, never entirely friendly." The author of those words also observed that Blaine's weak points were "nowhere more clearly to be seen than in the Bering Sea dispatches, and yet nowhere else did he make more brilliant use of his abilities in defence of a weak case. It may, however, be said with equal truth that in these negotiations he appeared more bombastic than in any other controversy."[7]

Bayard turned over his office to Blaine on March 4, but would take part in the Bering Sea dispute again during Cleveland's second term in the mid-1890's as ambassador to England. During the 1888 election campaign the Republicans claimed Bayard had been outwitted by British and Canadian diplomats. There was some irony in the charge because in London and Ottawa the governments of the day were accused of being outmanoeuvred by the Yankees.

Blaine turned first to Russia, the other major rookery owner, for support in his stand against Britain in the Bering Sea dispute. He worked out an agreement with the Russian envoy in Washington, Baron Rosen, under which the two governments would issue regulations about the number of skins to be taken from the Pribilof and Commander Islands each year and the enforcement of a closed season at sea. They would apply to foreign vessels hunting around the rookery islands the same restrictions imposed on their own citizens. While contending Russia and the U.S. had a property right in the seals, Rosen admitted in a memo to the State Department that the steps the two countries were proposing went against "the generally recognized principles of international law in regard to the high seas." Rosen's superiors in St. Petersburg apparently felt the same way and vetoed the proposal. They did so without explanation, but Rosen later learned that the Russian Minister of Marine Affairs had persuaded the government the proposal would lead to complications with other maritime powers, particularly Britain, whose naval might the Russians could not match.[8]

The nature of his diplomatic power play had been acknowledged by Blaine when he told Rosen their right to protect seals would not be conceded by other nations until the U.S. and Russia had affirmed the principle and declared their intention to enforce it. Blaine's approach to the issue was also made clear in a note to Harrison critical of Bayard's softness toward the British. He bluntly refused to give assurances to Britain that the U.S. would continue the policy of not seizing schooners while negotiations were taking place.

On July 30, 1889, word reached Victoria of the seizure of the *Black Diamond*, the first seizure in two years. When intercepted 35 miles south of St. Paul, the *Black Diamond* had at first refused an order to heave to, but the winds were too light to enable her to escape. She surrendered after an hour's chase when the *Rush* steamed across her bow with guns levelled. Captain Owen Thomas showed the ship's papers to Lieutenant Francis Tuttle but refused to hand them over. Tuttle returned briefly to the *Rush* to confer with Captain Shepard, then came back with a five-man boarding party and proceeded to Thomas' cabin. A crewman from the cutter unscrewed the hinges of the captain's chest and removed the papers. Seventy-six salted seal skins and 20 Indian spears were also seized. When Thomas refused to take his schooner to Sitka, seaman John Hawkinson of the *Rush* was placed aboard despite Thomas' "warning" to Tuttle that it would take a large prize crew to force him to go there.

Thomas set out instead for Unalaska, where he hoped to find a British warship. There was none, and Thomas ignored Hawkinson's order that he proceed to Sitka, setting sail for Victoria. He later blamed the Indians, a common tactic of the schooner skippers, for his action. The natives had threatened to throw everyone overboard if the *Black Diamond* headed for Sitka, Thomas said.

After dropping off the 20 Indian hunters at Ahousaht, the schooner entered Victoria harbour on the evening of August 3, anchoring near the

Customs House. The *Colonist* was gleeful: "As soon as the news travelled through the city there was general excitement, and the plucky action of the skipper was the general theme of conversation." Everyone was glad he had outwitted the American cutter, whose mission was regarded as one of "legalized piracy." One of the schooner's owners, Alexander Frank, demanded that Hawkinson be arrested for piracy, but Attorney-General Theodore Davie wisely squelched that idea. Frank also tried unsuccessfully to have the Treasury Department pay for Hawkinson's board during his enforced voyage.

Hawkinson said he had put up no resistance after being told by a crewman that the Indians would murder him if the schooner went to Sitka. He had naively given his papers to Thomas for safe-keeping and the captain wasted no time in making copies for use in future legal actions. Hawkinson said he had been well-treated during the forced voyage and spent most of his time in his bunk reading Rider Haggard adventure yarns.

As news of other seizures spread, Canada's newspapers united in a chorus of indignation as U.S. policy in the Bering fostered a new spirit of nationalism. A number of editorials, expressing indignation at British sluggishness, called for Canada to be given the right to conduct more of her own foreign affairs. The Ottawa *Citizen* said American politicians seemed "intent upon forcing issues with a country whose people are rapidly learning to despise, not fear them." The Toronto *Empire* loftily accused the U.S. of taking advantage of the reluctance of more civilized nations to resort to force.

The New York *Times*, labelling pelagic sealing "an utterly barbarous business," said it was up to Britain to contest the actions of the U.S., which was merely upholding its own laws. That amounted to a curious concept of international law. The *Times* also noted that Captain Shepard had intended the *Black Diamond* should escape, as well as the *James Hamilton Lewis*, which made a run for its home port of Seattle. Even the London *Times* noted a "curious want of seriousness about the Bering Sea seizures . . . it appears to be intended to frighten away the Victoria sealers by sham formalities of capture."

It was true. There were more than 40 schooners in the Bering that summer, half of them American, and the *Rush* did not have enough men to put a prize crew on each vessel seized. Six were simply warned to get out, and of the five others seized, two more — the *Minnie* and the *Pathfinder* — fled to Victoria, each with a prize crewman aboard.

One of the schooners which made a clean escape from the cutters was the *Sapphire*. As the morning mist lifted, Captain John Cox saw the *Bear* approaching from three miles away. The steamer gained for almost an hour, but Cox set all the canvas the schooner could carry and the cutter was soon left behind. The *Sapphire* had 2,500 skins aboard.

The *Triumph*, under skipper and part-owner Dan McLean, was spotted by the *Rush*, but had time before the cutter reached her to skin 30 dead seals on deck and hide the pelts with another 72 under a deep layer of salt in the hold. After a warning from the *Rush*, McLean left hurriedly for Victoria.

There was another war scare when it was reported erroneously in the U.S. that seven British warships and two torpedo boats had rushed out of Esquimalt headed for the Bering. In Port Townsend Captain Shepard said he was unaware of threats made against him in Victoria, adding that he would take the U.S. flag and shake it in the faces of the city's angry citizens. At this point even the bellicose *Colonist* felt compelled to write a sober editorial declaring it was reckless to talk of war. It proposed arbitration to settle the dispute.

Meanwhile, a group of Victoria vessel owners headed by J. D. Warren met soon after the *Black Diamond*'s arrival to organize an association of sealers. They called for a mass meeting of citizens to register a protest. On Saturday night, August 31, Victoria City Hall was jammed for a public meeting chaired by Mayor John Grant to discuss the motion: "Resolved that the citizens of Victoria protest against the usurpation of jurisdiction by the government of the United States over the waters of the Bering Sea outside the three-mile limit and express their indignation at the repeated outrages to the persons and property of their fellow citizens . . . causing great loss to the commerce of our city and financial ruin to our fellow citizenry." The motion was enthusiastically approved, along with another resolution urging the Canadian and British governments to compensate owners and crewmen. There was no mention of the Indian hunters.

Two months later a new Governor-General, Lord Stanley, met a delegation of sealers at the Legislative Buildings in Victoria. Britain cared about them, Stanley said, and "difficult and delicate negotiations" were proceeding. The sealers could help their cause, he said, if they could prove that not many seals were lost in the water and that the females were not being slaughtered.

The total catch of 26 Victoria-based schooners during the 1889 season was 35,000, worth $245,000, with about half coming from the Bering. There were 225 whites and 300 Indians employed at sea. Three of the schooners seized and confiscated in 1887 were disposed of by auction at Port Townsend. The *Grace* brought only $1,525, the *Dolphin* $1,250, and the *Anna Beck* $970. The *Grace* went to Seattle owners who renamed her the *J. Hamilton Lewis* and later sold her to Herman Liebes of San Francisco. The *Anna Beck* became the *James G. Swan*, operating out of Port Townsend and Neah Bay, and the *Dolphin* was transformed into the *Louis Olsen*.

Coinciding with the auction, Robert Ward and Co. of Victoria, agents for the Union Insurance Corp., ran large advertisements in the *Colonist* offering to insure sealing vessels against "SEIZURE AND CAPTURE!!!"

Meanwhile, the 20-year lease of the Alaska Commercial Company on the Pribilofs was about to run out, and Louis Sloss said the firm was reluctant to renew. It had hired San Francisco journalist Theodore Williams to study the effects of pelagic sealing. His report showed the seal population was dropping, Sloss said, and the company was being forced to take younger and smaller seals. "Unless we could be guaranteed absolute protection against illegal sealing," he said, "we would under no consideration renew the lease."

Sloss was being less than candid. The A.C.C. actually entered a bid offering to match that of any tender. Despite paying the government some $8,000,000 over the last 20 years— more than the purchase price for the whole territory—the business had been lucrative. Annual earnings had averaged close to $1,000,000. But the North American Commercial Company was awarded the new 20-year lease by offering 10 per cent above the highest bid. The N.A.C.C. ended up paying $100,000 annually to the government, plus $9.62 per skin, and was forced to accept much lower quotas than its predecessor because of the reduced number of seals. In 1890 the quota was set at 60,000, but the company took just 21,000 seals after Treasury Agent Charles J. Goff, alarmed by the half-empty rookeries, ordered operations halted on July 20.

The president of the newly-formed company was San Francisco furrier Isaac Liebes, backed by Rothschilds of London. Soon after the lease was awarded, ex-Treasury agent George Tingle charged that Liebes had an interest in a sealing schooner. This was not proven until many years later, however, and in the meantime Liebes had hired Tingle as superintendent after he agreed to drop the allegations.

Secretary of State Blaine kept a low profile during the summer of 1889. He repeatedly rebuffed British protests over the seizures and refused to order them halted. In October Blaine attempted to open negotiations with Britain through Sackville-West's successor in Washington, Julian Pauncefote. He proposed that a commission be set up on which the U.S., Britain, Russia and Canada would be represented. Its first assignment would be to report on the question of a closed season for seals in the Bering. If Britain agreed, Blaine said, the U.S. would consider the question of compensation for previous seizures. At the end of their meeting, Blaine took Pauncefote by the hand and said: "I know that England and Canada consider me unfriendly, but I can assure you it is not so. I am most anxious that we should be on the best terms with both England and Canada."

Lord Knutsford of the Colonial Office was receptive to the new Secretary of State's conciliatory approach and hoped Canada was prepared to agree to a "reasonable arrangement" for a closed season. But Ottawa proceeded to lay down four conditions: 1. The U.S. must abandon any claim to *mare clausum* in the Bering; 2. Canada must be represented on any commission dealing with the sealing dispute; 3. Canada must approve the proceedings of the commission, and; 4. Britain and the U.S. must agree on the amount of compensation for the seizures.

These terms galled Blaine. He now said he did *not* want Canadian participation in negotiations for a closed season. What was needed, Blaine said in reversing his field, was not a commission but a "diplomatic conference," which by definition would exclude Canada.

Halifax

*When the spring came in, and the fresh sweet winds, I thought of
the quick voyage north under full sails, the lowering of the boats,
the big catches, the gay times at the ports . . . it's the adventure that
counts, the daring and the hazard.*

—Sealer VICTOR JACOBSON

The Victoria sealing fleet grew rapidly in the late 1880s, bolstered by the arrival of men and ships from the Maritime provinces. Just as the New England states provided the backbone of San Francisco's seafaring trades, so did Nova Scotia, New Brunswick and Newfoundland for British Columbia. The expertise for building and manning sailing vessels had existed there for a century or more, and now the lure of prosperity on the other side of the continent spurred the long and dangerous passage around Cape Horn.

There were an estimated 225 schooners involved in pelagic sealing in the North Pacific from its beginnings in 1870 until the ban imposed by international treaty in 1911. Of these, 48 came from the Eastern seaboard, 16 built in U.S. and 32 in New Brunswick and Nova Scotia. Most had been fishing the Grand Banks for cod or mackerel.[1]

First to arrive in Victoria to engage exclusively in sealing was the *Pathfinder* in 1885. William Munsie, himself a Nova Scotian, borrowed $3,000 from businessman J. A. Bechtel to purchase the schooner, built in New Brunswick in 1879. She was sailed out by Captain William O'Leary, among the first of many Eastern skippers to come to the Pacific Northwest to enter the trade. The voyage took 145 days. Bechtel wrote off $2,000 of the loan for a share of the profits, which grew to a peak of $15,000 in the 1890 season.

In 1888, Captain H. F. Sieward, who had been sailing out of Victoria for some time, travelled to the East to purchase the *Araunah* for the trading firm of Hall and Goepel. He returned in March, 152 days out from Halifax. Indian hunters were quickly recruited and the *Araunah* crossed the Pacific to Copper Island, where she was seized by the Russians on July 1 and confiscated. The crew was jailed for a time in Siberia.[2]

Making the passage around Cape Horn in these small schooners was often harrowing. In 1888 the *L. Houlett*, under Captain William Grant of Cape

Breton Island, was wrecked in the Straits of Magellan while en route from Halifax, but the crew reached shore without loss of life. In 1890 the *Carmolite* was stalled in rough weather off the Horn for 50 days without gaining a mile. The time taken for the voyage ranged from 254 days by the big, 124-ton *Sapphire*, to the record 108 days for the *Geneva* under Captain Sieward in 1891.

Sieward brought four schooners in all around the Horn. In 1891 he left Hall & Goepel to organize his own company, purchasing the *Dora Sieward* in Nova Scotia. She was sailed out by Maritimer Captain Sprott Balcom, whose brothers Reuben and Sam, as well as his son Harry and nephew Berton, also became west coast sealing schooner masters. Sprott Balcom later went into the whaling industry.

Captain Robert Esdale McKeil was born in Nova Scotia in 1857 and like many there went to sea as a boy, aged 14. (Captain John G. Cox, member of another large Maritimes family active in the Victoria sealing business, had started when he was only 10.) McKeil arrived in Victoria in 1886, returning four years later to bring out the schooner *Maud S*.

He set sail from Halifax November 13, 1890, with a crew of 12, including five Nova Scotians and three Newfoundlanders. McKeil's brother Andrew was second mate. Three days out the schooner ran into a hurricane. It was the worst storm he had ever seen, McKeil wrote home later to his fiance Sara Ada (Sadie) Smith, of Maitland, N.S. The skylight was smashed and the cabin flooded as the *Maud S*. scudded for eight hours under bare poles.[3]

A few weeks later McKeil marked his 33rd birthday while the schooner was becalmed in the Doldrums, giving him time for reading. He told Sadie that he had read short stories in the *Family Herald* magazine, but had also been stimulated by picking up Milton's *Paradise Lost*. "I think it is beautiful," he wrote. "I never read anything like it before. I am going to read it again."

On December 16 the *Maud S*. crossed the equator and was moving swiftly southward again. Tierra del Fuego was sighted January 15. The schooner took on water at Good Success Bay and on February 10 rounded the Horn. The weather worsened, however, as the long northward leg began. There was an unexpected meeting with the schooner *Annie E. Paint*, which was also en route from Halifax to Victoria, under Captain Alfred Bissett.

As the *Maud S*. crossed the equator northbound she met a passing schooner en route to Chile from Victoria. "I had to ask for something," McKeil wrote Sadie, "so I thought I would take a couple of barrels and pretend we were short of water, (but) what I wanted was some newspapers."

In his journal-style letter, McKeil reported that the vessel's goat had died. Its diet consisted mostly of newspapers, he said, and the animal "seemed to prefer the Montreal *Herald* and Detroit *Free Press*." But two days before it took sick, the goat ate a Halifax *Herald* for breakfast, "and it never was the same goat after." There was a brief funeral service and burial at sea.

As well as the goat, there was much sickness among the crew, with one man confined to his bunk for seven weeks with consumption.

Soon after reaching Victoria, McKeil returned by train to Maitland to marry Sadie and bring her out to British Columbia, where he continued in the sealing business.

Other Maritimers who became prominent in pelagic sealing included Captain John McLeod, one of the best-known members of the community of Nova Scotia sealers in Victoria. He brought the 70-foot *Ariel* from Halifax after she had been purchased at St. Johns, N.B., by Captain S. W. Buckman of Victoria in 1888.

Captain Laughlin McLean came to Victoria in 1886 from Prince Edward Island. He started sealing with the *Favorite* in 1889 and commanded her for a number of years. Until 1894 *Favorite* was the only vessel in the fleet unmolested by the U.S. Revenue cutters. Captain McLean made a study of fur seal habits and was one of the most successful hunters on the coast.

Captain Melville F. Cutler, born in Nova Scotia, after bringing the *Carmolite* around the Horn in 1890 returned to Halifax to take charge as part owner of the handsome *Agnes McDonald*, which became one of fastest schooners in the Victoria fleet after her arrival in 1892. At 107 tons and spreading 1,800 square yards of sail, she had the lines of a yacht and was known as the "queen of the fleet." The *Aggie* was among the first of the Victoria-based schooners to seal off Japan, making an unusually fast passage to Yokohama in 1893. She logged a record 307 miles in 24 hours during that voyage. Her career ended in 1897 when she was wrecked off Japan.

The voyage to the Asian coast took an average of 50 to 60 days. Most captains chose to drop south to take advantage of the northeast trade winds. Others gambled on the more direct route, hoping to ride the easterly winds on the north side of low pressure systems whirling across the Pacific. It usually took two to three weeks to reach the Bering from Victoria, but was quicker coming home. Schooners returning from Asia came via the Aleutian Islands.

The *Agnes McDonald* was among 12 schooners added to the Victoria fleet in 1892, eight of them from the Maritimes. An unlucky 13th vessel, the *Warrior*, was wrecked near Montevideo while en route from Nova Scotia. Notable additions included the *Umbrina*, brought from Cape Breton by Captain Charles Campbell. Built in Shelburne, N.S., with a copper-fastened oak frame, *Umbrina* was 98 feet long with a 22-foot beam and 99 tons.

During her third sealing voyage, in 1895, cabin boy William George, 24, kept a diary.[4] There are few such records. As historian Bruce McKelvie has noted, "the average log of a sealing schooner was a masterpiece of non-information." Little more than data required by the laws of the sea was recorded.[5]

The *Umbrina* spent two weeks in Victoria harbour loading provisions and preparing gear. Tanks holding 5,000 gallons of water were topped up and 18 tons of coal stowed below. Since the schooner was to be away nine months, the grocery list was lengthy. It included twenty 200-pound barrels of beef, three barrels of pork, nine barrels of butter, 120 bags of flour, 20 cwt. brown sugar and 3 cwt. white sugar, 6 bags of rice, 8 bags of beans, 9 cases of table fruit and 4 of pie fruit, 9 cases of condensed milk, 200 pounds of tea, 8 cases of coffee, and canned vegetables. One ton of potatoes was taken on in Victoria and another 3 tons in Yokohama. Fresh vegetables and meat were also purchased in Japan. The quality and variety of the food reflected the fact that experienced hunters were hard to find by 1895 and demanded the best. (If there were any provisions left at the end of the voyage, some captains would spirit them home to their families.)

On January 15 a steam-powered tug put a line on the *Umbrina* and towed her out of the harbour past Race Rocks, clear of tides, to pick up the winds of Juan de Fuca Strait. (Coming home, steam tugs such as *Magic* and *Mystery* would meet the schooners at Cape Flattery and offer to take them in for $100.) There were 25 men aboard *Umbrina*, all whites — Captain Campbell, mate Charles Dahlberg, 12 crewmen, seven hunters, two officers, a cook, and George. Until the schooner reached the sealing grounds two months later, there were few jobs for the crew except an occasional change of sails. The hunters worked on their marksmanship by firing at birds, or bottles tossed into the sea.

The *Umbrina* was an uncommonly happy vessel. In the cool evenings crewmen gathered aft to play cards and gamble, while others sang and danced or just listened to accordions, harmonicas, guitars and mandolins. A few boxed, wrestled or exercised on a rope ladder. Some men sketched and painted, while others traded dog-eared novels. A few read aloud to their illiterate companions.

There were two cats aboard, and the usual complement of bedbugs. In the tropics the men slept on deck to avoid the bugs and the heat of their cramped quarters. During the day some swam beside the schooner, with one man posted at the rail to watch for sharks. Rain-water was collected for washing clothes, which in dry spells were trailed on a rope in the wake for cleansing. Bathing was usually restricted to landfalls, where a fire was lit on the beach and water thrown over hot stones in abandoned shelters. While ashore the men also hunted for fresh meat such as deer or bear, and cut firewood. When moving slowly against tides in the Aleutian passes they trolled for cod and halibut.

Arriving March 12 in Yokohama, the *Umbrina* found 15 other Victoria schooners already there, as well as six from U.S. ports. The men were given small advances to buy trinkets or frequent the many sailors' haunts. During the week-long layover more water was taken on, as well as bamboo for gaffs.

Sealing began off the Kuril Island chain on April 18 with a catch of 27. The best day was May 6 when 168 seals were taken. On June 10 the *Umbrina* went to the Japanese port of Hakodate to get attention for a sick crewman and unload skins to be shipped directly to London by Canadian Pacific liner. Four days later the schooner headed north toward the Commander Islands. They hunted for two more months there before returning to Victoria September 25 with 1,749 skins.

Weather was a constant concern for the schooners. The coastal waters were considered more dangerous than an ocean crossing. Fierce storms boiling up in the Gulf of Alaska shallows generated huge waves known as "greybeards" or "grandfathers," which would break over the schooner decks like a cliff of water. They carried away canoes, small boats and any gear not securely lashed.

In heavy seas, oil-bags or blankets soaked in dogfish oil were dragged off the bow or stern to smooth the roiling waters. The result "was instant and almost magical," in the words of one observer. "It is certainly astonishing to see the effect of a small drop of oil on large breaking seas," wrote the famed round-the-world sailor Captain J. C. Voss, who also commanded a number of sealing schooners. "As soon as the oil strikes the water it will spread itself over quite a large surface, and as soon as a breaking sea strikes that part, it appears to crawl under the oil, and loses its breaking top."[6]

If the hunting boats were caught in a sudden squall a couple of seal carcasses were often made fast to the painter to hold the boat's head to the wind and seas. Grease from the carcass helped keep the seas from breaking over the gunwales.

But all the oil bags in the world could not save schooners caught in a punishing storm with no sheltering island or bay within reach. Many simply disappeared without trace, all hands lost. In a few cases splintered wreckage was washed up on a beach a year or two later. Between 1886 and 1895 some 33 sealing schooners foundered, half of them with no survivors. The toll was 231 men, 130 of them Indian hunters.

The 1887 spring season, which had been unusually stormy, claimed a heavy toll of lives and ships. One of the first ventures by the Nuu-chah-nulths in schooner ownership ended in tragedy. The 42-ton *Active* foundered during the night in a gale 30 miles off Cape Flattery. The wreckage was spotted by the *City of San Diego*. All 28 Clayoquot Indians aboard, young men from the village of Yarksis on Vargas Island, had drowned, along with Captain Jacob Gutman of Victoria. The *Active* had been built on Mayne Island in the Gulf Islands in 1885 by Gutman and sold — or possibly chartered —to the Indians. The surviving residents of Yarksis abandoned the site and resettled at Cloolthtich on the west shore of adjacent Meares Island.[7]

Another Indian hunter, Cultus George, was drowned when the schooner *Champion* was wrecked near Nitinaht Bar. The other crew members reached shore safely. The *Rustler*, owned by J. D. Warren, was driven ashore and broke up in the same area, but there was no loss of life. Warren later denied allegations he had deliberately over-insured the *Rustler*. Three men were lost and presumed drowned when their small boat was separated from the *Pathfinder* in thick fog. During a gale all the small boats on the deck of the *Allie I. Alger* of Seattle were swept away.

When the schooners prepared to leave for the Gulf of Alaska and Bering Sea in following seasons they often found it difficult to recruit Indian hunters. The loss of the *Active* had caused concern, especially among the southern Nuu-chah-nulth tribes, about the safety of such voyages. When the *Adele* stopped at Port San Juan none of the men were willing to sign on.

Although there were no seizures during 1888, there was a brief threat of confrontation that was avoided by cool heads in London. When Rear Admiral Algernon C. F. Heneage, Commander-in-Chief of the Pacific Station at Esquimalt, learned the British schooners seized the previous year were to be taken from Sitka to Port Townsend to be put up for auction, he suggested to the Admiralty that the convoy be intercepted by H.M.S. *Caroline* and the vessels recaptured. The Colonial Office considered the proposal "somewhat startling." If any attempt at seizure was made outside British waters it would amount to "nothing less than an act of war." It would also put an end to diplomatic efforts to secure compensation for the original seizures and "effectively destroy any small chance the Fisheries Treaty may have of passing." Salisbury was most unlikely to approve the idea, the Colonial Office said. It told the Admiralty to order Heneage to leave the schooners alone if they were being escorted by a U.S. vessel.[8]

When the New York *Times* learned of the planned escapade it was incredulous: "A very curious story of a naval war barely averted comes from Ottawa, which is fast rivalling El Paso and Tombstone in the productivity of belligerent rumors in moments of local or individual excitement." That summed up the U.S. view of Canada as an excitable, bellicose little pest.

On August 20 the *Times* reported the cutters *Rush* and *Bear* had found no infractions by the Bering schooners during the summer and there had been no seizures, a fact the paper found "very curious." It was another month before the press learned that Captain Shepard of the *Rush* had been given secret instructions to leave the sealers alone.

The perils of pelagic sealing were tragically evident in 1892. Early that season the 71-ton *Maggie Mac* of Victoria vanished at sea with 23 men aboard. She had left port in January under Captain John Dodd. The crew included Dodd's 13-year-old son, and the average age of the all-white crew was 24. The last letter from Dodd was received in Victoria March 18 by

R. P. Rithet, dated Clayoquot. Nothing more was heard of her until February, 1893, when the schooner *Pioneer* called at Quatsino Sound and found that two storekeepers had recovered fragments of the ill-fated vessel in a small cove south of Cape Scott. The wreckage included one side of the hull and a considerable amount of gear. She had apparently been caught in a sudden, violent storm among a group of small islands between Cape Scott and Triangle Island.

The *Sea Lion* was hit by a gale two days after leaving Bering Island. Six sealing boats were washed overboard, as well as all the water casks. Hatch covers were swept away, the galley smashed, and cascading waves broke the fore and jib booms and tiller. The damaged schooner was given permission to make repairs at Sand Point, but was seized when it was discovered she had transferred 1,100 skins to the *Coquitlam* at Port Etches. The *Sea Lion* managed to slip away during a storm, however, the captain telling the marshal on board he could swim 200 yards to shore or be taken to Victoria. He chose to swim.

An Indian hunter was killed on the *Arietas* when a signal gun burst. The natives blamed the mishap on carelessness by white crewmen putting in too much powder and stone. They were also angry at Captain Abel Douglass for insisting they continue to seal. Later the Indians complained they were charged an exorbitant amount — $50 each — to be taken from Tonki Bay to Hesquiaht on the steam schooner *Libbie*, which brought down the *Arietas'* skins.

The *Laura* and the *Lottie* were wrecked during the 1892 season, without loss of life, and a number of other schooners were severely damaged. The captain and four crewmen of the *Oscar & Hattie* were drowned in the surf off Yaquina Bay while pursuing a deserter. Bad luck continued to dog the *Oscar & Hattie*. After taking on a new captain and crew members, the schooner proceeded to the Commander Islands, where she managed to evade seizure but was nabbed August 31 by the *Mohican* in the Aleutians. The schooner was anchored in Gotzleb Harbor on the north side of Attu Island to take on fresh water while en route home. Bad weather prevented her from landing on the south side of the island, which would technically have been outside the Bering. She was turned over to the British and ordered to Victoria, where a trial was held before Chief Justice Matthew Begbie.

After noting that entries in a ship's logbook, because they can be doctored, are admissible as evidence against the vessel but not for it, Begbie ordered the *Oscar & Hattie* and her cargo and gear confiscated. If the owners didn't like his judgement, the autocratic Begbie added tartly, "there is now a cheap and ready appeal court at Ottawa; it is no longer necessary to have recourse to the costly and tardy appeal to the Privy Council." The verdict, in January of 1893, appeared to be a miscarriage of justice and shocked the

Crewmen, hunters aboard *Pathfinder*

Crewmen, hunters aboard *Maggie Mac*, 1891

W. P. Sayward *Furling Jibs in Squall*

Captain Robert E. McKeil

Dora Sieward

Repairing barque *Majestic*, San Francisco, 1886

Raising sail on sealing schooner

sealing community. The *Oscar & Hattie* was clearly not sealing around Attu; there were few if any fur seals in the area.

On April 14, 1895, a number of schooners were caught in a sudden storm which blew up while they were sealing on feeding grounds just south of Cape St. Elias. The weather had been fine when the small boats went out in the morning, but the barometer plunged shortly after noon. The boats were quickly called in before the winds hit with full force as darkness fell.

The *Libbie* under Captain Fred Hackett and the *Favorite* under Alex McLean — both Cape Breton Islanders — were able to ride out the blinding blizzard and sub-zero temperatures during the night, but the *Walter A. Earle* was not so lucky. In the morning the *Favorite* came upon the *Earle's* mainsail, and a few hours later the schooner was found bottom up. Her masts were in place but the rudder was gone. There was no sign of Captain Louis Magneson, his crew, or 26 Indian hunters, including 12 from Victoria's Songhees tribe.

The *C. S. White*, a former Columbia River pilot boat converted to a sealing schooner, was caught in the same storm further to the southwest in the Gulf of Alaska. She lost her sails and fore topmast and was driven on a reef where she broke up. Three men were drowned but 22 struggled to shore. Of these, eight died of exposure or starvation and five of the surviving 14 had hands or feet amputated for frostbite after their rescue.

In the Bering during the brief summer sealing season, the weather was often unsuitable for hunting. In August of 1886 the *W. P. Sayward* in 24 days was able to lower her canoes on only 11. In 1887 the *Alfred Adams* had but 14 of 30, and the *Triumph* in 1888 had 17 of 45.

Fog was often the enemy. The schooners ran astern of the small boats like "an anxious hen following a brood of adventurous young ducklings." The schooner always attempted to stay leeward of the small boats because they had difficulty sailing to the windward. Hunting boats often went 10 to 15 miles from the schooner, but the Indians usually stayed within 4 or 5 miles. In clear weather they might venture up to 10 miles, or as far as they could still see the top of the masts.

The Indians were reluctant to launch their canoes when there was a danger of becoming separated from the schooner. On such days the mother ships every hour fired a small cannon or sawed-off shotgun, known variously as a "bum gun," "boom gun" or "bomb gun," to give a bearing to the hunters. Some used a special horn — a square wooden box with a bellows and projecting lever. By working the lever rapidly back and forth, a roar was produced. On clear days a "return flag" was hoisted by the schooner to call in the boats and canoes. If darkness fell before all the small craft had been rounded up, a flare of oil-soaked oakum wrapped around a strand of wire was lit on the main topmast head. The canoes and hunting boats seldom carried more than a day's food or water, but the men often survived for two weeks or more on seal meat before being picked up by their own vessel or another schooner. If they had been out many days their boots would sometimes have to be cut away to release the men because their legs were so severely swollen. Many perished, from starvation or drowning.

Two white hunters, Bill and Jack Hernebury, were out in a small boat from the *Ocean Belle* when they were carried away from the schooner by a swift current off Japan. After running out of food they tried raw seal meat, but found that it tainted quickly and made them sick. They needed the sustenance for strength to row, so set a fire in the boat using the seats and bottom boards. With this they were able to sear the meat to make it more palatable and prevent spoiling. After nine days they reached shore and were rescued by Japanese villagers after their boat capsized in the surf. While the brothers waited in Hakodate for the *Ocean Belle* to return, carpenters repairing their boat found that the boards where the fire had been lit were "thin as paper but hard as flint." The cold water underneath had prevented them burning through.[9]

Two Indian hunters from the *Thomas F. Bayard* were blown away from the schooner off the Queen Charlotte Islands with only five biscuits and no water because they needed the can for bailing out their canoe. One of them had three matches tucked in his hat. When they reached land they lit a fire and boiled moss gathered from rocks. It was seven days before they reached a small Tsimshian village and were taken to Bella Bella. They boarded a steamer but the purser refused to feed them. An Indian on board gave them $1.50 for food.

The fare aboard schooners with Indian hunters was not so grand as that described by William George on the *Umbrina*. A few tight-fisted owners or captains took only pilot biscuits and tea, forcing the natives to bring their own dried halibut, salmon or herring roe. The Indians lived apart in the forward section of the hold below the main deck. There was usually only one skylight, a stove, table and tightly stacked bunks. The few Indians who went reluctantly to the Asian coast were miserable in the hot, humid climate. Some died. Others got seasick from the unaccustomed roll. A stiff belt of sea-water was prescribed for that. But mostly the Indians suffered from homesickness, an affliction not so common among the footloose white crewmen.

In the long summer days of the northern latitudes the hunters would often be out 12 to 14 hours a day. If the Indians were using shotguns rather than spears, in the evenings they would prepare shells for the next day before climbing into their bunks. They often smoked while working with open 25-pound kegs of gunpowder and a hot stove for melting lead to cast the bullets. When tobacco ran short they mixed in tea leaves.

There were other hazards on long voyages. Medical care was rudimentary and men often spent long weeks confined to their bunks with pneumonia or other ailments. Victor Jacobson broke his jaw while trying to climb aboard the schooner from a small boat in pitching seas. "The mate and I patched it together with a bit of wire," he said, "using a brace and bit to bore through the bone." If someone died during the voyage the funeral arrangements were rudimentary. Jack London, a young writer-to-be who made one sealing trip aboard a San Francisco schooner, watched as one of his crew mates was sewed up in the blankets in which he died. A gunny-sack half-filled with coal from the galley was tied to the man's feet to ensure his body sank when it was consigned to the sea.

During one of Jacobson's voyages, in 1895, the wife of an Indian hunter on board as cook died. The Indians wanted to go home. The woman's death was a bad sign and they would not allow burial at sea or in a foreign place. Jacobson took matters into his own hands, cutting up the body and packing it in a canvas sack with salt. He then made a coffin which he secreted with the sack on a small island in the Aleutians. After picking it up on the voyage home, Jacobson tried to unload his bizarre cargo at Nitinaht, but the seas were too high and he proceeded to Victoria. There the Indian hunters proceeded to get drunk, he said, leaving the burial to him.

If sealing was slack the schooners were not above a little scavenging. When a dead whale was spotted, the Indians would work from their canoes to cut off large chunks of blubber for oil. In 1891 the *Penelope* recovered 800 pounds of whalebone from the carcass of a right whale, worth $5 a pound. The *City of San Diego* in 1906 found the carcass of a large decomposing walrus floating in the Bering. Despite the overpowering smell, the men managed to cut out the huge ivory tusks.

Such ventures were not always successful. When the *Diana* ran short of water while sealing in the Commanders, Captain Otto Buckholz went to the mouth of the Kamchatka River, where he anchored a mile offshore and sent in two small boats. When they saw walrus playing in the estuary it was decided to shoot one weighing about a ton "for a bit of sport." The tusks were hooked over the gunwales amidships, but the skinning knives used on seals wouldn't cut through the tough walrus hide. The men had no axe to cut out the tusk. As the carcass became heavier with water, the two men aboard went to the opposite side to balance their little craft. They finally abandoned the idea of retrieving the tusks, but in an attempt to release the carcass the boat flipped over. They were rescued by the other boat and taken back to the schooner to dry out.

Casual cruelty was commonplace among the sealers. One "amusement" was to drive a spear in a dolphin, killer whale or shark to see how long they could hang on to the thrashing beast. Dolphins and killer whales were also randomly shot from the schooner deck. The Orcas followed the vessels when they were sealing to feast on the carcasses tossed overboard. Lines baited with salt pork were trailed to catch albatross. The big, ungainly birds were tormented on the deck before being released or killed to make pipe stems or tobacco pouches out of their feet and bones. There was a lot of shooting at birds and fish, ostensibly for target practice but more often just for the satisfaction of the kill.

There was also the sport of outwitting the U.S. Revenue Service cutters assigned to enforce regulations protecting the Pribilof seals in a running game of cat-and-mouse. "Half the fascination of sealing was in dodging the gunboats," said Jacobson. The sealers kept a constant watch on the horizon for the tell-tale black smoke of the patrol vessels. If the wind was up they could high-tail it from the area, but when the canoes or small boats were out hunting, the schooners had no choice but to wait and submit to a search. Illegal skins were hidden quickly under floorboards and guns sometimes tied to a rope fastened to the mast and casually run over the side. Guns were also secreted in water tanks, chain lockers and sometimes stowed aloft in gaff-topsails.

The sealers became chronic liars from the conviction that what they were doing was legal and right.

It was a harsh life, but there was often liquor on board to humour the men after a long cold day of hunting in an open boat. More than a few deserted when an opportunity came. Sometimes this happened in California ports such as Monterey, where the schooners frequently stopped over at the beginning of the early winter hunt before following the seal herd up the coast. In the 1890s, when gold fever was at its height, men would take advantage of a free trip north and jump ship at Dutch Harbor or Unalaska in the Aleutians to make their way to Nome or the Klondike. In 1887 when the *Lillie L.* of San Francisco was close to shore near Cape Fairweather, two boats with six men pulled ashore and they made off. Ten years later Captain Dan Martin of the *City of San Diego* left in the middle of a voyage at Unalaska and the schooner was forced to return to Victoria.

Except for the hunters who received their share of the "lay" at the end of the voyage, based on the number of skins each was credited with, many crewmen had little to show for their long days at sea except a nominal $1 payment, required by U.S. law. Most had obtained advances which were quickly spent before sailing and were also in debt to the captain's "slop-chest" for articles of clothing purchased during the voyage. The advance cheques were cashed by boarding-house "crimps" or saloon-keepers and were redeemable only after the schooner had sailed with the man aboard. If he didn't go, the waterfront bars and rooming-houses were out-of-pocket, but they had ways of getting reimbursed. Sooner or later the men would have to sail to pay their bills in port.

The slop-chest was a profitable side business for the skippers. The markups on such items as shirts, pants, socks, oilskins and tobacco was as much as 100 percent. The captains who took out Indian hunters made the largest profits on their slop-chests — up to $700 a year. The markups were higher and the Indians could not resist the array of goods available without paying until the day of reckoning when the season ended. Slop-chest profits on the whites-only schooners varied between $150 and $400.

While Indians often stayed with the same vessel and a skipper they liked, many white hunters preferred to change schooners each year. Captain William Brennan of Seattle said the schooners tried to stay out of Victoria during the hunting season to avoid trouble with their crews. The work was hard and dangerous, the pay minimal, and many men ran away when they got the chance. "There are very few sailors among the crews," Brennan said, "most of them being green hands." Each vessel carried two or three experienced sailors to handle problems with the rigging or sails.

One of the few schooner logbooks which has survived containing more than the minimum information was kept for Captain Daniel Munroe of the *Onward* in 1886 by his mate, identified only as "Frenchie".[10] Some edited excerpts follow:

Monday, March 1: Hesquiaht to Kyuquot. Drop off Rev. Charles Seghers, Father Brabant and Father Timmis at Kyuquot. The next day hire 5 Indians to help unload cargo. Took on 5 casks water as well as firewood. *Kate* arrived at 3 p.m.

March 10: Take on 16 canoes and 32 Indians and set off. Canoes out at 2 p.m. on March 11, returning at 4:30 with 13 seals. Winds light, but heavy swells. Saturday, March 13: Very heavy sea and high winds — put reef in foresail. At 2 p.m. Indians said they wanted to go ashore so set gib, reefed mainsail and ran for Hesquiaht. Sunday was still windy and dropped second anchor to hold position in harbour. Monday: Rain, hail and snow.

March 16: More settled. At 3 p.m. lift anchors and set off. Saw seals on Wednesday but Indians afraid to go out in canoes in heavy swells. Put one canoe over and got one seal about 20 miles offshore. Weather better Thursday, canoes out, but seals scarce.

Saturday, March 20: Bad weather returns so head back to Hesquiaht with *Kate*. *Favorite* already sheltered there. Monday: Thunder and lightning, hail and heavy rain. Wednesday: Out of Hesquiaht again but driven back on Thursday. On Friday the winds were so light had to use canoes to help tow schooner out of harbour.

Canoes out much of the following week — from 11 a.m. to 6 p.m. on Monday, March 29, and 7:30 a.m. to 5 p.m. on Tuesday. Indians refuse to lower canoes on Wednesday morning but at 3:30 lowered five.

Thursday, April 1: Back in Kyuquot. Take skins ashore and resalt them. Left Kyuquot on Sunday but soon forced to return by heavy weather. Fog rolls in. Kept in until Friday, April 9, when head out again. No wind, and canoes towed her to anchorage. Saturday: Out again.

Wednesday, April 14: Back in Kyuquot and dropped off more skins. While in harbour on Friday the barometer dropped sharply and winds hit hurricane force. Put out second anchor.

Sunday, April 18: Steamer *Hope* arrives from Victoria with Charles Spring, who took skins back there. *Hope* tows *Onward* to sea on Tuesday. Thursday: Canoes out from noon to 10 p.m. Indians wanted to go ashore on Friday so stopped in at Clayoquot for short time.

Sunday, April 25: Hit by high seas just inside Barkley Sound which washed two canoes overboard and wrecked boat on the stern davits. Tuesday: Call in at Port San Juan for wood and water. Thursday: Snow and hail. Saturday: 40 miles off Cape Flattery, 12 canoes out from 2 p.m. to 6 p.m.

Head north again. May 5 in Kyuquot for wood and water. Saturday, May 8: Indians won't leave until ceremonies ashore ended.

Monday, May 10: Canoes out at 6 a.m. but return at noon when swells increase. Few seals around. Tuesday: Land skins at Hesquiaht. Head north.

Saturday, June 19: Squalls with rain and heavy cross seas. Shipping large amount of water. Reef mainsail and foresail.

Wednesday, June 23: Sight dead whale at 9 a.m. Got out canoes and Indians climbed on carcass to cut off chunks of blubber.

Monday, June 28: Sighted Shumagin Islands through break in fog. Saw many seals but fog too thick to put out canoes. Wednesday: sight the *Favorite*. Thursday, July 1, anchor at Unga Island. Indians bring water on board and rigging repaired.

Wednesday, July 7: Cross seas heavy. Take on water off Sanak Island. Sunday, June 11: Through Unimak Pass. Monday: Canoes out first time in Bering from 2 to 4 p.m. July 15: Sight the *Dolphin*. Canoes out 4 p.m to 7:30. Friday, July 16: Thick fog. Saturday: *Dolphin* reports boat with three men aboard lost 10 days before and no word of them. Tuesday, July 20: Spoke schooner *Alexander*. Wednesday: With *Thornton* at 55 north, 167 west. Canoes out noon to 7 p.m.

Tuesday, July 27: Transfer 508 skins to *Favorite*. Thursday: With *Favorite*, canoes out 5 a.m. to 9 p.m. Friday from 6 a.m. to 8:30 p.m. Sunday: With *Favorite*, canoes out 6 a.m. to 7:30 p.m.

Monday, Aug. 2, *Corwin* comes up at 5 a.m. with *Carolena* and *Thornton* in tow. Officer and crew come on board and towed to Unalaska, not telling me the outrage, only that looked as if she was fitted out for seal hunting. Tuesday: Guns, ammo, boats, canoes and ship's papers removed. Wednesday: Ordered by Cutter captain not to let more than 4 men ashore at one time. Thursday and Friday: Lie at anchor with watchman aboard. No word of how we are to be disposed of.

Sat, Aug. 7: *Corwin* crewmen take off some provisions — flour, butter, sugar. Munroe protests to Cutter captain for not informing him why seized: "I Daniel Munroe, master of the British schooner *Onward*, do hereby declare that I do not know wherein I have violated the laws of the United States in taking seals within the usual limits of shore within the Bering Sea and I therefore protest against the action of the United States Authorities in seizing the vessel under my command — together with the sealskins composing the cargo."

In 1891 Stanley Henderson signed on the schooner *Vancouver Belle* as a hunter on a sealing voyage to the Bering Sea. Henderson, a friend of Captain Harvey Copp, kept a diary during his six weeks at sea.[11] The 90-ton vessel, built by Copp in Vancouver's False Creek after he came west from New Brunswick, had 27 men aboard, all whites — including 14 seamen, nine hunters, a cook and a steward. Some extracts from Henderson's account of the voyage follow:

The *Belle* was towed out of Burrard Inlet by the tug *Earle* on June 13 at 5:30 a.m. A gun salute was fired by the schooner to honour the port of Vancouver, which sent out five sealing schooners that season, compared to 43 from Victoria. The tug took her as far as Race Rocks. She put in at Neah Bay to buy some lamp chimneys, which had been forgotten, and was checked out by the Revenue cutter *Wolcott.*

June 22: Reached Kodiak Island. Average speed during the voyage was 7 knots.

June 23: Heavy swells. Everything in little cabin shared with Capt. Copp was sent flying. A 1,000-pound trunk that was sliding around had to be lashed down; otherwise it was too dangerous to get out of the bunk. A cold and heavy rain. Lay all day under reefed foresail. Decide seals have left Portlock Bank at north end of Kodiak Island and so head for Bering. Met *W. P. Sayward,* which bound for Alitak Bay on south end of island to transfer 732 skins to the *Danube.* The *Minnie* had 540 skins. The *Minnie* and *Sayward* left Victoria in February with Indian hunters. The *Sayward* had picked up three men in a small sailing boat off Cross Sound north of Sitka which had been lost from the *Penelope.* They were almost dead when found and lucky to be alive. Also met the 90-ton *Sylvia Handy* of San Francisco, with 700 skins. She was also headed for Alitak Bay. The schooners lay off, afraid to go inside 3-mile limit with a Revenue cutter there, even though most of the skins had been taken well outside the limit.

June 25: Pass volcanic Shumagin Islands. As the sun set the fantastic forms of their mountainous peaks looked most weird in the declining day. It was the first time the setting sun had been visible since leaving port.

June 27: Saw Pogromni Volcano on Unimak Island belching steam and smoke. It was covered in snow from water's edge to 6,500-foot peak. Spotted pair of travelling seals, but too far away for a shot. Pursued the seals for two hours and then lost them. No seals taken that day — they were all travelling and only about a dozen were seen. Copp and the mate caught 90 cod.

June 28: Through Unimak Pass. A Sunday. Quiet on board — men reading, mending and loafing. Socks darned with sail needle. Total catch for month of June: 4 seals.

July 1: Dominion Day. Red Ensign run to masthead after breakfast. Got first seal 10 miles from schooner after missing one. Twenty-two skins in all that day. Expert hunter Pete Peterson got 8.

July 3: Head to Bogosloff Island, just north of Unalaska Island. Powder dirty and guns bucked if two shots fired from one barrel without cleaning. Weather bad so played whist and poker with matches.

Sunday, July 5: Go in to Unalaska Bay for water before heading for Pribilofs. 400 gallons had been ruined by paint leaking into tank. Ten miles from shore, off Cape

Cheerful, intercepted by Revenue cutter *Corwin* and ordered out of Bering Sea, "by authority of United States and British governments under the *modus vivendi.*" Crewmen bitter, although *Corwin* officers polite. Just 28 skins for long voyage. Copp decides to look for British man-of-war at Unimak Pass to ask if Americans bluffing. If U.S. gets Bering closed for seals, cod and whales will be next. [In his own journal of the voyage, which he kept for his children, Copp recorded that the captain of H.M.S. *Nymphe* told him there was no alternative but to return home.][12]

Met the *E. B. Marvin*, under Capt. McDougall, who was also warned out. Schooners were given 48 hours to leave the Bering. If they did not, would be confiscated and lose chance of being compensated by Britain. The Cutter *Rush*, whose officers were brusque and unfriendly, towed the *Marvin* to Unalaska. Met the *Mary Ellen* under Captain Jacobson, who had sent the *Minnie* back to Victoria and was following in the *Ellen*.

On passing through Unimak Pass saw hundreds of whales and had a number of shots at them. Caught more cod and halibut. Days get shorter as move south. [In summer in the Bering. daylight lasts from 3 a.m. to 11 p.m.]

July 22: Pass Cape Flattery.

July 25: Arrive at Brockton Point. Met by friends. Henderson wanted something fresh to eat, and chose mutton chops with a bottle of port.

The men were paid off with between $100 and $350 a few days later. Henderson got $250.

CHAPTER SIX

LONDON

It is very difficult to persuade an American that he is not superior to the rest of creation.

—JULIAN PAUNCEFOTE

London was caught in the middle in the Bering Sea dispute and there was no easy way out. On one side were the bellicose Americans; on the other the intransigent Canadians. Britain's primary concern was to maintain the principle of freedom of the seas, but she also had an interest in preserving the seal herd to protect her large investment in the treating, dying and marketing of furs.

The man called upon to carry out British policy was Robert Arthur Talbot Gascoyne, 3rd Marquis of Salisbury. Salisbury had entered the House of Commons in 1853 at the age of 23. Family wealth had not been able to provide him a happy childhood. Shy and reclusive, he hated his school days at Eton. A brooding, melancholy nature manifested itself at an early age and lasted the rest of his life. Despite a lack of taste for the political arena, he spent the next half century in public life. Salisbury served three terms as prime minister, switching the position with William Gladstone. His chief interest was always foreign affairs and he continued to run the Foreign Office from Downing Street.

In his early days Salisbury had acquired a reputation for caustic wit and bitter sarcasm. He was a Tory of deep conviction, with a cautious attitude toward change, suspicious of democracy, parliamentary reform, and the popular press. "Politics brutalize and degrade the mind," he once lamented. With age his manner became more calm and reserved, inspiring trust with what one biographer described as an "imperturbable and almost Olympian detachment."[1] An impressive figure, with luminous eyes, a bold forehead and full beard, he coolly held his hand until the moment demanded action, an effective tactic in diplomacy. With patient, subtle persistence he was able to defuse dangerous confrontations.

The goal of Salisbury's diplomacy was to avoid war, which was often brought on by entanglement in foreign alliances. His approach to foreign affairs was flexible and pragmatic. He never sought diplomatic "victories" because a humiliated rival could become a bitter enemy. His best work was accomplished through secret diplomacy, removed from the disruptions of press and Parliament.

His style did not endear Salisbury to the Canadians, obsessed with and fearful of the growing giant to the south. Ottawa looked to Britain to stand up to what Canadians regarded as American bullying. The thankless task of attempting to mediate Canadian-American differences often frustrated Salisbury. "Both Canada and the United States are rather unreasonable in the matter and it is no easy task to bring them together," he complained to Queen Victoria. Lady Gwendolen Cecil wrote of her father that "it is difficult to say whether he was more tried by the crudities of the American diplomatic style or the refusal of his own clients (Canada) to face the facts of the situation."[2]

Considering the gravity of some of Britain's concerns in the 1890s in the Middle East, China, Africa and India, the amount of time Salisbury devoted to the far-off Pribilof Island fur seal herd is astonishing. This was particularly so in the first three years of the decade when he was kept busy rebutting James Blaine's imaginative and aggressive moves. Up to that time Britain paid little attention to North America.

But Salisbury quickly recognized the potential dangers of the Bering Sea dispute. After appointing Julian Pauncefote to succeed Sackville-West, Salisbury told the new minister to Washington it was "the only really black point on the Anglo-American horizon." He added: "I feel that we may have trouble any day, because the views of the two parties — the American and Canadian — are so very far apart. And the awkward part of the question is that if the Canadians have their way the seal must disappear; or, to put it another way, any effective rule for the preservation of the species must begin by forbidding the only kind of seal-catching in which the Canadians can take part."

If Britain was the nation caught in the middle, then Julian Pauncefote was the man at the squeezing point. It was his responsibility to relay Salisbury's messages to the irascible Blaine and transmit in turn the American Secretary's often outrageous proposals. Although he found it difficult to get along with Blaine, Pauncefote was an ideal man for the job. Lady Gwendolen praised his "imperturbable calm and strong sense of humour," both essential in dealing with the crusty Secretary of State.

A former barrister in Hong Kong who had gained a reputation for expertise in international law, Pauncefote joined the Foreign Office in 1874. His friendly, open personality and diplomatic skills soon became apparent. Promotions followed rapidly. "His uprightness and honesty reflect all that was best in the Victorian age."[3]

Pauncefote's appointment by Salisbury to the U.S. was a shrewd move. Like the Prime Minister, he favoured the conduct of diplomatic relations by legal means rather than force. An ardent supporter of arbitration, he was the first lawyer appointed by Britain to Washington and so was able to work well with the many lawyers in the State Department.

But Washington was not an easy posting. Unlike Salisbury, Pauncefote had to deal directly with the vagaries of the American system of government. He had difficulty accepting the fact that power was shared by the President, Congress and the press. He found the jingoistic newspapers especially troublesome. The Irish-Americans and their sympathizers were constantly trying to frustrate good relations between London and Washington. Pauncefote kept a low profile, never giving interviews to the press, making as few speeches as possible, cautiously avoiding public controversy. Pauncefote vented his frustration at times in private letters to Salisbury in which he complained about the press "raging and lying outrageously." American self-righteousness tried his patience: "It is very difficult to persuade an American that he is not superior to the rest of creation."

After Pauncefote had convinced the Canadians it would be best to stay in the background, the British decided to respond to Blaine's overtures. In January of 1890 Salisbury said Britain, the U.S. and Russia should get together in Washington to discuss the general question of the seals and Bering Sea access. Compensation could be the subject of separate negotiations, but the U.S. must agree to stop the seizures. The pursuit of seals in the open sea had never been considered piracy, Salisbury said. Even in the case of the slave trade the right to arrest vessels of another country could be exercised only by international agreement. No country had ever been granted the right to police international "morality" as claimed by Blaine for the U.S. Salisbury also argued that the right to catch seals in the ocean could not be held to have been abandoned by a nation because it had not chosen to exercise it for a number of years.

Blaine agreed, but only half-heartedly. He asked the approximate amount of the British claims and balked when told they would total about $500,000. Blaine then set off on a new dialectic course, once again attempting to bolster his case with Latin. Instead of violating *mare clausum*, the Canadians were now guilty of pursuing a trade that was *contra bonos mores*. They were disregarding international morality by taking seals in a manner that was sure to result in the extermination of the species, while providing only "temporary, immoral gain" to a few persons. "The law of the sea is not lawlessness," Blaine wrote in his best newspaper editorial writer's rhetoric.

After Blaine had proclaimed proprietory rights for the U.S. to control sealing in the Bering, Salisbury confided to Pauncefote that Westminster was "disturbed." He was unsure whether it was merely a ploy on Blaine's part to spur the Canadians to speed up negotiations. "We cannot tolerate a renewal of the captures," Salisbury wrote Pauncefote. It was too early to say what form British resistance would take, he said, but the country would not permit U.S. cruisers "to treat Bering Sea as if it were their private property."

Salisbury concluded sombrely: "I confess that the attitude, both at Washington and at Ottawa, makes me somewhat apprehensive of the result. The Canadians have the strict law on their side; the Americans have a moral basis for their contention which it is impossible to ignore. If both sides push their pretensions to an extreme, a collision is inevitable."

When Blaine attacked the Canadians for thwarting an agreement, the focus of his anger fell on the Canadian minister of fisheries, Charles Hibbert Tupper, son of the controversial Sir Charles Tupper. Tupper the elder had been unseated in a Nova Scotia election bribery scandal and posted to London as High Commissioner. The U.S. consul in Halifax described him to his superiors in Washington as "bold and politically unscrupulous . . . ingenious in explaining inconsistencies."

The younger Tupper had been sent to Washington to act as technical adviser to Pauncefote on the sealing issue. When Blaine shrewdly produced the statistics gathered by Canadian fisheries inspector Thomas Mowat showing that females were preponderant in the catch of pelagic sealers, Tupper disavowed the figures. Blaine then raised the question of a closed season outside the 3-mile limit, the need for which Tupper sharply questioned.

Tupper raised U.S. eyebrows by suggesting that if a closed pelagic season was agreed to, there should be corresponding curbs on the land kill. It was unreasonable, he said, to ask Canadian sealers to make a sacrifice to preserve the herd while the U.S. lessees continued to kill seals.

When Tupper questioned the need for any curbs on pelagic sealing and boldly challenged Blaine to prove his argument, the Secretary sputtered angrily: "I did not expect to meet a Canadian representative. I understood that the British Government and the United States would agree upon a closed season and then submit the agreement to Canada for approval."

Tupper complained in a note to Macdonald that Pauncefote was taking it for granted that some form of closed season should be agreed upon and was too willing to make concessions to the Americans: "There is always present on his part a desire to make his future residence in Washington as pleasant as possible," Tupper said. Pauncefote had also suggested outside arbitration if no agreement could be reached. In the meantime, for the next 2½ years if necessary, no sealing schooners would be allowed within 15 miles of the Pribilofs. Tupper told Macdonald that Canada could concede a 20-mile zone, but should object to any arbitration which would "put us at the mercy of a foreign government." Canada would be better off in future conducting its own foreign affairs, he added.

Tupper's reports on the Washington proceedings strongly influenced Governor-General Stanley, who told the Colonial Office the Canadians were prepared to "acquiesce in general the principle of protection of seal life, but are most anxious that an enquiry by experts may precede a permanent Treaty, as we believe the facts to be incorrect on which U.S. proposals are based."

Canadian fears were summed up in an Ottawa speech by Senator William J. Macdonald of Victoria: "I have long thought that the whole matter will be brought to sudden maturity by some act of bloodshed on one side or the other. Some bold captain with a shipload of valuable skins, and feeling himself legitimately in possession of them, will defend his property, and the diplomats will regret they did not use more expedition in bringing about a termination of the dispute."

On April 29, 1890, Pauncefote, despite Canadian opposition, submitted a draft proposal which included a 10-mile cordon around the Pribilofs and provision for outside arbitration. After observing that "the respect which the sealing vessels would pay to the ten-mile limit would be the same wolves pay to a flock of sheep so placed that no shepherd can guard them," Blaine nevertheless replied that with a few minor changes the draft could be the basis for a settlement. Two weeks later, however, the agreement collapsed when President Harrison and his cabinet rejected the draft and issued orders that seizures be resumed.

Blaine had been undercut by his own colleagues, but took out his frustration on the British. He complained that Salisbury should have admitted at the start of the talks that "no arrangement could be made unless Canada concurred in it, and that all negotiation with the British Government direct was but a loss of time." Blaine added, however, that he still supported negotiation and asked Britain to keep the sealers out of the Bering during the summer so as not to exacerbate the situation.

When Pauncefote replied that Britain could not enforce such a ban without enacting legislation, which would take too long, Blaine said Salisbury should issue a proclamation requesting the vessels to keep out. The Prime Minister said he would do so only if the U.S. agreed to arbitration of the question of the legality of U.S. seizures between 1886 and 1889.

On May 24, in a bluntly worded report to Queen Victoria on her birthday, Salisbury referred to a "grave telegram" from Pauncefote warning of the present danger. "It was agreed unanimously," the Prime Minister said, "that, whatever the consequences might be, the Cabinet could not recommend Your Majesty to allow your North American subjects to be interfered with, on the open ocean, in the prosecution of their legitimate industry; and that the claim of the United States to treat Bering's Sea as if it were their own territorial water could not be tolerated." Salisbury told the Queen she had, "under our advice, already carried patience and long-suffering to a point which is arousing much discontent on both sides of the Atlantic; and you could not submit to this quite unjustifiable assumption without a serious loss of reputation and power."[4]

The situation was becoming tense again. The Admiralty was told to be prepared to send warships to the Bering. Salisbury told Pauncefote on May 29 that more seizures could result in "the most serious complications," but kept

British intentions secret. Salisbury told Lord Knutsford of the Colonial Office on June 26 that, "my ground for disliking to give Canada at present any information as to what protection the Canadian vessels may look for is simply this: that, *unless* they allow it to be known, such information is worthless to them; and *if* they allow it to be known, it will be repeated in every newspaper throughout the Union, and will almost drive Blaine into an aggressive policy."

When Pauncefote was informed that seizure orders had gone out to the U.S. Revenue cutters, a cypher telegram was dispatched to the British admiral in command of the China squadron at Hong Kong. Four Royal Navy warships set off on a "summer cruise" of undefined duration. A news agency noted their departure but said they were going to South America. On arriving in the Bering they began patrolling "with leisurely aimlessness" the area of Canadian sealing activity. There was no word on either side to break the official silence. All seemed calm.

The fact was that seizure orders had not been sent to the Revenue cutters. Either the Americans had been bluffing, or British firmness had made them back away from a confrontation. In either case, Governor-General Stanley told London the British show of force had done "untold good" among Canadians sceptical of British resolve.

While the Royal Navy put a number of warships into readiness at Esquimalt, Salisbury exchanged broadsides with Blaine. The pursuit of seals in the open sea had never been considered piracy by any civilized state, Salisbury said. Pelagic sealing could not be regarded as *contra bonos mores* unless and until it had been banned for special reasons by international arrangement. The Prime Minister trotted out a bit of Latin himself. The seals were indisputably *ferae naturae* or *res nullius* until they were caught — wild animals belonging to no one.

The New York *Times*, a political foe of the Republicans, poked fun at "Mr. Blaine's agile mind" for coming up with the argument that the fur seals were "American-born" and therefore entitled to U.S. protection beyond the 3-mile limit. "This view has not yet commended itself to the dull Britishers. They seem to think Mr. Blaine is like a farmer who should claim to own a turnpike, or a neighbor's pasture, because he had chased a runaway calf over them."

Blaine then reached back in history once again to the 1821 ukase of Czar Alexander. He said John Quincy Adams' protest was not against the Russian claim of jurisdiction over the Bering, but merely its extension southward below the Aleutian chain to 51° north latitude. Blaine also advanced the dubious claim that the phrase "Pacific Ocean" in the treaties of 1824 and 1825 did not include the Bering Sea. He sent Salisbury 105 maps dating from before 1825 which showed the Bering Sea with a separate name from the Pacific Ocean. That proved nothing, Salisbury retorted, because names such as the Bay of Biscay or Gulf of Lyons did not separate them from the Atlantic or Mediterranean. One historian has observed that Blaine's blustering argumentiveness had little more effect on Salisbury "than the plea of a brilliant prosecuting attorney on a staid judge."[5]

Although the U.S. Revenue cutters had gone to the Bering, there were no seizures during the summer of 1890. The only action taken that year was in March when the Victoria schooner *Pathfinder*, which had run for home after being seized in 1889, was arrested in Neah Bay while taking refuge from a storm to repair a broken tiller.

But there had been a few scares during the summer. In July the New York *Times* published a report from Victoria that two "clipper schooners" were being fitted out in Maple Bay north of Victoria to take on the Yankee gunboats. They would be armed and disguised as sealers to tempt seizure and provoke an incident. The plan was "Mephistophelian," said the *Times*, which also recalled a report from the previous year that the schooner *Sapphire* had gone out with 60 "fully armed" Indians. (Sixty was the usual complement of hunters of the big *Sapphire* and their "arms" consisted of no more than the usual sealing spears and shotguns.) The *Times* partially redeemed itself for this nonsense by pointing out that too much time was being wasted arguing about treaties signed in the 1820s, while the only thing that mattered was protection of the seals. And when a suggestion arose in the Canadian press that purchase of Alaska by Canada would effectively end the sealing and boundary disputes, the *Times* noted scornfully that U.S. policy in North America was to "buy but never sell."

The London press also joined the fray. "England is strong enough to be calm and courteous," counselled the smugly Tory *Telegraph*. But the opposition *Chronicle* said "Mr. Blaine proves himself an abler man in controversy than Lord Salisbury, although having a worse case to defend. The representatives of England seem mere babies in the hands of Mr. Blaine." The *Times* noted the "sinister influences of party pressure" in the U.S., as if it did not also exist in England.

By December, Salisbury had grown weary of jumping to counter each of Blaine's shifting positions. Despairing that the two nations could ever negotiate an agreement, he again suggested arbitration. Blaine replied that the dispute could be reduced to a single point: If Britain was able to sustain her position that the treaties of 1824 and 1825 included the Bering as part of the Pacific Ocean, then the U.S. would have "no well-grounded complaint against her." Otherwise, the American case against Britain was "complete and undeniable."

Realizing the entire dispute would thus rest on one contention that might be lost, Blaine then advanced five separate questions for arbitration. The first four related to the jurisdictional rights of Russia in the Bering and their transfer to the U.S. by purchase. The fifth involved the right of the U.S. to protect the fur seals outside the 3-mile limit through "ownership of the

95

breeding islands and the habits of the seals in resorting thither and rearing their young thereon and going out from the islands for food." If the arbiters found that Britain must concur in measures to protect the seals, then they should also determine the regulations. Blaine concluded by dropping, at last, the claim of *mare clausum* in the Bering. The U.S. "has never claimed it and never desired it," Blaine blithely declared. "It expressly disavows it."

In February of 1891 Salisbury proposed some minor modifications to Blaine's five questions. While the two governments were working out details of the arbitration a *modus vivendi*, a restriction on sealing in the Bering, was agreed upon until the dispute had been resolved.

There was some powerful behind-the-scenes lobbying in the U.S. to derail the Bering negotiations. One of the principals was Stephen B. Elkins, Blaine's financial adviser and friend for many years and manager of his campaign for the Republican nomination in 1888. The New York *Times* described him as "bland, oily and effusive." Elkins had been one of the unsuccessful bidders for the second lease in 1890, but was invited into the winning N.A.C.C. because of his valuable political connections. Pauncefote reported that Elkins was delegated by the N.A.C.C. to look after its Washington affairs and had "an influence with the president that no other one person can in the least degree approach."

The N.A.C.C. was pressing for an increased harvest despite discouraging reports from the Pribilofs. Treasury Agent Charles Goff had told a Senate Committee studying the fur seal industry that the herd was decreasing at an "alarming" rate. Even the natives were concerned about the decline of the seals. Goff said that on the drives to the killing grounds up to 85 percent of the bachelor seals were being turned away because they were too young. The usual figure was about 15 percent. Where Elliott had found 1,200,000 seals on the Northeast Point rookery in 1872, Goff counted only 250,000, a dramatic decline even allowing for Elliott's over-estimation. The Agent recommended a full closure for an indefinite period.

On June 15, Britain agreed to prohibit its subjects from sealing in the Bering until the following May. The U.S. also agreed to ban land killing, excepting 7,500 seals to feed the Aleuts. Under pressure from Elkins, however, Blaine had persuaded Secretary of the Treasury Charles Foster to allow the N.A.C.C. to take 60,000 skins "if they can be found." Foster explained he had given his approval because Blaine authorized it "and has told me that Salisbury is ugly and will not stop his people from killing."

Blaine fell ill in May and President Harrison took over his duties for the next six months. He promptly cancelled the 60,000 quota for that year, although the lessees did take more than the 7,500 allowed for food. Pauncefote was grateful to deal with someone other than the cantankerous Blaine. He told Salisbury: "It is most important if possible to settle matters before Mr. Blaine's return to the State Department."

Charles H. Tupper

Rosie Olsen

Indian hunters and crew aboard *Favorite*, 1894

Hunters and crew on *Saucy Lass*, 1910

Elliott had pressed the government to have the *modus vivendi* declared by March 1 so as to give sufficient warning to the pelagic sealers, but it stalled until June 15 when the agreement was signed in Washington by Pauncefote and Acting Secretary of State William Wharton. By then there were an estimated 79 sealing schooners out, including 47 Canadian and 30 U.S. Knowing the *modus* was coming, they wanted to get as many seals as possible before being warned.

The *Corwin* under Captain C. L. Hooper was ordered to the Pribilofs with copies of the President's proclamation of the *modus* for distribution to the sealing schooners and commanders of the Revenue cutter fleet. The warships *Thetis, Alert* and *Mohican* were also sent to the sealing grounds to halt further pelagic sealing.

A number of schooners used passes between the outer Aleutian Islands to enter the Bering, avoiding the heavily-patrolled Unimak Pass. Forty-one of the Canadian schooners were eventually warned to leave the Bering. A number went across to the Asian coast.

The first schooner seized under the *modus* was the *E. B. Marvin* under Captain Caleb McDougall. She was apprehended by the *Rush* and turned over to H.M.S. *Nymphe*, which ordered her to proceed to Victoria. At least seven other schooners were merely warned to leave the Bering.

Feelings ran high in Victoria against Britain for agreeing to the closure. The schooner owners raised the possibility of switching the entire fleet to German or Italian registry. The sealers who had not yet left for the north were shown the Proclamation in the *Colonist* of June 16 but refused to accept it as an official warning. A total of 89 schooners went to the North Pacific that summer, a record number. Many which gave Victoria as their home port were owned in San Francisco, Portland, Seattle and Port Townsend. The New York *Herald* speculated that the increased number of vessels was based on the assumption that the tough U.S. proclamation was designed to placate the American public and that neither U.S. nor British warships were going to interfere with the pelagic sealers. The *Herald* also pointed out there was a rumour circulating among the sealers that compensation would be paid to the owner of every schooner stopped from hunting, another incentive to send vessels out. For some, the tactic worked. In 1892 the British government paid $100,000 to the sealers because it had failed to provide sufficient warning of the *modus.*

After the *modus* agreement was signed, the two countries appointed commissioners to study seal habits on the Pribilofs and related issues involved in the preservation of the herd. Their reports would be used by the arbitrators in determining what regulations were necessary. The investigations were to be separate from the arbitration proceedings, but the results would be submitted to the arbitrators as a joint submission. Britain chose Sir George Baden-Powell, brother of the Boy Scouts founder, and George

Mercer Dawson, a Canadian scientist with wide-ranging interests. He was a geologist by training but also became an accomplished botanist and ethnologist.

The U.S. selected Dr. Clinton H. Merriam and Professor Thomas C. Mendenhall, considered by Blaine to be far superior to the the British choices. In a letter to Pauncefote he said the American commissioners were "gentlemen who were especially fitted by their scientific attainments" and, unlike Baden-Powell and Dawson, had not publicly expressed their opinions on the issue before or after their appointments. Pauncefote retorted that the Americans had previously published papers opposed to the British position, but he did not hold that against them. All four men were "equally entitled to the confidence of both Governments," he told Blaine.

Despite the temporary absence of Blaine, who was ailing again, negotiations toward an arbitration treaty did not go smoothly. The main stumbling block was the question of compensation. London wanted the U.S. to pay if it was found to have wrongfully seized the Victoria-based schooners, but would not accept liability for damages if the arbitration went against Britain. Eventually a compromise was reached whereby the arbitrators would rule on questions of fact relating to the claims, but any question of liability resulting from that finding must be dealt with in further negotiations.

Harrison gave in reluctantly, believing Britain should accept binding arbitration on damages. But Salisbury maintained his government could not be liable for alleged losses resulting from the activities of the pelagic sealers, who sailed under her flag but outside British jurisdiction on the high seas. Salisbury insisted the arbitration agreement should not be binding until accepted by other maritime powers, but Blaine, now back on the job, pressured him into dropping that demand. Blaine also sought to have the number of arbitrators limited so as to exclude Canadian participation. Britain got around that gambit, however, by making room on her delegation for a Canadian.

After much haggling, the Arbitration Treaty was signed by the two governments on February 29, 1892. Special "Agents" were appointed by each side, international lawyer and diplomat John W. Foster by the U.S. and Charles Tupper Jr. by Britain. But then Blaine, fearing the arbiters might go against the U.S. position, attempted to have the four-man special commission empowered to draw up regulations to control pelagic sealing.

That move was doomed to failure when the commissioners issued a brief non-committal communique March 4 in which they admitted irreconcilable differences. This was followed by detailed reports to their own governments which were subsequently exchanged. There was no consensus on what had caused the decline of the herd since 1867. Baden-Powell and Dawson blamed raids on the rookeries by American schooners and the lessees' method of driving the bachelors to the killing fields. Mendenhall and Merriam said it was the Canadian pelagic sealers who were responsible.

The arbiters would obviously not finish their work by the end of the 1892 season, so another *modus vivendi* was required. Blaine said it must be more stringently enforced this year, because the previous *modus* had been "very ineffective." But Canada favoured sealing as usual, because the U.S. had broken the 1891 agreement by killing more than the 7,500 quota for Aleut food.

This argument was complicated by the fact it was an election year in the U.S. There was a suggestion that Harrison was willing to risk war with Britain, or at least provoke the threat of one, because the country had never changed presidents during a war. In a letter to Harrison March 6, Blaine warned that strategy could work both ways: "If we get up a war cry and send vessels to the Bering Sea, it will re-elect Lord Salisbury."

The President dropped all the diplomatic niceties in a blistering note to Salisbury over his rejection of a second *modus vivendi*. Canada believed Harrison was bluffing in his threats of war, but Pauncefote took them seriously. Describing Harrison bitterly as "that obstinate and pugnacious little president," he urged Salisbury to accept the *modus* to avoid a perilous situation.

Not all Canadians were convinced Harrison was bluffing. Warned the Ottawa *Journal*: "If the dispatches from Washington are to be trusted, there is a great danger of very serious trouble between Great Britain and the United States...one cannot contemplate without shrinking, the possibility of war between the two most powerful and determined nations in the world, particularly when the brunt of war must fall on ourselves." The London *Times* echoed that concern: "If the *modus vivendi* is not restored it is believed America will hurry men-of-war to the Bering Sea and sweep off Canadian sealers."

Despite these forebodings, and another N.A.C.C. protest against a ban on land killing, a new *modus vivendi* agreement was signed on April 18, just 13 days before expiry of the existing pact. Nevertheless, 65 schooners with 952 whites and 495 Indians aboard were cleared from Victoria and Vancouver for sealing voyages along the coast or to the Asiatic side.

In June, Blaine suddenly resigned. The reasons for his sudden departure have never been clearly defined. It was known that he was suffering from a serious illness, the nature of which was not disclosed, and that he was grieving over the deaths of two sons and a daughter within the space of a year. He had been especially close to his eldest son, who had assisted him in the State Department. Despite his physical and emotional difficulties, rumours persisted after his resignation that Blaine intended to make one last run for the Republican nomination against Harrison in the summer of 1892. As a result his relations with the President, never close, became more strained. Blaine did not contest the nomination, however, and died the following year.

He had failed to solve any of the important issues dividing the U.S. and Canada. "His handling of the fur seal question was clumsy, lacking in finesse, and was his most conspicuous failure."[5] In fact, Blaine's aggressive tactics had brought Britain and Canada into a closer relationship.

CHAPTER SEVEN

Petropavlosk

You never mind limits; no catch seal. You can navigate these waters, but no seal. You came here to steal seals. Your government stopped sealing on your side; we stopped sealing on this side.

—Captain BORIS DE LEVRON

The seizures of 1887 caused some Victoria sealers to avoid the eastern Bering Sea the following year and set out instead for the Asian coast. One of the schooners which crossed the Pacific in the spring was the *Araunah*, owned by merchants Richard Hall and John Goepel. They instructed Captain H. F. Sieward to proceed north off Japan to the Commander Islands, being careful to avoid territorial waters.

But on July 1 while located, according to Sieward, six to eight miles off the south end of Copper Island, the *Araunah* was seized by the Alaska Commercial Company steamer *Alexander II*, which carried Russian naval officers when on patrols. It was believed the seizure was made at the request of the A.C.C. on the Commander Islands. The Governor of the Islands, Nicholas Grebnitsky, who was also aboard the *Alexander*, ordered 133 sealskins seized.

Sieward signed a statement admitting the offence and there was no official protest. He said the schooner drifted with the current to a position about six miles off the island and one of the canoes might have been within three miles. The captain, crew and 12 Indian hunters were taken first to the district capital of Petropavlosk, then moved to Vladivostok. From there they went to Yokohama, where they boarded the Canadian Pacific liner *Batavia* for Vancouver.

The legal issue boiled down to the question of whether the Russians had the right to seize the schooners when they were outside the 3-mile limit but their canoes and small boats were within. Lord Salisbury agreed they did and two years later admitted to the Russians that the *Araunah* had violated the law, justifying the seizure and confiscation. But in 1898, a decade after the event, a petition to Queen Victoria was drawn up by the Victoria legal firm of

101

Tupper, Peters and Potts. It was signed by Hall, Goepel, Sieward and able seaman Caesar Doring — the only white crew member who could be located. Damages of $21,852 were claimed from the Russians.

The petitioners claimed they had only lately become aware of Salisbury's statement to the Russians eight years before. They said Sieward's confession had been signed under duress while he was a prisoner. There had been no intent to violate Russian laws, the petition said. "At the most, from all the facts, it might reasonably be argued that one or two of the canoes, owned or controlled by Indians and not belonging to the *Araunah*, accidentally drifted within the jurisdictional waters of Russia." It was the same ploy attempted by Captain Olsen of the *Anna Beck* in 1887 — the specious argument that the Indians were working under contract and the schooner was not responsible for their actions.

Crewman Doring said the *Araunah* had been 20 to 25 miles offshore the previous day, but had drifted closer to the island in fog overnight. The 12 Indian hunters had been sent off at 6:30 a.m., unaware of the schooner's position. Captain Gronberg of the *Alexander* said the Indians had gone inside the three-mile limit after seals.

One of the Indians said he tried to stay seven miles offshore, but when he saw the island clearly he knew he was only four miles away. He said the schooner was seven miles from land and the canoe, with no skins aboard, six miles offshore at the time of seizure. Sieward claimed Russian estimates of the distances involved were even more conflicting than those of his own men. He conceded that one of the canoes was inside the 3-mile limit, but said there was no evidence it was hunting at the time. The captain blamed the current for taking the schooner closer to the island than intended.

Grebnitsky said two of the canoes were seen only a half mile offshore. He noted there had been no entries in the schooner's logbook for almost a month, usually an indication the vessel was involved in illegal activities.

In the end the petition failed because Salisbury stood firm on his original position that the Russians had acted legally. The government did not support the *Araunah*'s claim.

The North American schooner fleet was more careful around the Russian islands after the *Araunah* seizure and there were no further incidents until 1890. In that year Dan McLean, who had previously been sailing under the British flag, took charge of the San Francisco-owned schooner *J. Hamilton Lewis* — the former steam-schooner *Grace* operated by J. D. Warren. While off the Commander Islands he was apprehended by the *Alexander* and ordered to turn over his papers. When McLean hoisted an American flag, however, and refused to give up his sealskins, he was allowed to go free. The Russians considered themselves allies of the Americans in the seal dispute at the time, so this was the first instance of a flag benefitting those sailing under it.

Unchastened by his brother's experience, Alex McLean took the *J. H. Lewis* back in 1891 under her new owner, furrier Herman Liebes of San Francisco. Liebes had hired Alex McLean in 1891 to advise him on the purchase of sealing schooners because McLean was so knowledgeable about the fleet. After McLean bought the *J. H. Lewis* for $4,500 in Port Townsend, Liebes made him master. McLean set out for the Commanders and landed on a Copper Island rookery August 2, "in order to test the chronometer," he later claimed.

McLean's raiding party was surprised by Russian guards, who opened fire. McLean was wounded but was helped to one of the small boats by the other crew members, none of whom had been hit. One man became so frightened while frantically attempting to get back to the schooner, however, that he fell overboard and was drowned. The sails were quickly hoisted on the schooner and she attempted to escape. But the Russian gunboat *Aleut* suddenly emerged from the fog disguised as a schooner. She caught up to the *J. H. Lewis* about 12 miles — McLean claimed it was 20 miles — off Copper Island. When he was ordered to heave to, McLean yelled back that he was in neutral water where nobody had the right to interfere with his business. The *Aleut* fell back a short distance and loosed a volley of shots across his bow. But the veteran sealer was not easily intimidated. He made a run at the *Aleut*, attempting to throw a hawser or chain to foul her propeller. The *Aleut* turned suddenly, however, and rammed the bow of the *Lewis*, knocking down her fore-rigging. A boarding party was sent over the railing.

The crew members were transferred to the gunboat, which towed the schooner to Petropavlosk. The rigging was repaired and with a crew of nine Russians and six Americans she sailed for Vladivostok, accompanied by the *Aleut*. The crew was confined at night but had the run of the town each day until 8 p.m.

Petropavlosk, which had a population of 300 in 1892, is located near the southern tip of the Kamchatka Peninsula, on the east side about 300 miles southwest of Bering Island. It lies at the head of a pretty little harbour flanked on both sides by high hills. Clapboard buildings housing the Governor, mayor, two policemen, two Orthodox Greek Churches and a trading post were grouped on 30 acres of flatland behind the beach at the head of the harbour. The peasant population lived in log huts thatched with hay or straw. David Starr Jordan later observed that while the Aleut cottages on the Pribilofs were all "puritanically white," the Russians allowed various shades of blue, green, yellow or scarlet to suit the tastes of the Petropavlosk peasants and brighten up the bleak winter landscape. They lived on fish in the summer and game in winter. There were a few cows and horses and many dogs. In 1892 the remains could be seen of ruined fortifications dating from the period before the Crimean War when Petropavlosk was the headquarters of the

Russian whaling and sealing fleets in the Pacific. English and French naval forces which attempted to capture the little port were defeated there in 1854. The town is also remembered as the starting point of the ill-fated Vitus Bering expedition in 1741.

McLean's crew complained that conditions in the town jail were miserable. Two men contracted smallpox, one fatally. The others were released in January of 1892 and sent to Korea, where they were transferred to another Russian vessel which took them to Nagasaki. From there the American consul sent them to Yokohama and then home to San Francisco.

McLean got out of jail after four months by bribing the guards. After reaching Nagasaki, he wrote up a new logbook to show the *J. H. Lewis* was outside Russian territorial waters when seized. McLean later also admitted obtaining bogus affidavits from the crew, which were sent to the State Department in Washington. John Hay, a Department lawyer later to become ambassador to Britain, was fooled. He took the case before The Hague International Tribunal in 1902, along with the claims of the *C. H. White* and *Kate & Anna*, which had been seized later in the Commanders. Arbiter Tobie Michel Charles Asser rejected the Russian defence of "hot pursuit" and found that the seizures outside territorial waters were illegal. He awarded $28,588 plus interest from January, 1892, to the *J. H. Lewis* and $32,440 to the *C. H. White*. Asser ruled that the *Kate & Anna*, which had been released by the Russians, could have continued sealing instead of proceeding to San Francisco, so was not able to claim for the loss of a prospective catch. He allowed $1,488 for 124 seized skins.

The antics of the McLean brothers and other rookery poachers did not improve the already poor reputation of the pelagic sealers. The newly-formed Sealers' Association in Victoria wrote to Sir Charles Tupper in London protesting that they should not be regarded as "adventurers engaged in an illegal pursuit." Rather, they were "law-abiding citizens, desirous to do nothing which might conflict with the maritime laws." Association president John G. Cox said the group represented 63 schooners, 250 members and capital of $750,000. A total of 1,300 men were employed by the schooners, of whom one-quarter were Indians. (The proportion of Indians would increase sharply in later years.) Money spent annually on wages, insurance and provisions totalled $400,000. An estimated 5,000 people in all were dependent on the business, Cox said. The Association expressed concern about recent Russian actions, asked what the regulations were on that side, and whether they could expect protection by British gunboats against harassment.

Tupper replied that the Association should be wary of the risks involved in going to the Commander Islands in view of the current unstable situation. Russia had not joined the U.S. and Britain in the *modus vivendi* of 1891 and 1892 and appeared to make no claim prohibiting sealing outside the 3-mile limit. The seizures had taken place, however, and the Russians had reiterated their determination to combat rookery raiding.

Ignoring Tupper's warning, some 40 sealing schooners, 32 of them from Victoria, crossed to the Asian coast in 1892. They paid the price when five schooners were seized off Copper Island between July 16 and August 12. They were the *Willie McGowan, Rosie Olsen* and *Ariel* of Victoria, the *Vancouver Belle* of Vancouver, and the *C. H. White* of San Francisco. The schooners were taken into custody by the 16-gun Russian cruiser *Zabiaka* under Captain Boris De Levron, and the A.C.C. steamer *Kotik* ('The Seal'), which had been commissioned by the government for patrol duty. Governor Grebnitsky was aboard the *Kotik* so that arrests could be legally authorized.

Captain John McLeod of the *Ariel* provided an account of the seizure of his vessel. She had left Victoria May 14 before the impending notice of the *modus vivendi*. On her way north, near Chirikoff Island in the Gulf of Alaska, McLeod was warned by the British warship H.M.S. *Daphne* and the U.S. Revenue cutter *Rush* that the Bering was closed to sealing. He proceeded to the Russian side where, at 4:30 a.m. on July 28, he was stopped by the *Zabiaka*.

"We were alone with no vessels in sight," McLeod said. "The cruiser came alongside and the captain hailed me, asked me, 'What are you doing there?' I told him, 'You can see for yourself what we are doing.' He said, 'but — in Russian waters.'"

During their exchange a boat lowered on the opposite side of the steamer suddenly came around her stern carrying sailors and marines with fixed bayonets. The boarding party went below and drove the crew on deck. There had been no entries in the *Ariel's* logbook for two days. Marks and calculations made in pencil on her charts had been half rubbed out, but showed that bearings had been taken when "quite close" to shore, the Russians said.

The 39-ton *Rosie Olsen* managed to get outside the 3-mile limit before being caught, but four of her small boats were picked up inside, one only a mile from Aria Island. Under Captain Michael Keefe, she carried a crew of six whites and 16 Nootka hunters from Esperanza Inlet. Keefe claimed De Levron tried to take away his nautical instruments but he hung on to them despite the threat of a flogging. Logbook entries had not been made for several days and the chronometer was out of order. Of the 379 skins aboard the *Rosie Olsen*, 96 percent were female.

The Russians claimed the *McGowan* tried to escape despite a warning shot from a 9-pounder gun. Capt. John Daley finally heaved to after a second shot whistled across her bow.

The *Vancouver Belle* was seized by the *Zabiaka* two weeks later. She was one of the few sealing schooners which listed the new town of Vancouver on the British Columbia mainland as home port. She was built and owned by Captain W. H. Copp, who had taken his schooner to the Bering in 1891 and made a successful raid on a Pribilof rookery. John Kraft, a Victoria hunter, said the men drove the seals to the water's edge to be killed so that the tide would wash the blood away. They got 400 in one night. "I do not think the U.S. Government has the right to allow a company to kill all the seals," Kraft said, "and I and my companions, since we had been prevented from taking seals in the Bering Sea, thought it was not wrong to take them ashore."

Copp made another voyage to the Bering in 1892, but when he found it was closed again, went across to Copper Island where he was seized. The *Vancouver Belle* was alongside the schooner *Anaconda* at the time, but the U.S. vessel was not apprehended.[1]

The *Belle* had been sighted by Russian guards on the shore who signalled the *Zabiaka*. While in pursuit of the schooner the cruiser stopped to pick up three small boats from the *W. P. Sayward* and the *Belle* fled, but was soon caught. Men aboard the three *Sayward* boats had been killing seals on the rookery when they were spotted and made a run for the schooner, throwing the dead seals overboard. They were caught with eight seals bearing head wounds, showing they had been killed with clubs on shore and not shot in the water.

The skippers later claimed they were at least 25 miles from shore when seized, but De Levron told them he would have made the arrests even if they were 1,000 miles out. He claimed that jurisdiction to the mid-Pacific boundary was agreed to in the 1867 treaty with the U.S. The captains signed statements admitting they had been sealing within Russian waters, although the schooners themselves were all outside the 3-mile limit. Later they alleged they had signed the affidavits — written in Russian and verbally translated into English — under threat of banishment to Siberian prison camps.

The *C. H. Tupper* of Victoria was also stopped and boarded by the *Zabiaka*, but allowed to go free. "The Russians were a formidable looking crew," said Captain Wentworth E. Baker. "Each man was armed with a cutlass and a revolver and carried a box of cartridges at his belt." When Baker asked De Levron what were the limits of Russia's jurisdictional claim, he replied sharply: "You never mind limits; no catch seal. You can navigate these waters, but no seal. You came here to steal seals. Your government stopped sealing on your side; we stopped sealing on this side."

De Levron gave a similar answer to John B. Brown, master and part owner of the *Walter P. Hall*, which was stopped and warned. When Brown asked the limits of Russians waters, De Levron drew on the schooner's chart a line from Cape Chalutka on the coast of Kamchatka to the most southerly point of the Aleutian Islands.

The *Zabiaka* had attempted to tow the *Ariel*, but when the towline broke a Russian crew was placed in charge of the schooner and sailed her to Petropavlosk. McLeod later claimed his men had been mistreated by the

106

Russians. He accused the boarding crew of raising a Russian flag on the *Ariel* masthead after hauling down the Union Jack and trampling it on the deck.

The first captured sealers to arrive in the town were 38 men from the *C. H. White* and the *Willie McGowan*. They were jammed into a 10-foot by 18-foot jailhouse. Some preferred to sleep outside and others took turns. There was no furniture and the dirty little room was crawling with lice and vermin.

The men were helped by John Malowansky, a Russian-born former resident of Victoria who had been involved in the sealing trade on the Commander Islands since 1869, first as agent for the Hutchinson-Kohl leasing interests and then for the Russian Seal Skin Company. Malowansky had become a U.S. citizen with a winter residence in San Francisco, but spent the sealing season in Petropavlosk. He was also involved for a time in the fur trade in Vladivostok.[2]

Malowansky persuaded government officials to give the crew members seven cents a day each for food, an amount which did not buy much in a remote town where food prices were unusually high. He also gave extra food to the men from his store and found work for them in the harbour loading ballast on the U.S.-owned, steam-powered barquentine *Majestic*.

When the *Ariel* crewmen reached Petropavlosk August 3, they were marched through mud and wet grass behind the beach to a dilapidated former hospital building, where they found the crew of the *Rosie Olsen* already confined. Because of the crowded conditions, some of the men chose to sleep in the open on the beach, despite lacking warm clothing which they claimed had been stolen from the schooner by the Russian boarding crew. The Russians said later, however, the weather was so hot the crew of the *Zabiaka* slept out on her decks by choice. The prisoners admitted it was warm during the day, but said it was damp and foggy at night. A few white crewmen were allowed to sleep in Malowansky's warehouse. Some sold extra items of clothing for food.

The British Ambassador to St. Petersburg, Sir R. B. D. Morier, later protested that some of the seamen would have starved "but for the kind-heartedness of some poor moujiks (peasants), who shared with them their black bread and salt fish." And Copp complained that he and his crew had been treated "in a most barbarous way" at Petropavlosk by Governor Grebnitsky, who refused to turn over money for food promised by De Levron. The only concession made by Grebnitsky was to provide Copp with the *Rosie Olsen*, the oldest and least seaworthy of the seized schooners, on which to return home.

When Copp pleaded with De Levron to have the *Vancouver Belle* returned, he was refused. De Levron said he had been lied to by the crews of the small boats. Copp said he had otherwise been well-treated by the Russian captain: "He considered from what he had read in my book of sketches of my own life that, as I had not been a sealing captain long, I was really ignorant that I was trespassing in Russian waters . . . he treated me with much kindness and gave me a cabin and treated the crew well."

Meanwhile, negotiations were taking place between the Governor and Captain De Levron with Captain Lorentzen of the *Majestic* to return the prisoners to Victoria and San Francisco. After prolonged haggling about how their fares were to be paid, 69 whites and Indians left Petropavlosk on August 8 aboard the tramp trading ship. Soon after, 36 more men left Petropavlosk for home aboard the *Rosie Olsen*— 18 from the *Vancouver Belle*, nine from the *W. P. Sayward*, six from the *Annie C. Moore* and three from the *E. B. Marvin*.

Lorentzen's daughter, who sailed with her father, wrote up the agreement. Provisions for the passengers were taken from the schooners. They asked for enough food for a 45-day voyage, but the Russians allowed only 30 days. To a request for small boats in the event of a mishap, the Russians permitted them to take eight sealing boats and two canoes aboard the *Majestic*. Lorentzen later claimed he had bought these small craft from De Levron and gained ownership of them when they reached Victoria. He was also reluctantly granted two stoves taken from the schooners, as well as the unconsumed provisions.

The men had no blankets and only light clothing. They slept in the ship's hold, while the four schooner captains were given accommodation in the carpenter shop and hatch house. Captain McLeod said conditions for the 84 men between decks was "wretched and dangerous." Mate James Stratford of Victoria broke two ribs in a fall.

The sealers distrusted Lorentzen, believing him to be working with the Russians and responsible for foiling their attempt to flee in the *Ariel* and *Willie McGowan*. The *Majestic* was owned by D. Hirschfield of San Francisco, who later sued Ottawa for the crewmen's passage money.

The headline in the Victoria *News* after the *Majestic's* arrival August 30, read: "Startling Story of Outrage, Insult and Pillage." The *News* said the captured crews had been turned "heartlessly adrift." The *Colonist* headline read: "Intense Excitement in the City and Province Over the High-Handed Outrage." Without waiting to determine the facts of the seizures, the *Colonist* urged Britain to "bring the Russians to their senses and teach them a little respect for the old Union Jack." Premier Theodore Davie sent a protest to Ottawa. The sealers called for the dispatch of a British warship to the area to protect the remaining schooners. The Royal Navy cruiser H.M.S. *Leander* was in fact sent from Yokohama to Petropavlosk to pick up the sealers stranded by the seizure of their vessels, but found they were already on their way home. There were no reprisals. Salisbury had decided to deal with the matter through diplomatic channels.

A week later the *W. P. Sayward* arrived in Victoria with nine of its 28-man white crew left behind, captured by the Russians in three small hunting boats close to or on the shore. Then the *E. B. Marvin* returned, also short-handed three men. One of her boats had been seized by workers on a Copper Island beach as the crew began slaughtering seals. The *Annie C. Moore* left two small boats behind in evading Russian pursuers. Some of these men had been caught in their boats close to the islands, while others were captured on the rookeries.

The *C. H. White*, under Captain L. M. Furman, had four Aleut hunters on board when seized. They were left stranded in San Francisco after the *Majestic* arrived there, then transported to Port Townsend where the citizenry grudgingly cared for them until they could be returned to their Aleutian Island homes.

Some time after reaching Vancouver September 21, the *Rosie Olsen*, renamed by the Russians the *Priz,* was turned over to the Dominion government. Copp had lost the *Vancouver Belle* and her cargo of skins, worth a combined total of about $40,000, and gave up sealing for the more peaceful trade of stevedoring.

As the *Rosie Olsen* was entering Juan de Fuca Strait near the end of her long Pacific crossing, Copp, lying in his cabin during the night, heard some of the crew members making plans to seize control of the schooner from him, take her into Victoria, and claim a share of the anticipated salvage money from her owners. These were the same men, Copp said later, "that I had kept from starving, got them liberated, supplied them with clothing, and even the luxury of a few pounds of tobacco." He nipped the mutiny in the bud and proceeded to Vancouver, where the *Rosie Olsen* was placed in trust under the government even though Captain Keefe had offered Copp $1,500 for her recovery on behalf of the owner, Andrew Spratt of Spratt and Gray, a Victoria machinists' firm. Ottawa eventually returned the schooner to Spratt, a move hailed by the Victoria industry.

The 37 crewmen of two other seized schooners, the *Carmolite* and *Maria*, came home in style. The *Maria*, under Captain Sprott Balcom, was seized by the *Kotik* with 10 unskinned seals aboard while seven miles off Copper Island after two small boats were sighted and captured one and a half miles from shore. The *Carmolite* attempted to escape after being sighted three miles off a rookery. Her logbook had no entries for the past two days. Captain William Hughes of the *Carmolite* and his men were taken first to Petropavlosk, then sent on a Russian warship to the mainland port of Vladivostok, where they saw the *J. H. Lewis* up for sale. They remained there for 17 days on the warship before being sent to Nagasaki, where all but three boarded the *Empress of Japan* for Victoria. The others signed up as crew on the U.S. man-of-war U.S.S. *Palos* in Japan.

The seizures put money in the pockets of a number of Russians. Malowansky profited by purchasing 1,124 of the seized skins. The government held on to 1,028 others. Both lots were taken on the *Kotik* to be sold in San Francisco. There were a number of American-built schooners working out of

Vladivostok which had been purchased by traders and fishermen at the prize court auctions. A share of the proceeds from the sale of the seized skins and vessels went to the officers of the Russian cruisers. Malowansky also bought the Indians' canoes for $3 to $6 each.

Word of the Russian seizures was well-received in Washington. The government now felt it had an ally in its dispute with Britain. The New York *Times* noted that previous Russian action had been taken only against rookery raiders who came ashore. Now a closed area for seal protection was being claimed, which meant Russia was "entering the lists on the side of the United States."

Pelagic sealing had been unknown on the Asian coast before 1891. Until that year the few North American schooners on that side had simply sent their men ashore to slaughter the seals on the inadequately guarded rookeries. When larger numbers started going over, the schooners began taking seals in the water, although many adopted the practice of staying just outside the 3-mile limit and sending their small boats and canoes into the rookeries. The scale of the killing in 1891 and 1892 was disastrous to the herd, which was much smaller than that of the Pribilofs and so took longer to regenerate.

M. Chichkine, the Russian Foreign Minister, told Ambassador Morier that Britain, by engaging in negotiations with the U.S., had in effect admitted the propriety of a departure from the general rules of international law in order to protect the seals. He pointed out that the *modus* had put great pressure on the Russian herd and the number of skins from it had greatly increased on the London market. Ninety percent of the these skins were females, Chichkine said, while the skins harvested in the normal fashion on the rookeries were always surplus males. The destructive nature of pelagic sealing was also shown "by the number of seals wounded or abandoned on the shore or within territorial waters, and afterwards found by the local authorities."

The Russians, meanwhile, vigorously rebutted the pelagic sealers' version of their treatment. Chichkine said the conduct of the crew from three of the seized schooners in Petropavlosk had been "scandalous." The schooner crewmen, who were free to come and go in Petropavlosk, had behaved in a disorderly manner. Captains John Daley of the *Willie McGowan* and Michael Keefe of the *Rosie Olsen* had gone to see De Levron on the *Zabiaka* while intoxicated, "and used such abusive language to him that the sailors of the cruiser had to turn them out of the captain's cabin."

The official St. Petersburg gazette, *Pravitelstvenny Vestnik*, protested an article printed in the London *Times* quoting the schooner crewmen which was critical of the Russians. The gazette pointed out the Canadian sealers had come to Russian waters because their activities had been curbed on the American side with the approval of the British. It also claimed the schooners were captured as far as 40 miles offshore only because they had been chased for up to 90 minutes at speeds as great as 13 knots. Marked charts on the schooners showed they had been much closer than they admitted and were planning raids on the rookery.

"The small yield of the seal fishery on Copper Island this year confirms the rookeries have been half ruined by pirates, chiefly English," the gazette said. "The conduct of our officers during the search was in every case irreproachable."

The Russians set up a special commission to investigate the seizures. It found that in the case of four of the schooners—the *Maria*, *Rosie Olsen*, *Carmolite* and *Vancouver Belle*—there was clear evidence their canoes had either landed on the rookeries or were seen within three miles. As for the *Willie McGowan* and the *Ariel*, the evidence was not so clear-cut and the Russians said they would consider paying some compensation. The Commission said there was no truth to the *Ariel*'s flag-trampling charge, an accusation which impugned Russian honour. Theft of clothing was also denied and $100 in cash alleged by Captain McLeod of the *Ariel* to have been stolen was later found behind the drawer of a chest.

As for conditions on the *Majestic*, the Commission said the deck of the hold on which most of the men slept was above the ballast and was covered with dried branches upon which mattresses had been laid. Captain Lorentzen had wanted $10 a head for passage, the Commission said, but he had agreed to be paid out of the supply of small boats, canoes, food and ovens.

The Russians *were* scrupulous and conscientious about such matters and there was no cause to doubt their word, despite the horror stories told in Victoria. Ambassador Morier, in fact, later conceded to Chichkine there had been considerable "exaggeration on the part of men smarting under a sense of hardship and injustice." It was also true, however, that while the sealers had been well treated by the Russian Navy, the civil authorities ashore had not been so considerate after Governor Grebnitsky denied responsibility for their welfare.

A rumour gained circulation in late 1892 that Captain De Levron had been declared insane and relieved of his commission. This was interpreted by the sealers as a backdown by the Russians. The truth was that De Levron had been replaced because his superiors believed he was not assiduous enough in catching poachers. It was alleged that on two separate occasions he had taken his ship into harbour during the height of the season, once for 10 days and once for 15 days, while the poachers were allowed the run of the rookeries.

St. Petersburg indicated it was willing to enter negotiations with the British on the dispute, but in the meantime laid down unilateral rules for the 1893 season. No vessel without a licence would be allowed to hunt within 10 miles of the Russian mainland, i.e., the Kamchatka Peninsula. In addition, there would be a 30-mile wide zone around the Commander Islands, preventing schooners passing between Copper and Bering Islands.

Britain admitted the eastern Bering *modus* had forced matters to a head and agreed to these "exceptional and provisional" measures by the Russians. But under a new agreement British vessels seized by the Russians for violating the regulations would be tried by British courts. The Victoria sealers generally approved of the restrictions and the *Colonist* urged their observance.

The sealers were advised of the new measures, but once again left early to avoid the official warnings. Some 50 were gone by March 17, with 25 cleared for the North Pacific and 24 for the Asian coast. Another 11 crossed to the other side later. Only two schooners were left in port when official word of the British-Russian agreement reached Victoria. A number of U.S. schooners had also already cleared for the western Pacific.

As part of the agreement Russia agreed to reduce its Commander Island and Robben Reef rookery kill from 50,000 to 30,000. Britain in turn said her cruisers would cooperate with the Russian navy in patrolling the area.

Only one Victoria vessel, the *Ainoko*, was apprehended by the Russians in 1893, but she managed to escape. Stopped by the Russian cruiser *Yahout* off Copper Island, Captain George Heater was ordered to Yokohama to face a British court. But Heater claimed the 15 Indian hunters aboard refused to go to Japan and so he made a run for Victoria instead, dropping the Indians off at Hesquiaht. He was subsequently cleared by Judge Henry P. Crease at a court hearing in Victoria.

Victor Jacobson had two vessels on the Asia side in 1893. He sent the *Mary Ellen* with a crew of white hunters to Japan, then set out himself as captain of the *Minnie*, a small vessel he had built himself. There was considerable merriment on the Victoria waterfront during the *Minnie*'s construction. She was described as "merely a flat box, put together in a very shaky manner," but nevertheless sealed successfully for a number of years.

On learning at Sand Point that his wife was ill, Jacobson returned home on the schooner *Borealis* and sent on the *Minnie* under the command of Captain Morehouse. Morehouse was seized three miles inside the new 30-mile zone and ordered to Yokohama. He also went instead to Victoria, but in this instance the schooner was confiscated and put up for auction by the Admiralty. There was considerable sympathy for Jacobson in the industry, however, and he was permitted to buy the *Minnie* back for the bargain price of $650.

Ainoko *Boarded from Russian Patrol Ship*

Steam schooner *Mischief* of Yaquinna, Oregon

Casco

CHAPTER EIGHT

Port Etches

The idea of anyone daring to execute our laws seems more than the Canucks can stand.

—Captain ROBLEY D. EVANS, USN

Despite the existence of another *modus vivendi*, 1892 was marked by one of the most controversial U.S. actions in the long history of the pelagic sealing dispute. For the first time, a non-sealing vessel was seized. She was a large commercial steamship, the *Coquitlam*, chartered by the Sealers Association of Victoria. Her job was to take skins from the schooners before they risked seizure by entering the Bering, and deliver additional supplies to the fleet.

The practice of chartering a steamship was not new. In 1890 the auxiliary steam schooner *Mischief* of Yaquinna, Oregon, had been hired by a syndicate of 29 sealing vessels — 25 from B.C. and four from the U.S. — to rendezvous with the fleet near sheltered Sand Point harbour on Unga Island, a favourite anchoring spot of the sealers.[1] Captain J. G. Cox of the Association was on board to supervise the transfer operation.

The *Mischief* arrived in the Shumagin Islands July 4 to find the schooners flying British flags but holding a gala Independence Day celebration. One of the main events was a prize fight between crewman Jack Burke of the *Henry Dennis* and John Couley of the *Walter L. Rich*. Couley knocked Burke out in the 14th round and a lot of money was said to have changed hands as a result. Consul Levi Myers commented on the day's festivities in a report to the State Department: "Can it be that there were American hearts beneath these British jackets, and that there is quite as much American money employed in the fitting out of these vessels as Canadian?"

On July 16 nineteen Victoria schooners met the *Mischief* 15 miles offshore to make the transfer. Bad weather delayed the operation and the vessels were forced to seek shelter. As a result the *Mischief* missed her rendezvous with the four U.S. schooners — the *Henry Dennis, San Jose* and *Lillie L.* of San Francisco, and the *Allie I. Alger* of Seattle — but took a total of 13,000 skins from the others.

Another 6,000 skins were transferred to the schooner *Aurora*, which was forced to return to Victoria because her Indian hunters would not enter the

Bering. They protested they had not been paid for skins previously seized on the *Aurora* and were owed two years' wages by the firm of Munsie and Cox, which had chartered her for sealing.

In 1891 the Sealers Association leased the S.S. *Danube* from the Canadian Pacific Navigation Company to meet the fleet at Alitak Bay at the south end of Kodiak Island. The *Danube* had made two historic voyages before being acquired by Canadian Pacific. She was the first merchantman to make the east-to-west voyage through the new Suez Canal with a cargo of tea from the Orient, and four years later she brought the body of the missionary-explorer David Livingstone home to London from Africa.

Besides taking off 17,267 skins valued at $300,000, the *Danube* delivered mail and supplies to the schooners. To help defray her charter cost of $10,000, she delivered goods to canneries along the coast on her voyage north.

At Alitak Bay the *Danube* had stayed 10 miles offshore for the three-day transfer to avoid contravening U.S. customs laws. The U.S.S. *Thetis* had tailed her toward the rendezvous but apparently believed she was going to Sand Point. The warship then proceeded to Unimak Pass, where she delivered warnings to a number of schooners becalmed at the entrance of the narrow, tide-ripped passage. A few returned to Victoria; others headed for the Asian coast.

Robert McKeil wrote Sadie that he had first learned of the *modus* from the *Danube*. Since no schooner was to be seized until after it had received an official warning, the fleet hurried into the Bering to get as many seals as possible before being intecepted. Some captains said they would recognize no warning but that of a British officer, and most of the owners were cautious. Three of them — E. B. Marvin, J. G. Cox and William Munsie — had come north on the *Danube* to supervise. Since McKeil was an owner of the *Maud S.* he decided to take no risks and sent 394 skins back on the *Danube*. He entered the Bering July 2 and despite thick fogs had taken 476 seals by July 23. Intercepted by the *Mohican* on the 23rd, McKeil tried to slip away in fog but failed. The *Mohican* officers were courteous and friendly, saying, "don't blame us, it's the work of Blaine and Salisbury." The *Maud S.* saw lots of seals the next day but did not lower her boats. McKeil said he later regretted his decision on learning the 76-ton *Carlotta Cox* got 158 that day.

The *Danube* arrived back in Victoria July 6. Later that month she was chartered by the government to take Baden-Powell and Dawson to the Pribilofs on an investigative field trip for the arbitration commission. On the earlier voyage a correspondent for the London *Times* had been aboard, sending back misleading dispatches for British readers. Without going near the Pribilofs and using material probably fed to him by Sealers Association officials, he wrote that the land kill was entirely to blame for the decline of the herd, which he said had been driven to other breeding areas in the Bering.

114

The A.C.C. and N.A.C.C. were accused of killing nursing mothers before their pups were weaned. It was all nonsense, and only added fuel to the emotional content of the dispute.

The Americans also chartered a steamship in 1891, but for a different purpose. The Navy leased the *Alki* from the Pacific Coast Steamship Company of San Francisco. She was placed under the command of a naval officer and outfitted with a detachment of U.S. Marines and a surgeon. The *Alki* was to be a prison ship for crew members of seized schooners. As it turned out, the crews of only three schooners — two of them American — spent time aboard her.

Captain McDougall of the *E. B. Marvin* grudgingly allowed a boarding party from the *Thetis* on his vessel near Unga Island July 1. He was duly warned but proceeded into the Bering anyway. Four days later the *Marvin* was stopped by the Revenue cutter *Rush* just north of Unimak Pass. A prize crew was put on board and she was ordered to Unalaska, where McDougall and his crew were locked in the hold of the *Alki*. They were soon released to H.M.S. *Nymphe* and sent to Victoria. The Americans had assumed they would be tried there, but the British decided not to prosecute. McDougall claimed the official warning served upon him was not binding because only a British naval officer could endorse his log. The official *modus* warning document also referred to "William" Pauncefote instead of Julian, which McDougall said, unconvincingly, indicated it was a fake. Meanwhile, crew members from the seized U.S. schooners *La Ninja* and *Ethel* were transported to San Francisco on the *Alki*.

In the spring of 1892 the Americans prepared to intercept the transfer of skins and supplies by sending undercover agents to Victoria to question sealers on the rendezvous site. The captains had not been given details of the operation by the Association, however, and would not learn the site of the meeting place until opening sealed orders after leaving port. The Treasury Department agents left empty-handed, reporting to their superiors only that the *Danube* would be the steamship involved again. They were wrong. The Association had gone to the Union Steamship Company of Vancouver to charter the *Coquitlam* instead.

Captain Cox had chartered the new steamship before her outfitting was completed in May. The bonds had been signed by R. P. Rithet and Thomas Earle, two Victoria financiers active in the sealing industry. The schooner owners were assessed $100 for each vessel participating in the operation.

The *Coquitlam*, under Captain Edwin E. McLellan, sailed from Victoria at 4 a.m. June 9 with a crew of 16. Also on board were reporter Ashmun N. Brown of the Victoria *News*, and Captains William Grant and Cereno J. Kelley of the Sealers Association. The Association had approved Brown's passage, but his city editor had made a deal allowing Kelley to approve Brown's reports. Kelley and Grant were actually in charge of the voyage, giving orders to McLellan on where to go. The skipper rebelled, however, when they tried to interfere with the actual sailing of the ship, which was his responsibility alone.

McLellan and the Association executives had been warned by Customs Agent A. R. Milne to make the transfers on the high seas in order to avoid complications with the Americans, who he said were claiming a 12-mile limit. Cox prevailed on Milne to let the *Coquitlam* sail without a manifest because she was running late.

But it didn't matter what precautions they took — trouble was waiting in the person of Captain Robley D. "Fighting Bob" Evans. Evans was commander of the *U.S.S. Yorktown*, the Navy's new white-hulled frigate. He had been ordered to head up one of the largest concentrations of American warships since the Civil War to police the sealers. Strictly speaking, the *modus* applied only to the Bering Sea and Evans should have limited his operation to it, but he was not the kind of man to be bound by silly rules drawn up by striped-pants diplomats.

Evans was stocky and pugnacious, like his pet bulldog Jowler. Ruggedly handsome and arrogant, Evans was later promoted to admiral for his heroic exploits during the Spanish-American War. He was commonly referred to as "Old Gimpy" because of leg wounds suffered during the Civil War. Doctors had wanted to amputate both legs, but he is said to have stopped them by pulling a pistol from under his pillow.[2]

The *Yorktown* had sailed from Port Townsend May 13 with the Navy steam sloops *Adams* and *Mohican* and the Revenue cutter *Rush*. Evans was now on his own. Port Townsend was the last telegraph point in contact with Washington and there was no radio communication at sea. The cutters *Corwin* and *Bear* and Navy ships *Albatross* and *Ranger* were to follow, joining the *Yorktown* at Unalaska.

Evans had decided the supply ship must be captured, whatever her position when located. He confided in his memoirs: "I read plainly between the lines of my orders that the Washington authorities considered it was of vital importance that she should be captured, and I made up my mind to get her, legally if I could, illegally if I must. If I took her at sea, the Department could disavow my act and punish me; but in the meantime my mission in the North would be accomplished and sealing broken up, at least for that year."[3] Naturally, Evans did not convey his intentions to Captain A. A. Chase-Parr of H.M.S. *Melpomene*, the senior Royal Navy officer in the area and his British counterpart in the *modus* patrol.

The area was described as a lawless "nest of pirates" by Evans, who later dismissed protests by Canadian newspapers over his arbitrary actions: "The idea of anyone daring to execute our laws seems more than the Canucks can stand."

He was convinced the schooners would have to return to Victoria for provisions, ending their sealing. But most were outfitted for the full season. The supplies delivered by the steamer were more in the nature of luxuries, such as fresh meat and vegetables.

On the way to Unalaska the *Yorktown* and the cutters boarded a number of schooners to deliver copies of the *modus* regulations. By the end of the season U.S. and British patrol ships had intercepted 107 of the estimated 110 schooners in the area. Evans fired warning shots at some to bring them to. He seized the Indian-owned, 23-ton *Mountain Chief* of Port San Juan and turned her over to Royal Navy officers, telling them to keep her out of the area in the future, "or we will blow the stuffing out of her." A few weeks later the little schooner was stopped by the Navy sloop *Adams*. The boarding party found seven freshly killed seals on the deck, six of them females. The *Adams* attempted to take the *Mountain Chief* in tow but had to give up because of heavy seas. The schooner made her own way to Unalaska where she surrendered to the *Melpomene*. Captain Parr ordered her to Victoria, where she was restored by Customs Agent Milne to owner Jim Nawassum after the Indians pleaded ignorance of the *modus*.

Three rendezvous points had been picked for the *Coquitlam* in the Gulf of Alaska, making it difficult for Evans to intervene. Tonki Bay on Afognak Island, Port Etches on Hinchinbrook Island, and McLeod Bay on Montague Island all were uninhabited anchorages in Prince William Sound. The steamer arrived at Tonki Bay on June 18 to find 12 schooners waiting. The next day six of them—the *Brenda, Umbrina, Sea Lion, Venture, Maud S.* and *Walter A. Earle* were towed out of the harbour beyond the 3-mile limit to take on provisions, including coal, and transfer a total of 6,035 skins.

One of the schooners, the *Sea Lion*, unloaded 629 skins and took on coal, eight sacks of potatoes and a sack of onions. Captain Otto Buckholz later claimed he had not gone into the bay to meet the *Coquitlam* but was there only to prepare for the long voyage across the Pacific to Asia. Buckholz said he acted on his own initiative in transferring skins because the schooner owner trusted him to make such decisions.

Captain Campbell of the *Umbrina* said he ducked into Tonki Bay on June 18 because of a storm. He went outside the bay to transfer 707 skins because he thought they would be safer on the *Coquitlam* in view of the long voyage ahead.

Captain Hooper of the *Corwin*, meanwhile, had been ordered to keep watch on Alitak Bay, where the *Danube* transfer had been made the previous year. Hooper arrived June 10 and pulled out three days later after leaving a steam launch and party of men to patrol the harbour. The *Corwin* returned on the 15th and boarded three schooners. The next day Evans anchored in the bay after a storm blew up, thinking sealers might seek shelter there. On one of three schooners there he found instructions fixing a rendezvous at Port Etches and Evans ordered the *Corwin* to proceed there.

The *Coquitlam* arrived outside Port Etches on the 22nd. Seventeen schooners were gathered in the bay. The *Mohican* was also in the area and the sealers were on guard.

Evans thrived on subterfuge and derring-do. He ordered Hooper to haul his vessel close inshore, set down the topmasts, and cover his lower masts with bushes, so that he would be "well hidden from inquisitive eyes." Meanwhile, Lieutenant J. H. Quinan of the *Corwin* had been sent ahead into the harbour in civilian clothing aboard the little coasting steamer *Elsie*, which carried mail from Sitka to Unalaska. Quinan's assignment was to keep watch on the *Coquitlam* and the schooners. Evans himself sailed into the bay briefly, posing as a tourist aboard a chartered yacht in the area with a group of sightseers.

As the *Coquitlam* approached Port Etches, Captain McLellan sent his mate and some men in a small boat with a letter for any U.S. patrol vessel that might be in the harbour, declaring the steamship was out of water and asking permission to enter. When word got back that there were no cutters in the bay, McLellan took the *Coquitlam* inside the next morning.

When the schooners had clustered around her, the *Corwin*, lurking outside the bay, moved in to make the seizure two hours after the *Coquitlam* had entered. Exactly what the steamship was doing at the time became a matter of controversy in the legal case that followed. "I did not receive anything but water in Port Etches," McLellan told a hearing. "There was no transfer of supplies to anyone in that port." Lieutenant Quinan testified the steamship had her cargo pennants flying, but McLellan insisted there were none. The steam winch was merely shifting coal in the ship's bunkers to level her, the Captain said, and the schooners were only getting mail.

McLellan also insisted the 6,000 sealskins aboard his vessel had been obtained in an earlier transfer outside Tonki Bay, beyond U.S. jurisdiction. He was certain the *Coquitlam* had been beyond the 3-mile limit there, but could not say whether she was 12 miles out. It seemed unlikely, since the schooner captains testified they had been towed for only 15 minutes. There was also convincing testimony on this point from Fred DeWales, a boat puller on the *Brenda*. DeWales said he had kept a diary since he was seven years old, making entries every night before turning in. His diary located the *Coquitlam* seven miles offshore at the time of the transfer. He knew the exact distance just by sight, the seaman said.

Captain A. K. St. Clair of the *Ocean Belle* in a later newspaper interview seemed to confirm, as the Americans claimed, that the *Coquitlam* was involved in more than shifting coal. St. Clair boasted that some crewmen had managed to get off a number of kegs of Jamaica rum just before the American

118

boarding party took control of the ship. "While the U.S. officers were coming on board on one side," he told a reporter, "we were taking one out from the window of the steward's room on the other."

On one aspect of the seizure both sides seemed to be in agreement: the Indian hunters aboard the schooners were thrown into a panic. They had learned to fear the Revenue cutters from their own experiences or those of fellow tribesmen during the seizures of 1886 and 1887. As soon as they realized the *Coquitlam* had been taken into custody, the Indians launched their canoes from the schooners and headed for shore. It took much persuasion to get them to return.

The *Corwin* gave the schooners time to take on water and then ordered them out of the bay. After transferring more skins to other schooners heading back to Victoria, most decided to cross the Pacific to the Commander Islands. Some were forced to abandon their voyages, however, because their still-nervous Indian hunters insisted on being taken home.

On July 5 Captain Hooper laid charges against the *Coquitlam* for violation of revenue laws. In his report to Washington he said the vessel had "entered a harbor of the United States, not a port of entry, without a permit from the customs authority, transferred and received a cargo in violation of law, and was engaged in towing within the jurisdiction of the United States, and for these acts subjected herself and cargo to confiscation."

Captain McLellan was ordered to take his ship to Sitka for a court appearance. Crew members were held in custody in their quarters. All agreed they had been well treated, but expressed indignation over the affair in strong terms after returning home.

The *Coquitlam* arrived in Victoria September 20 after being released on bond. A total of $64,000 had been put up by the schooner owners and $22,000 by Union Steamships. This had left them still short $1,660, which was raised by Captain McLellan with the help of some new friends in Sitka who identified with the sealers. He later expressed appreciation for the hospitality of the Sitkans during his enforced stay.

Comment by Victoria's newspapers, surprisingly muted on first learning of the seizure, became louder as the men told their stories. The *Colonist*, no doubt because it had been scooped on the story, initially declared the incident was not a high-handed act like the earlier schooner seizures and advised its readers to stay calm. Captain McLellan had failed to take precautions which would have precluded the ship's capture, the newspaper said.

Lawyer E. C. Hughes, acting in the U.S. courts for the Sealers Association in seeking the return of seized sealskins and provisions, said the law under which the *Coquitlam* was seized was intended only to prevent smuggling. He noted the regulations gave half the seized property to officers making the arrest and one-quarter to the collector of customs, a strong inducement to seize on any technicality. Hughes also said international law recognized the jurisdiction of nations only within one marine league (three miles) off-shore, not the four leagues claimed by the U.S.

This was the issue on which the case hung. The 12-mile cargo unloading limit on which the U.S. based its argument was an old Act of Congress the defendants said was unconstitutional. They also argued that the manifest was adequate under Canadian law. After the Territorial Court in Sitka ruled in favour of the government, the *Coquitlam* owners and the Sealers Association immediately launched an appeal in Circuit Court in San Francisco, setting in motion a legal wrangle that would drag on for 39 years.

The U.S. Government challenged the jurisdiction of the San Francisco court and it was not until May 18, 1896, almost four years after the seizure, that the U.S. Supreme Court upheld the lower court's right to hear the appeal. On November 19 the appeal was upheld by the Circuit Court, thereby quashing the forfeiture. After prolonged negotiations, Secretary of State John Hay advised British Ambassador Sir H. M. Durand in Washington the government was prepared to recognize liability and pay a reasonable indemnity, but required proof of damages. Britain failed to provide the information and the case went on.

An arbitration hearing on the damage claims was finally held in January, 1914. The U.S. began by denying liability on grounds that Captain Hooper had acted in the *bona fide* belief that revenue laws had been violated and the evidence showed probable cause for that assumption. The damage claim by Union Steamship Company for $104,709, including $40,000 for legal costs, was said to be "grossly exaggerated" and "practically amounting to fraud." It covered alleged losses arising not from the seizure itself but from other unrelated causes, the U.S. said, adding that the *Coquitlam* owners and the Sealers Association were squabbling among themselves in a legal action over freight charges, and were attempting to have the legal costs of that dispute paid by the Americans.

Union Steamships wanted to be reimbursed before the skins were released to the sealers. The 6,000 skins were in good condition and valued at $64,000. The company was seeking $8,000 for its services and $1,000 for the detention. In a counter action R. P. Rithet, Thomas Earle and Carne & Munsie sued the company to recover the skins. They put up $9,000 security pending the outcome of the hearing.

Rithet and Company claimed for interest on bonds it had posted, and the estate of William Munsie, who had owned three of the schooners involved in the Port Etches transaction, claimed $30,000 for loss of prospective profits as a result of the seizure of provisions on the *Coquitlam*. Another $10,700 was claimed for deterioration of the detained sealskins which were said to have disappeared or been chewed by rats. Harry Darling, Union Steamships Manager, sought $30,000 for loss of business by the company, but supplied no vouchers to back up his claim.

The U.S. pointed out that Captain McLellan admitted leaving Victoria without a manifest in order "to save time," and wrote out an invalid one after the seizure. McLellan had also failed to report to a customs officer in Alaska, as required by law.

The Court of Appeals decision was criticized at this hearing for basing its decision on a technical construction of the language of the statutes applicable to the case. The government said the seizure was made in the belief there was a 12-mile limit for the collection of customs and to prevent illicit trade. Although this was admittedly a grey area, as much a political as a judicial question, the *Coquitlam* and the schooners had clearly attempted to evade customs laws.

In 1913 the Americans offered $48,000 compensation, which the British accepted. But no money changed hands for another 13 years, when the U.S. paid a total of $60,000 — the award plus interest — into Canada's Exchequer Court. Specific amounts for the two surviving claimants were not fixed, however, and in 1931 there was another lawsuit to determine how the money should be divided. The survivors were upset because the Dominion government deducted $1,000 in costs from the $60,000 and paid no interest for the five years it held the money.

There was another sequel to the *Coquitlam* affair which created a brief stir in Victoria. In 1901 Robley Evans published his memoirs, *A Sailor's Log*, which mirrored its author — headstrong, indiscreet, pungent. Evans' highly-coloured version of what took place in and around Tonki Bay and Port Etches in 1892 prompted a reply in the Seattle *Times* by Ashmun Brown, the newspaperman who had been aboard the *Coquitlam* during the seizure. His article, accusing Evans of "absolute falsehoods and absurd conclusions," was gleefully reprinted in the *Colonist*.

Brown challenged Evans on a number of "facts" in his book: The steamer had on board only the 6,000 skins transferred at Tonki Bay, not 30,000 as claimed by Evans; the weather was clear in Port Etches, not foggy as Evans described conditions; and no supplies were transferred to the schooners because Captain McLellan insisted they wait until next day and go three miles out.

"What a world of trouble is caused governments by those officers of the Evans stripe," Brown concluded, "who insist on reading their orders between the lines rather than on the lines."

Although only a handful of schooners sailed out of Seattle, the press in that city was generally sympathetic to the Victoria sealers and strongly opposed to the A.C.C. monopoly on the Pribilofs. The newspapers had been critical in March of 1892 when the schooner *James G. Swan*, (formerly the *Anna Beck*), had been ordered forfeited by a Seattle court for sealing in the Bering. The vessel was owned by a Makah Indian at Neah Bay, Chestoqua

Peterson. On July 24 the Port Townsend Chamber of Commerce presented a memorial to the federal government urging the North Pacific and Bering be made free areas for fishermen, including sealers, as in the North Atlantic.

In the fall the *Post-Intelligencer* carried a surprising interview with Lieutenant John Clyde Sullivan, paymaster on the U.S.S. *Mohican*, who said seizing pelagic sealers was wrong. "We haven't the shadow of a right to declare Bering Sea a closed sea," Sullivan added, "and we will be knocked out entirely by the International Commission." The *Colonist* was pleased again to reprint the interview.

A total of 27 American-owned sealing schooners, the majority from San Francisco, were out during the 1892 season. They took 23,695 skins, of which 3,381 were delivered to fur buyers in Victoria. There was a record number of 65 B.C. schooners, employing 952 whites and 491 Indians. A total of $300,000 was paid out in wages and another $300,000 spent on food and gear. Their total catch was 45,000. Of these, 24,531 came from the Gulf of Alaska, 4,479 from the lower coast, and 14,804 from the Asian side.

Despite extra patrols on the rookeries, with signal rockets and a new telephone line around St. Paul to sound the alarm against raiders, a few schooners still succeeded in taking seals ashore. The *Mollie Adams* of Seattle got away with 1,600 skins in one raid.

In April, Britain announced she would pay $100,000 in compensation to vessels which claimed for loss of earnings because of the *modus* agreement in 1891. U.S. liability for the seizures was to be determined later and the British reimbursed. Forty-four claims totalling $640,000 were gone over by two special British investigators in 1892. G. Y. Gledowe, a Treasury Department official, and Arthur J. Ross, a marine claims adjuster, were in Victoria from May to August making a detailed examination. Thirteen claims were rejected outright because their earnings on the coast covered their outfitting costs for the year and any prospective losses in the Bering. The *E. B. Marvin* claim was rejected because she had ignored a warning to leave the Bering, and that of the *Otto* because her papers were not in order. The biggest award of $10,047 went to the steam-powered *Thistle*. The *Vancouver Belle* was next with $7,210. The awards to the vessel owners were generally double those to the captain, crew and hunters. Nevertheless, most seem satisfied to receive any amount of compensation, even though the total was less than one-sixth the amount claimed.

In a precedent that would be followed in later compensation awards, Indian hunters got less than whites doing the same work. Most of the Indians received an amount under $100, while the whites got over $200 each.

Also in April, the N.A.C.C. filed a court action claiming $1,500,000 from the U.S. government for the sharp reduction in the number of seals it was able to harvest. Instead of its 60,000 quota in each of 1890 and 1891, the company took a total of only 34,477 for both years. The suit was withdrawn when the government adjusted taxes and other levies. But another claim of $1,600,000 was filed in the fall when the quota was reduced from 100,000 to 75,000 and only 32,000 skins were actually taken. The lawyer for the N.A.C.C. in these actions was none other than the ubiquitous Noah L. Jeffries.

Meanwhile, U.S. "investigators" were busy in Victoria in 1892 gathering information to support the American arbitration case. The U.S. Consul, Levi W. Myers, was assigned to make an evaluation of the schooners and check into their ownership. Since it was widely believed the final outcome of the dispute would be the purchase of the fleet by government, the owners believed Myers' estimates could be a factor in how much they would eventually receive. As a result, they were circumspect and evasive when approached. "The exceeding sensitiveness of the sealing interests can hardly be appreciated by one who has not touched it," Myers told Assistant Secretary of State William Wharton in a report dated April 29, 1892. He was compelled to be cautious and prudent in his inquiries, he added. Myers also accused Customs Collector A. R. Milne of withholding information on the vessels and their catches.[4]

When the Consul went to shipbuilder Samuel Turpel to certify his evaluation list, he was rebuffed. And when Turpel advised the sealers of Myers' inquiries they claimed his estimates were "utterly ridiculous." They had previously got on well with the Consul, but now there was an open breach. Myers eventually persuaded W. J. Stephens of Spratt's Shipyard to confirm his schooner evaluations.

Myers' investigation of ownership turned up the fact that most of the schooners belonged to outside investors rather than the sealers themselves. His list included grocers, real estate and insurance agents, building contractors, saloon-keepers, a druggist, and the registrar of the Supreme Court. Only a few owned a schooner outright; most held a number of the 64 shares into which each vessel was divided. Myers reported there were also hidden owners, including American investors whose mortgages were not always registered.

In addition to Myers, the U.S. had other investigators digging up information in Victoria and along the west coast of Vancouver Island, where the steamship *McArthur* visited a number of villages to interview Indian hunters, storekeepers and others involved in the industry. Major W. H. Williams, a former Treasury agent in the Pribilofs, set up an office in Victoria's Driard Hotel to interview seamen. The sealers noted scornfully that the best men were already out at sea and Williams was paying $2 to waterfront hangers-on who knew little about the business. Another Treasury Department sleuth, a "Mr. Day," posed as a correspondent of the New York *Herald* to gain information from the sealers. They later denied being paid by Day for their cooperation but admitted being treated to dinner by him.

A. J. Henry of San Francisco was appointed as a special agent by the State Department to make investigations in Victoria. He pretended to be interested in making a sealing voyage in order to get crewmen and masters to talk. Henry later reported to his superiors that he had found public sentiment in the city to be "very bitter against our government." The citizens he interviewed sympathized with the sealers and were cautious in what they said about the industry. "The Sealers Association has among its members some prominent citizens of the city and has a great deal of influence, and the residents seem to be afraid to incur the displeasure of the Association . . . I at once saw that it would be utterly impossible to obtain written testimony in Victoria contrary to the interests of those engaged in the sealing business, because any person giving such testimony would be boycotted by those in sympathy with the sealers and probably ruined financially."

Restrictions on the land kill resulted in higher prices and better profits for the pelagic sealers. A dozen schooners were added to the Victoria fleet during 1892. A stylish addition was the *Casco*, a luxurious yacht built in San Francisco in 1878 for dentist Samuel Merritt at a cost of $40,000. She became famous after Merritt chartered her to Robert Louis Stevenson, who wrote about her in his South Seas stories.[5] A Victoria syndicate headed by Captain Dick Folger acquired the *Casco* for $7,000 in 1892. She had a number of owners over the years, including Victor Jacobson. Between 1898 and 1901 the *Casco* was owned in Anacortes, Washington, smuggling Chinese immigrants and opium. Later she made amends for this nefarious trade by serving as a training vessel for Sea Scouts in Vancouver. Her colourful career ended in 1919 when she was wrecked during a trip to Siberia with a party of gold hunters.

Despite expansion, there was growing pessimism about the industry. The owners complained they were taking all the risks, while the crews took chances by hunting in forbidden waters in order to increase their catch and wages. Many boats were for sale at low prices. On November 9 the 117-ton *E. B. Marvin*, the second largest schooner in the Victoria fleet, was sold at auction for a mere $6,800. She was built of oak, only eight years old, and in good condition.

Other seizure victims of the American cutters in 1892 were the 30-ton *Henrietta*, built on Lopez Island, which was apprehended by the *Yorktown* on September 2 just inside the Bering. The schooner refused to take the line that was thrown, hoping that rough seas would thwart a boarding party. But the dogged Robley Evans managed to get a boat in the water and towed the *Henrietta* to Unalaska, from where she was sent on to Sitka. Her trial was delayed and in December the crew — four whites and 24 Kyuquot Indians — were still stuck in Sitka without money for passage down the coast. They were unable to find work and were forced to camp out on the beach. The *Coquitlam* refused to take them home. The captain and two officers were confined in jail for nine months awaiting trial.

Also noteworthy was the seizure July 19 by the cutter *Rush* of the schooner *Winifred* near Amak Island on the Bering side of the Aleutians. She was considered a prize catch by the Americans because her skipper was Captain Gustave Hansen, the notorious poacher who had made a number of raids on the Pribilof rookeries. In 1890 on the *Adele* he had raided them twice in late fall. The following November Hansen was in charge of the *Borealis* when 400 seals were killed on the beach at a St. Paul rookery.

In June of 1892 the *Winifred* had been stopped by the *Mohican* and warned not to enter the Bering, but Hansen had been able to conceal his identity to the boarding party. When Captain Washington C. Coulson of the *Rush* boarded the *Winifred* in July her sealing boats were still in the water and there were freshly killed seals on the deck. This time Hansen was identified and Evans made sure his prize prisoner would pay for his sins. He sent the *Corwin* to St. Paul to pick up Treasury Department agents to appear as witnesses at Hansen's trial in Sitka. Evans also insisted that because the *Winifred* had participated in the cargo transfer at Tonki Bay, she did not have to be turned over to the British since the seizure was made outside the terms of the *modus vivendi*. Captain Parr of H.M.S. *Melpomene* reluctantly concurred. Because of involved advance preparations, Hansen's trial was also delayed nine months while he and his two chief officers languished in the Sitka jail.

CHAPTER NINE

Paris

It was a contest of forensic talent by the foremost lawyers of the English-speaking world, and such a contest as had never before been seen.

—JOHN W. FOSTER

While Robley Evans policed the Alaska side and Boris de Levron the Asian waters, the diplomats of Britain and the United States were busy ironing out the details for an arbitrated settlement of the fur seal dispute.

One of the stumbling blocks in these negotiations, as it would be in years to come, was Canada. Both major powers considered Ottawa's demands a nuisance. "The difficulty of this triangular negotiation is extreme," Lord Salisbury complained. James Blaine, as usual, had been more outspoken. He said Salisbury should have admitted at the beginning that "no arrangement could be made unless Canada concurred in it, and that all negotiation with the British Government direct was but a loss of time."

The man doing most of the behind-the-scenes work for the U.S. was John Watson Foster, a lawyer who specialized in international cases. A life-long Republican, Foster served as Secretary of State for nine months in 1892 during Blaine's illness and after his resignation. (A grandson, John Foster Dulles, would later serve in the same post.) It was a controversial appointment. The New York *Times* alleged Foster had taken diplomatic assignments in foreign countries as a means of advancing his legal practice.

When the Harrison administration was defeated later in the year, Foster returned to his law firm and continued his work as the "handyman" of the State Department, with a special assignment to work on the Bering Sea case. Controversy dogged him in this role too. Foster had a business connection with the North American Commercial Company, which succeeded the A.C.C. as lessees of the Pribilofs in 1890. His critics said his concern for the preservation of the seal herd was motivated by a desire to improve N.A.C.C. profits.

The controversy that surrounded Foster during most of his career was not dampened by his abrasive personality. As John Hay, a subsequent Secretary of State, noted: "Foster's worst enemy would never accuse him of any tendency to mercy or tenderness to an opponent." He was blunt and unyielding in negotiations, haggling over every detail. One biographer described him as "nationalistic and partisan throughout...a conservative, inflexible, fundamentalist Presbyterian."[1] His attitude was one of moral rectitude and self-righteousness.

This was especially so in any dispute involving Britain. Foster viewed the British as commercial rivals and the main threat to the economic and military interests of the U.S. In some instances he took a harder line toward Canada than Blaine had done. The British and Canadians regarded him as unmannerly and boorish when he took his rough, country-lawyer manners to the negotiating table.

But they learned never to underestimate Foster's abilities. He was meticulous when preparing a case, mastering every detail of complex issues. His strength lay more in backroom bargaining than the gentlemanly atmosphere of formal proceedings.

In the first week of September, 1892, Britain and the U.S. exchanged the cases which they intended to present to the Arbitration Tribunal. When the U.S. protested that the British had not dealt with the habits of the seals, the British insisted that aspect came under Article 7, the regulations which would follow if the U.S. lost the verdict. They did agree, however, to hand over the report of Baden-Powell and Dawson, which covered the details of seal life, and to extend the deadline for the U.S. counter-case.

The counter-cases of the two countries were exchanged in February of 1893. The first formal Arbitration meeting was held in Paris March 23, then adjourned until April 4. It was agreed the sessions should be open to the public.

The hearings continued much longer than anticipated. The French thought they would take only a few weeks, but they went on for almost five months. The oral argument began April 12 and ran until July 8. The hearings were closed after July 10 until the verdict was rendered August 15.[2]

There were seven men on the Tribunal—two each from Britain and the U.S. and the other three from France, Italy and Norway-Sweden. The Americans were Mr. Justice John M. Harlan of the Supreme Court and Senator John T. Morgan of Alabama; the British side was represented by Lord Hannen and Sir John Thompson, the Canadian Minister of Justice who later served a brief term as Prime Minister. The others were Baron Alphonse Chandron de Courcel of France, a financier and railway magnate who had served as ambassador to Berlin and was now a Senator; Marquis Emelio Visconti Venosta, a former Prime Minister of Italy; and Gregers Gram, Minister of State for Norway-Sweden. The chairman was Baron Courcel of the host country.

Counsel for the U.S. were James C. Carter, Edward J. Phelps, Henry W. Blodgett, Frederick R. Courdet, Robert Lansing and William Williams. They were appointed by the outgoing Harrison administration but were approved by Walter Q. Gresham, the Secretary of State in the second Cleveland administration, which had succeeded Harrison. Gresham was a former Republican colleague of Foster who had supported him in his bid for the GOP presidential nomination. Gresham later switched to the Democrats. Of the seven men chosen to represent the Administration at Paris, four were Democrats — Phelps, Carter, Courdet and Morgan — and three Republicans — Foster, Williams and Lansing. Despite opposing political loyalties, they were a tightly knit group with some intriguing connections.

Lansing, a lawyer for the State Department was Foster's son-in-law. Williams was the son of C. A. Williams, a former official of the A.C.C. Phelps, the impetuous U.S. ambassador to Britain, like Foster had a legal practice that did business with the principals of the N.A.A.C. Phelps had worked closely with Foster and Lansing in preparing the U.S. case during the summer of 1892. Phelps was a strong speaker and understood politics, while Carter had read law more widely and was noted for his ability to clearly elucidate an abstract legal principle. Carter had been recognized for some years as the leader of the American Bar. Courdet was a prominent New York lawyer who had been recommended by Phelps primarily because he was fluent in French. Blodgett was a close friend of Harrison, who persuaded him to serve despite failing health. Blodgett contributed little to the Paris hearings.

Agents and counsel for the British were Attorney-General Sir Charles Russell, Sir Richard Webster (Russell's predecessor as Attorney-General), Charles Hibbert Tupper, the Canadian Minister of Marine, and Toronto lawyer Christopher Robinson. Foster later praised the work of the two Canadians at Paris. He described Tupper as "a good lawyer and a very alert politician." Robinson was "a lawyer of fine ability and high character, who made one of the most cogent and able of the arguments delivered before the Tribunal."[3]

Despite a dispute over the official language to be used, the French were pleased to have the Tribunal sit in Paris. The government placed at its disposal the entire lower floor of the Ministry of Foreign Affairs on the Quai d'Orsay, which had an extensive garden at the rear. On their arrival the participants were welcomed at a luncheon given by the President of France, M. Sadi Carnot, at the Elysee Palace. There were a number of other social events during the course of the hearings, including elegant garden parties for the delegates' wives. One of the most popular hosts was Lord Dufferin, the former Governor-General of Canada who was now British ambassador in Paris. A gregarious Irishman, Dufferin was a friend of Foster's from 12 years before when they were both envoys in St. Petersburg.[4]

A dour Presbyterian, Foster still liked a good party. The American delegation lodged at the Continental Hotel was described by Foster as "a merry company." A bit too merry for some of the folks back home as it turned

128

S.S. *Danube*

USN research ship *Albatross* and Revenue Cutter *McCulloch*

Dora Sieward *Footing Down Juan de Fuca Strait*

out later when the entertainment bills were scrutinized by Congress. Foster was bitterly defensive about allegations of extravagance.

On the language issue, the French Foreign Minister, Alexandre Ribot, commented sourly that it was bizarre to designate Paris as the site of a court proceeding at which a French judge (Courcel) was to sit and to ask him to render his decision in English. The U.S. had insisted on such a procedure, however, because it felt it would be at a disadvantage if French was used since it was much easier for Britain to find jurists fluent in that language. (Ironically, the leader of the British delegation, Sir Charles Russell, was weak in French and likely would not have participated had the proceedings been in French.) A compromise of sorts was worked out to satisfy the French. The proceedings were to be in English but a protocol of each day's session would be prepared in French, accompanied by an English version. The verdict was rendered and signed in both languages. Courcel had no trouble with this arrangement, being almost as fluent in English as in French.

The British case had been prepared under Webster's direction while Attorney-General and he had expected to be chief counsel at Paris. But in one of the sudden changes of government which occurred in Britain in this period, Gladstone returned as Prime Minister and named Russell as his Attorney-General. And so Webster became Russell's junior at Paris.

It was not the first time he had been upstaged by the flamboyant Russell. The two men had clashed dramatically before a historic commission in 1888. Russell had taken the case of Charles Stewart Parnell against the London *Times*, which had accused the Irish leader of sympathizing with rebel perpetrators of violence against Britain. Webster acted for the *Times*. Although Irish himself, Russell was a moderate who had never taken up the cause of Home Rule. But his passionate defence of Parnell was described as "noble, inspired" and "one of the most remarkable speeches ever made in an English court of justice."[5] Russell spoke for eight days outlining the historic grievances of Ireland against the English. This forensic *tour de force* routed the suave and conciliatory Webster.

The fur seal arbitration hearing in Paris was the last great case in which Russell appeared as an advocate. In May of 1894 he was raised to a life peerage as Lord Russell of Killowen and soon after became Britain's Lord Chief Justice. Webster succeeded to that post on Russell's death and was elevated to the peerage as Baron Alverstone, gaining notoriety in Canada as the man who surrendered her interests in the Alaska Boundary Tribunal in 1903.

Russell was described as having "a clear head, a strong will, an imperious temper, and an independent spirit … action was the principle of his life."[6] Russell said one of the secrets of his success was not allowing himself to be distracted. He did not read much other than the law. His favourite off-hour pursuits were sailing, chess and horse-racing. The latter passion led to embarrassment in Paris when his eagerness to gain a better view of the Grand Prix violated track rules and he was arrested. Because his French was so poor, Russell was not released until a junior member of the British staff arrived and explained to police his official position.

Foster was bemused by Russell's "peculiarities," particularly his habit of snuff-taking. "His sneeze often echoed through the tribunal chamber," Foster later wrote, "accompanied by the flourish of a huge red bandanna handkerchief which he carried."[7]

The dominant figure at Paris was unquestionably Russell. The Americans were often angered by his icy, aggressive manner, but they grudgingly admired his skill. Williams described Russell as "a man of great distinction at the bar, he was of a forceful and aggressive nature, with a rapid and incisive delivery which expressed his thoughts with great clarity."[8] Russell was famed as a cross-examiner. When he rose to question a witness his defiant bearing, haughtiness and piercing deep-set eyes had a mesmerizing effect. As one observer described it, he had the same effect on a witness "that a cobra produces on a rabbit."

There was accommodation for a small number of spectators, but the arcane legal arguments that ran on for hours must have been tedious for most. As Foster observed, however, "it was a contest of forensic talent by the foremost lawyers of the English-speaking world, and such a contest as had never before been seen."[9]

In opening the hearings Courcel said the establishment of the Arbitration Tribunal "put a happy end to a dispute which it seemed at one time could only terminate in war."[10] And so the historic debate began, far removed from the teeming herds of the Pribilofs, the waterfront haunts of the pelagic sealers and the isolated villages of the Nuu-chah-nulth hunters.

Although Blaine had attempted to assert American sovereignty over the Bering, his successors realized this claim was not likely to stand up in an international tribunal. As a form of insurance they advanced the new argument that the U.S. had the "right of protection and property" in the fur seals even when they were outside the 3-mile limit. This assertion became the central issue of the case.

The British effectively squelched Blaine's *mare clausum* argument by declaring that rights of navigation in open seas could not be taken away by decree of one country: "They are natural rights, and exist to their full extent unless specifically modified, controlled, or limited by treaty." The Bering was described as a "common highway" to the Arctic Ocean fisheries and the mouth of the Yukon River.

The British had been helped in this argument when the Americans became the victims of a bizarre intrigue. It began in a basement room of the State Department in Washington where the Archives of the Russian-American Company had been gathering dust since the 1867 Purchase of Alaska. The five boxes contained bound volumes of orders and general correspondence.

They had been looked at only once in the intervening years, by a Russian emigre known as Ivan Petroff who had worked on Hubert Howe Bancroft's *History of Alaska*. During the preparation of the American case to be presented at Paris, Petroff was hired to hunt through these Russian-language documents for relevant material to support American claims of jurisdiction over the Bering. He translated 30 of the papers, "purporting to show instances, some of them striking ones, of what our government hoped it might be able to prove."[11] References to fur seals were inserted in the documents where none existed. (The seals were not considered important at the time the papers were written early in the century; sea otters were still the big prize).

His employers were delighted with Petroff's discoveries and gave facsimiles of the original documents to the British. But the coup turned into disaster when it was learned that Petroff's translations were fakes. There are conflicting accounts of how his perfidy was discovered. In his *Memoirs* Foster says a clerk in the State Department Library, William C. Mayo, stumbled on the fraud while practising his Russian by checking the Petroff translations against the originals. Mayo reported his findings to Williams, who told Foster it appeared to be an act of "treachery" by Petroff.

But Williams, writing 50 years later, claimed the credit for himself. He said he knew a little Russian, at least enough to recognize Russian capital letters. Going over the Petroff documents one night, he noted that most of the "striking passages" had proper names such as Kamchatka, Bering, Aleutian, Okhotsk. But he could not find them in the originals. His suspicions were aroused and, before the evening was over, "became satisfied that a fraud of the first order had been practised on the government."[12]

Confronted with the evidence, Petroff broke down and signed a full confession. Charges were considered but the Attorney-General said there was no statute applicable in the unusual case. Petroff drifted into obscurity and liquor. Around Wrangell, Alaska, he had been known in his early days as "Hollow Legs" for his prowess as a drinker.

The Petroff affair occurred in the fall of 1892 after the Americans had presented the British with their case containing the false information. Foster immediately advised Julian Pauncefote of his government's embarrassment. He said correct translations would be made and the U.S. case amended.

John Bassett Moore, a State Department employee who helped prepare the American case and later wrote monumental histories of international law and arbitrations, including the fur seal dispute, speculated on Petroff's motives. He believed Petroff had tried to ingratiate himself with the government and impress upon it the importance of the Alaska archives in the hope that he might be employed to classify and translate them.[13]

The U.S. maintained at Paris that the Russians had established a fur seal industry on the Pribilofs which they attempted to protect against intruders, and that the same policy was followed by the Americans after the 1867 purchase. The fur seals were among a class of animals "susceptible to ownership." The U.S. was entitled to a property interest in the herd because it had practised restraint in protecting the seals on their rookeries. Skins from the surplus males were supplied to the rest of the world through trade.

Canadians had no right to destroy the herd by hunting at sea, the U.S. argued. While conceding the general rule of freedom of the seas, the Americans said that did not condone actions injurious to the interests of any nation bordering the world's oceans. The invasion of such interests for the purpose of private gain was not permissible.

The British said that when all the novel legal sophistry of the Americans was put aside, the U.S. case was based on a claim of property in the seals. They noted the U.S. could not find a precedent to back its claim, but was calling for a new international law to meet the special circumstances of the case. Everyone had the right to fish on the high seas, Britain said. (Sealing was actually hunting, not fishing, however.)

Britain's case also included a number of factual errors, such as the claim that the seals at first did not fear humans but now "dread the approach of man, and endeavour to flee from him." In fact, nothing other than a drop in numbers had changed on the Pribilof rookeries after a century of ritualized harvest. Britain also put forward the dubious argument that since sealskins were a luxury item, and the seals consumed large quantities of fish, it might be beneficial to mankind to kill them. But fish were only a small part of the fur seals' diet, and those they did consume were seldom harvested by man. The British mistakenly claimed the mothers did not go to sea for some weeks after giving birth to their pups, and fasted on the rookery like the bulls.

Even more blatant was the British claim that use of shotguns instead of spears had reduced losses because they made it necessary to get closer to the seal. The introduction of firearms had actually resulted in a greatly reduced rate of recovery. A speared seal seldom escaped because the harpoon-head was attached to a line, whereas a seal riddled with buckshot often sank before the hunter could reach it. If the seal was shot in the head while the rest of the body was under water, it was almost certain to sink before it could be gaffed.

Brazen too was the British claim that females constituted less than 40 per cent of the catch. The U.S. said the figure was closer to 80 or 90 per cent and that three-quarters of these were either gravid or nursing. Research carried out after the Paris Tribunal proved the U.S. contention. Later studies also confirmed that, contrary to British claims, the Pribilof seals do not give birth

132

at sea or at any land location other than the islands, except perhaps a small percentage that joined the Asian herd and hauled out on the Commander Island rookeries.

Responsibility for these errors in the British case rested ultimately with the Victoria sealers. They were interviewed in great detail during preparation of the case and simply lied in their answers in the hope of preserving their industry. As a result, the British counsel at Paris "became at once and remained throughout, partisans and champions of pelagic sealing, sacrificing the principles of science to political expediency."[14]

Britain also contended that the capital invested by Canadians in the sealing fleet exceeded that of the Americans in the Pribilofs. That too was a misleading argument. The U.S. correctly pointed out that the British themselves had $5,000,000 invested in the processing of sealskins and that the number of people engaged in the industry in the U.S., England and France was more than 6,000. Canadian investment was "insignificant" in the over-all picture, amounting to less than $300,000. If the seal herd was wiped out by unrestricted pelagic hunting, the greatest loss would not be felt by the schooner owners and crews.

Although the British were the worst offenders, the American arguments were not free of error. The most entertaining, if irrelevant, aspect of its case revolved around what is known as *animus revertendi*, the regular return of animals to a particular location and the possession implied thereby. The precedents cited went back to Roman and ancient English law. James Carter said the regular return of animals to the same place made them domestic in law. The fur seals were actually land animals, he said, domestic in their habits and readily controlled by man, even to the extent of "voluntarily placing themselves when on the islands within the control of man." They thus became the subjects of "ordinary husbandry as much as sheep or any other cattle." In laboured support of this argument, the U.S. reached into Gaius' *Elements of Roman Law* to liken seals to bees, deer, pigeons, swans and geese.

Russell replied by quoting from the British legal writer Thomas Chitty on *The Prerogatives of the Crown* dealing with the ownership of fish and birds by royalty. Chitty said the state can regulate its own citizens but not foreigners outside its territorial jurisdiction.

Lord Hannen interjected: "If a Royal swan at large in the country where the King had the right to swans escaped to another country where the other King had the same right to swans at large, which King would the swan belong to?"

"Quite so, my lord," Russell replied. "For myself I should be prepared to back the right of the King in whose territory it was found."

Russell said *animus revertendi* did not refer to migratory animals, but only those that returned in a matter of hours or days, induced by man through

133

confinement or training. Wild animals such as the fur seals were *res nullius*, "and therefore a thing which anyone may capture; a thing which the man who first possesses and captures may acquire the property in." If the seal was a domestic animal, Russell asked, why was it not branded, as American law required cattle on the prairies to be branded? He was being sarcastic, but branding was actually attempted a few years later on the Pribilof seals.

Destruction of the herd was avoidable, Carter said. "It can be easily, certainly preserved, either by an award of property to the United States, or by the establishment of regulations tantamount to such an award of property." Permitting anyone to destroy a useful breed of animals because they happened to move freely in the sea would be a "crime against nature," Carter said. Subsistence hunting by Indians could carry on without danger to the herd, but "it will not do, under cover of that pursuit ... to employ these Indians and man large vessels with them upon the high seas there to attack these seals for the purpose of furnishing them to commerce." It was one thing to hunt for meat and clothing, but when the Indians "want to engage in commerce and clothe themselves in broadcloth and fill themselves with rum in addition to their original wants ... a different problem is presented."

Carter concluded the American case by declaring: "The doctrine maintained by us simply amounts to this, that whenever a vessel is caught red-handed, *flagrante delicto*, in pelagic sealing, the Government of the United States has the right to seize her and capture her; that is to say, it has the right to employ necessary force for the purpose of protecting, in the only way in which it can protect, its property in the seals, or its property interest in the industry which it maintains upon the islands. That is the extent of our claim."

Russell replied that international law was based on rules of conduct which nations have agreed should govern their relations with one another. It rested on the principle of consent and could not be created by the Tribunal. But Russell's position begged the question: Why didn't the British consent in this instance to curb the wasteful activities of the pelagic sealers?

The dilemma was alluded to by Courcel after Russell said sanctions required to enforce any regulation of pelagic sealing were the "moral obligation" of the countries involved and not the responsibility of the Tribunal. "If we leave the case in such a situation that the two nations are left to do things which we know they will not do," Courcel protested, "we shall have done nothing."

For all his reputed no-nonsense approach to the law, Russell was not above engaging in a bit of anthropomorphic rhetoric. At one point he suggested that if the seal was given a choice of being knocked on the head on land or taking its chance of being shot in water, it would opt to make a target of itself for the pelagic hunter. The seals had a sporting chance at sea, Russell said.

134

Both Carter and Russell in their arguments, unwittingly or presciently, forecast problems that would arise in the salmon fishing industry in future years. When the habits of fish were better understood they might lend themselves to the same methods of protection as fur seals, Carter said. Russell wondered what the result would be when fishermen from other nations catching salmon outside territorial limits damaged the local canning industry.

During the Tribunal hearings an event occurred outside its halls which had a bearing on the debate within. It resulted from the ongoing negotiations between Britain and Russia over seizures of Canadian schooners around the Commander Islands. The Russians took the position that the *modus vivendi* agreed upon by the U.S. and Britain had increased pressure on her rookeries because of the larger number of schooners there. Consequently she imposed, in the interests of "legitimate self-defence," a ban on sealing within 10 miles of all her coasts and creation of a 30-mile zone around the Commander Islands. Russia also agreed to restrict her land kill to 30,000 annually, and to pay damages for British schooners previously seized.

Although Britain refused to formally concede Russia's right to interfere with her ships outside the 3-mile limit, she agreed "to afford all reasonable and legitimate assistance to Russia in the existing circumstances." Britain therefore accepted a pact establishing the protective zones for seals. Concluded in May, the treaty was read to the Tribunal by Webster on June 21.

The Americans were furious that the British would make this concession to Russia while taking such a stone-wall position in negotiations with them. There was little the U.S. could do, however, since it had vetoed Russian participation at Paris.

A British proposal that the Pribilof land kill be limited to 50,000 annually, and that pelagic sealers be banned within a 20-mile zone around the Pribilofs, was emphatically rejected by the U.S. The Americans said the rookery quota was its own business and a 20-mile zone would not protect nursing females, which often travelled 100 miles or more from the rookeries to feed.

The U.S. estimated that 480,000 pelagic skins were taken between 1872 and 1891, mostly females with young, and that 60 per cent had been lost. The aggregate loss to the Pribilof herd in those 20 years was 1,430,000, counting pups and the unborn. Two-thirds of this loss occurred in the seven years preceding 1892.

Robinson retorted that pelagic sealing was "a perfectly justifiable and proper industry...respectable employment." He conceded, however, that it did have objectionable aspects. The British concluded their argument by declaring once again they were being compelled to stand up to defend freedom of the seas. But freedom of the seas was *not* the crux of the dispute. Britain was employing legal rhetoric to obscure the real issue, which was preservation of the seal herd. Her case amounted to a defence of slaughtering female seals at sea with their unborn pups.

Nevertheless, the Americans became increasingly pessimistic about the outcome as the hearing progressed. Phelps wrote on April 2 to Bayard, now the American ambassador in London: "I fear the case will be much protracted and with arbitrators holding the balance who understand neither the English language nor English law, the result cannot be predicted." Phelps also complained of the "crudeness and imperfections" of the treaty setting up the arbitration hearing. The majority of American newspapers were also convinced the U.S. had a weak case. Of the American claim to property rights in the seals, the New York *Evening Post* commented: "It is difficult to decide whether this should be treated as law or natural history. In either view it is as novel as erroneous."

A number of prominent Americans were critical of the U.S. performance at Paris. Writing to President Cleveland, Bayard complained that Phelps "always exhibited a disposition for small aggressiveness against Great Britain, which I did not consider politic, wise or self-respecting in the United States." John Bassett Moore, in a letter to Bayard, deplored Phelps' petulant interruptions during the debate and his threat that the U.S. might refuse to pay compensation if the decision of the arbitrators went against it. Such a position "was not in good taste and was scarcely defensible," Moore wrote.

Foster continued to be optimistic, however. He wrote Gresham on June 20: "I feel very confident that if we do not secure a recognition of property, we shall obtain regulations which will be an effective protection to the seals and save to our Government the large revenues from them."

Phelps began the closing argument for the U.S. on June 22, concluding: "We contend that this case of ours, this right of property in protection, call it what you please, is as completely established by the just principles of international law as it is by the consideration of ethics and morality."

It came as no great surprise, however, when the arbitrators ruled against the U.S. on all the major points, largely because they conflicted with the accepted doctrine of freedom of the seas. The arbitrators regarded regulations as the best way to settle differences between the two nations.

The regulations, which were regarded as favouring the Americans, were destined to become more important than the award itself. The first forbade sealing at any time within 60 miles of the Pribilofs. Other regulations provided for a closed season north of the 35th parallel from May 1 to July 31, and a ban on the use of shotguns or rifles in the Bering at all times. Firearms could be used outside the Bering, however, during the legal period. The Tribunal said the two governments should review the regulations in five years.

The Tribunal also declared that "in view of the critical condition to which it appears certain that the race of fur-seals is now reduced ... the Arbitrators

Edgar Crow Baker

Jennie Thelin (aka. *Carmencita, Acapulco*), under tow, *circa* 1905

H.M.S. *Pheasant*

Bering Sea Arbitration Tribunal members in Paris, 1893

John W. Foster

Sophia Sutherland in drydock, San Francisco

think fit to recommend both Governments to come to an understanding in order to prohibit any killing of fur seals, either on land or at sea, for a period of two or three years, or at least one year." This recommendation was not acted upon.

Although he voted with the majority on each, Visconti-Venosta expressed concern that the regulations nullified all that the Tribunal had conceded on the question of rights. He emphasized that he did not intend to suppress pelagic sealing altogether.

In respect to damages arising from the treaty and the *modus vivendi*, the arbitrators decided to let the two sides negotiate their differences.

On August 15 the seven arbitrators signed the award in triplicate, on parchment. Chairman Courcel summed up the proceedings: "We know that our work is not perfect, we feel its defects... we had to base our action on circumstances necessarily liable to change. Our desire is that this voluntary engagement may not cause regret to either of them, though we have required of both sacrifices which they may, perhaps, regard as serious. This part of our work inaugurates great innovation... our work is a first attempt at a sharing of the products of the ocean... if this attempt succeeds, it will doubtless be followed by numerous imitations, until the entire planet — until the waters as well as the continents — will have become the subject of a careful partition."

Morgan regretted that the Tribunal had not been able to create a new international law that would preserve the seals. The U.S. would however accept the final award as the best possible result under existing conditions, he said. "We hope for still broader results from the foundations we have laid in this new field of international agreements."

Morgan also submitted a written minority opinion which declared that Canada, without diplomatic power or responsibility, was able to control and embarrass British diplomacy "even in antagonism with the interests of the British people." Morgan said Britain, as the result of Canadian recalcitrance, had changed her attitude on the questions at issue "without changing her views of what was right."

American sealers were sheltering under the British flag and Canadian registry to evade American laws, Morgan said, and the blame lay with Canada: "If Canada had passed any reasonable laws for protecting these interests of the United States, even during negotiations, a serious disturbance of neighborly feeling could have been avoided... the policy of Canada has made it impossible for Congress to restrain the people of the United States from participating in this reckless destruction, and from this defiance of her public policy and laws."

On the subject of regulations, Morgan said restrictions on the use of firearms by pelagic sealers were inadequate. Guns should be banned outright because they doomed the seals. "The genius of man, in killing the seals, is almost infinitely superior to the instinct of self-preservation in the seal."

Gresham expressed fears that Britain would not strictly enforce the regulations to save the herd. "The Canadians will doubtless endeavor to induce the British Government to consent to nothing which will make pelagic sealing more hazardous or difficult than heretofore," he told Bayard. "I fear that whatever is done, Canadians, and perhaps Americans, will transfer the ownership of their sealing vessels to citizens or subjects of other Powers, thus avoiding the effect of the regulations. It remains to be seen whether other Powers will now give their adhesion." Gresham said the U.S. would deal only with the Imperial Government on the regulations. "If the Canadians are permitted to have their way," he told Bayard, "no agreement of any kind will be reached, and the seal herds will speedily disappear." The regulations set down at Paris were binding, Gresham said, but required a convention because they were not "self-executing."

Relations between Britain and the U.S. deteriorated in the months after the Paris ruling as the result of what the Americans charged was stalling by the Canadians. But the situation improved when Gladstone resigned, Lord Rosebery took over as Prime Minister and Lord Kimberley became the new Foreign Secretary. Bayard advised Gresham that Kimberley was a "straight-forward man of ability and experience" who would not "permit the Canadians to be tricky in relation to the Bering Sea." His judgement seemed to be confirmed when in April of 1894 both countries passed legislation implementing the regulations.

There was still the matter of compensation to be negotiated, however. The British had submitted claims at Paris totalling $542,169.26, plus interest of seven percent. Pauncefote estimated that, with interest, the claims amounted to $786,000, including $62,847 in legal costs for taking the appeal of the *W. P. Sayward* to the U.S. Supreme Court. Some members of Congress, urged on by Senator Morgan, strongly opposed paying anything to the British. Morgan held to his position that the seized schooners were "hovering" with the intent of depredating the property of the U.S., even though the Tribunal had ruled the Americans had no property rights in the seals.

When Gresham offered a $425,000 settlement in August, the British complained it was far below their claims, but reluctantly agreed to the amount. The compromise proved academic, however, when the appropriation was voted down, 142 to 113, by Congress, an action Bayard found "humiliating and painful." Cleveland and Gresham apologized privately to the British. George Baden-Powell suggested Britain should pay the $425,000 to the sealers and thereby put a "moral claim" on the U.S., but his advice was not taken.

Reaction to the Paris arbitration was predictably mixed. Moore wrote later that the ruling against the U.S. did not reflect on the ability or effort of the American delegation. It was, he said, the result of historical and legal antecedents, including the original U.S. claim of *mare clausum* when it seized the three Victoria schooners in 1886. Moore said the U.S. had also erred in arguing that Russian pronouncements and treaties in the 1820s had specifically excluded the Bering Sea in the phrase "Pacific Ocean." Like Morgan, Moore was critical of the Canadians. "Colonies, like small children," he wrote Bayard, "sometimes think it pays to be bad, but their parents ought not to encourage them in such conduct."

Foster at first tried to claim a victory for the U.S., but later admitted it had suffered a "technical defeat" at Paris. Nevertheless, "it was far better that we should submit our rights and interests in the seal herd to the arbitrament of an impartial tribunal than risk the horrors of a war between the two kindred people." Foster said the regulations were inadequate, and eventually pelagic sealing would have to be banned outright. It had been a mistake by the U.S. to couple the question of the right of the protection of property with the matter of concurrent regulation necessary for the preservation of the seals. This had led to regulations designed both to allow profitable pelagic sealing while at the same time protecting the herd, an impossibility.

Theodore Roosevelt, a New York City Police Commissioner at the time of the Arbitration Tribunal, later to become an imperialistic President, said Paris "should teach us to beware, beyond all others, of peace-at-any-price men. It should teach us to be extremely cautious about entering into any arbitration."

Henry W. Elliott confirmed that he was not a true conservationist by observing that preservation of the seal herd was "an idle aim" at Paris. "We want to preserve the commercial interests," he said.

One of the most biting comments was made some years later by Gresham's wife Matilda: "After the hearing was over," she wrote, "Messrs. Carter, Phelps and Coudert said the case had been badly made up and badly prepared, and they differed amongst themselves as to what had been done and what should be done. But in true lawyer style, they united in cursing the court."[15]

A correspondent for the London *Times* said of the U.S. claim that Britain's heart was not in the dispute: "The cause of the Colony is Great Britain's cause, and Great Britain's cause the Colony's; that the cousinly relationship extends to the whole family."[16] The *Times* said in an editorial the regulations were not desirable from the British point of view, but "the reference of an international dispute to such an arbitration is a triumph of morality and civilization." This sentiment was echoed by the London *Daily Telegraph*, which rejoiced in the "triumph of a new and peaceful international principle — reason in place of force." Said the New York *Herald*: "The country may well be satisfied . . . the most this country had reason to expect from the arbitration was an arrangement for the protection of seals, and this we have got."

In Victoria the *Colonist* expressed confidence there would be compensation, but the sealers were not so sure. John Cox of the Sealers Association was disappointed that compensation had not been agreed upon at Paris. He said the "ruinous" regulations were "more than the clever Yankees had ever dreamed of asking." The *Colonist* also noted with satisfaction that the U.S. would have to bear the heavy cost of enforcing the regulations, which correctly implied that the sealers would try to get around them. The Ottawa *Citizen* called the decision "an empty award" and said the industry had now been handed over to the Americans through the new regulations. The Victoria *Times* noted what seemed to have been ignored by everyone, that other nations were still free to seal in the Bering right up to the 3-mile territorial limit around the Pribilofs. This flaw in the Paris settlement would have devastating consequences in the future.

The most perceptive observations on the Paris proceedings were made by naturalist David Starr Jordan, president of Stanford University and a future participant in the fur seal dispute. Jordan said the U.S. had "claimed too much and proved too little" at Paris. The hearing involved questions of law on one hand and problems of natural history on the other, and the arbitrators "showed very little interest in any aspect of the case not purely legalistic or diplomatic."[17]

Jordan concluded: "At Paris it was evident that no existing canon of international law covered the case, there being no other valuable animal with similar habits, and so no adequate precedent for protection; the seizure of any wild creature anywhere in the open sea had always been assumed as a universal right. In the unquestionable absence of applicable international statute, it lay within the province of the Tribunal to make new law. This, in fact, it did by its limitation of pelagic sealing, though in such an ineffective way that the action was valueless except as a legal precedent."

The British historian R. B. Mowat perhaps summed it all up best. The Paris Award, he said, "was good for everyone except the seals."[18]

CHAPTER TEN

San Francisco

*It was manifestly absurd to suppose that men engaged in a
business like pelagic sealing would take the trouble to report
accurately facts which must injure their business.*

— DAVID STARR JORDAN

On January 20, 1893, a large three-masted schooner was towed out of San
Francisco Bay through the Golden Gate to begin a seven-month Asian coast
sealing voyage. At 148 tons the *Sophia Sutherland* was the largest vessel in the
San Francisco sealing fleet. It would not have been a noteworthy voyage
except for the presence of her youngest crew member, a young "wharf-rat"
from the Oakland waterfront. Jack London was just a few days past his 17th
birthday when he signed on the *Sophia Sutherland*. He had never been to sea
before. It was a turning point in his short, turbulent life.

There were 12 seamen in the fo'c's'le where London bunked, 10 of them
Scandinavians, and 10 white hunters quartered elsewhere. Because of his
swaggering manner and small size — he was only five foot seven — London
was soon called upon to prove his manhood to the hardened crewmen. His
autobiographical writings picture a game little scrapper winning respect by
triumphing over a huge bullying opponent. As usual with London, it is
difficult to distinguish between truth and fancy.

Taking a southerly course to catch the trade winds blowing toward the
western Pacific, the *Sophia Sutherland* skirted the southern shore of the big
island of Hawaii before making her first landfall in the Bonin Islands after 51
days at sea. There the schooner made repairs and took on fresh water while
the crewmen took turns revelling on these exotic little volcanic islands.

The *Sophia Sutherland* then sailed north off the Japanese coast past
Robben Reef, following the herd toward Kamchatka. She sealed a total of 12
weeks. As well as serving as a deckhand on the schooner, London worked as
boat-puller on one of the small skiffs. After a day's hunting he would remove
the skins from the seals and salt them away. "The deck was a slaughter-house,
week in and week out," London wrote. He also noted that "the brutality of the

occupation produced brutal fun" — such as placing a greasy and bloody seal carcass in someone's bunk.

Then it was back to Yokohama to spend some of his money carousing during another two-week layover preparing for the return voyage to San Francisco. The shorter trip home, helped by the north Pacific westerlies, took only 37 days.

Not long after his return, London entered a contest for aspiring young writers sponsored by the San Francisco *Morning Call*. He won first prize of $25 for his graphic description of riding out a typhoon aboard the *Sophia Sutherland* in the China Sea. Despite his youth and inexperience, London claimed to have been assigned the helm during the worst of the storm. In any case it was London's first payment for writing and the start of a spectacularly successful career.

London was asked to go out the following season on the sealing schooner *Mary Thomas* but declined. She vanished at sea on that voyage with the loss of all aboard.

As well as the $25 prize, London's experiences on the *Sophia Sutherland* spawned one of his his best known novels, *The Sea Wolf*. London had originally planned a book based closely on the voyage. "It will be almost literally a narrative of things that happened on a seven-months voyage I once made as a sailor," London wrote his editor-publisher, George Brett, in 1902. "The oftener I have thought upon the things that happened that trip, the more remarkable they appear to me."[1] The novel was to be called "The Mercy of the Sea." Although notes and a rough draft were drawn up, it was never completed.

Instead, London turned his attention to the improbable story of Captain Wolf Larsen and Humphrey Van Weyden and their epic struggle aboard the schooner *Ghost*. While not nearly as accomplished, the *Sea Wolf* bears some comparison to Herman Melville's *Moby Dick* in its exploration of the darker side of man and a preoccupation with the superman theories of Nietzsche.

After its publication the rumour was spread that the character of Wolf Larsen was modelled on Alex McLean. That myth has had a long life, and more than 70 years after his death in 1914 McLean is still being linked in articles and books to London's fantastic tale.

Both men strongly denied the connection. "I never personally laid eyes on Captain Alex McLean in my life," London wrote in 1914, saying only that the *Sophia Sutherland* had crossed paths with McLean's schooner on a number of occasions during his 1893 voyage, and that he also knew about Alex' brother Dan.[2]

As for Alex McLean himself, he always resented any suggestion that he resembled the brutal Wolf Larsen. With typical bravado, he told a friend that if he ever met the author he would knock his head off.[3] Although McLean was

142

hard on his crewmen and enjoyed a good scrap, he possessed none of Larsen's diabolical cruelty. He was more often described as suspicious and secretive. Others who suggested that Dan McLean was a model for the infamous "Death Larsen," brother of Wolf Larsen, were equally mistaken. The rivalry between Dan and Alex was keen but friendly and they worked together at various times.

The Larsen brothers clearly emerged from London's fertile imagination and could not have been based on any real-life individuals. A San Francisco newspaperman named Joseph Noel claimed he had been given the dramatization rights to *The Sea Wolf* in return for having supplied London with the conception of Larsen. Noel said he got the idea for the character from a book called the *The South Sea Pearler*.

Frank Tooker, editor of *Century Magazine*, which serialized *The Sea Wolf*, has suggested that in Wolf Larsen London created a fanciful version of himself. "In his mental apprehension of himself as intensely masculine, a radical, a protestant, a believer in evolution, and a lover of accepted literature," Tooker wrote, "he created Wolf Larsen in the likeness of his own image."[4]

The McLean myth has persisted because in a trade filled with colourful characters, the brothers stood out in their personal style and exploits. Both were instantly recognized in the waterfront bars they haunted by their magnificent matching handlebar moustaches. Alex' was red and said to measure two feet from tip to tip. It could be tied behind his neck. He was a dapper dresser ashore, favouring Stetson hats, Prince Albert coats and starched collars. He was a gin drinker. Although taciturn in manner and spare of build, Alex McLean was an imposing figure, with bold, blue-grey eyes under bushy brows and a mass of thick wavy hair.

In order to maintain the imaginery "Wolf Larsen" connection, the newspapers tried to portray Alex McLean as a piratical figure who spent much of his time in jail for various brawls and misdemeanours. In fact, except for his four-month stay in a Russian prison for poaching seals, he had been jailed briefly only twice for minor dust-ups in Halifax and San Francisco.

Dan was born in 1851, Alex eight years later. Both had gone to sea at the age of 14 on Cape Breton sailing ships and came to the west coast in 1880. Alex shipped as first mate of the *Santa Clara* on a voyage from the Maritimes around Cape Horn to California. He spent a few months in San Francisco before moving on to Victoria in 1881. His first job on the coast was crewman on the steamer *Gertrude*, which travelled between the Fraser River and Victoria. Next he signed on the Dominion Government coastal vessel *Sir James Douglas*, which served as a lighthouse and buoy tender, working his way up to mate. He left in 1883 to go mining in Alaska. Meanwhile, Dan bought the 7-ton sloop *Flyaway* and also went on a prospecting trip to Alaska, where he staked a claim near the Treadwell mine site at Juneau. On future sealing voyages, the enterprising McLean brothers continued to hunt for gold along the coast while en route home from the Aleutians.

In 1882 and 1883 the brothers shipped together in the schooner *San Diego* for a north coast sealing voyage, with Dan as captain and Alex mate and navigator. For the next two years Alex worked for Charles Spring on the *Favorite*, with an assignment to get information on the transfer and sales of skins on sealing vessels plying the coast. He was also hired by prospective purchasers to inspect vessels offered for sale at San Francisco. In the late 1880s most San Francisco-based sealing schooners were transferred to Victoria registry.

In 1889 Dan McLean sailed the *Mary Ellen* out of San Francisco bound for the Bering. During a stopover in Victoria the seven-man crew went ashore to protest to the authorities about mistreatment by the skipper. Complaining that they moved around the decks too slowly, McLean had put them on short rations of corn meal and water. When seaman George Cumming did not grab a rope quickly enough, McLean hit him with a belaying pin. On learning the men had taken their grievances ashore, Dan attempted to get out of the harbour with the *Mary Ellen* but was apprehended and placed under arrest. He appeared before Judge G. A. Walkem in Supreme Court on a charge of attempted murder, later reduced to assault. Walkem imposed a $100 fine and ordered McLean to pay Cumming $50, plus court costs of $20.

Later that season Dan McLean went to the Bering on the *Triumph*, the larger of two schooners which went by that name. Built in Shelburne, N.S. in 1887, she was 106 tons, 85 feet long, with a 29-foot beam. McLean was a joint owner with Victoria businessman Edgar Crow Baker and two others. They bought her new for $8,250, had her copper-bottomed and outfitted in San Francisco for $2,938, and spent a total of $1,429 on additional gear in Victoria, for a total investment of $15,245. Two years later she was sold to ship chandler E. B. Marvin of Victoria for only $9,000.

The *Triumph* was warned out of the Bering by the cutter *Rush* on July 11 and left immediately, according to a declaration made later by McLean in Mexico. No skins were found by the boarding party from the *Rush*, but McLean had managed to hide 72. The *Triumph* was lost off Vancouver Island in late 1894 with 35 men aboard. Earlier that fall she had brought a record 4,560 skins to Victoria from the Bering. Because of her size she was able to carry as many as 43 hunters and 19 canoes. McLean declared he was "one of the most successful of all those engaged in the business," but conceded there was an element of luck in finding and tracking the main herd of seals.

Dan McLean had more troubles with his crew in 1894 in the *Edward E. Webster* of San Francisco. Near the end of a Pacific crossing to the Asian coast, 14 men who belonged to the new Sailor's Union mutinied. When he reached Yokohama a week later McLean said the men were "scum" trying to get an advance on their wages. The crew claimed they were concerned about their safety and refused to go out in the small boats in fog and a 6-knot wind. The schooner had no foghorn, they said.

Disputes over their citizenship constantly dogged the McLeans. They claimed both British and American, depending on which was more favourable to their situation at the time. A sister and brother lived in Boston and both Dan and Alex stayed with them occasionally. Dan McLean made at least five different declarations of citizenship at various times. Eventually the U.S. Government proved, at least to its satisfaction, that both were Americans.

According to the evidence amassed by the Government to establish they were not eligible for compensation, Dan had become an American citizen in October, 1882, under terms of the 1870 Naturalization Treaty between the U.S. and Britain. He went through a form of naturalization in Canada in 1886 but the U.S. said the procedure did not conform to the terms of that treaty. A number of occasions on which Dan had lied about his citizenship were documented. At Halifax in 1887, in order to register the *Triumph* in his name, he denied in an affidavit that he had ever taken the oath of allegiance to a foreign state. In 1889 McLean made a formal claim for compensation for the seizure of the *Triumph*, declaring he was master and one-third owner of the Victoria-registered vessel. But in September of 1892, while giving evidence to be presented to the Paris Arbitration Tribunal, he stated that he was a naturalized American citizen residing in San Francisco.

A ticket to a "Grand Complimentary Party" to be held on Tuesday evening, January 19, 1886, was an indication of Dan McLean's standing on San Francisco's waterfront. Sponsored "by his Scottish friends," the affair was held at the Music Hall, 927 Mission Street. Dancing commenced at 8:30, with Auld Lang Syne at 1 a.m. Gents' hats were checked for 50 cents.[5]

In the case of Alex, the U.S. said there was "no question whatever" of his American citizenship. He had become a naturalized citizen by order of a Circuit Court in Massachusetts on December 1, 1882. There was no evidence that Alex had ever owned property in Victoria other than an interest in ships registered there. He had lived in the city between 1884 and 1889 but had shifted back and forth to San Francisco and was based in California between 1889 and 1896.

His wife and small daughter went with McLean on the *Mary Ellen* in 1892 on a sealing voyage. He had sold his catch in advance to a Victoria buyer for $8 a skin, then discovered the price had jumped during the season to $10. He made a run to San Francisco to try and sell his catch there at the higher price, but the original buyer got wind of the move and was waiting when the *Mary Ellen* entered the Golden Gate.

Alex embarked on his last great sealing adventure in 1904 after persuading a group of San Francisco businessmen to finance a raid on the Commander Islands. McLean told them the rookeries would not be well guarded because the Russians were involved in a war with Japan. For $800 the syndicate bought and refurbished a big old schooner, the *Jennie Thelin*, which had been allowed to settle in the mud of an Oakland creek mouth.

McLean was able to recruit only six experienced crewmen, but shanghaied 21 others from San Francisco boarding houses. Eight had never been to sea before. The "cook" was so inept he made coffee with sea-water. One man who claimed to be a doctor turned out to be a quack who was arrested at the end of the voyage for previously practising medicine without a licence. Seaman William O'Rourke later complained he had been forcibly dragged on board and kept in irons for three days. The 27 men were told they were going cod-fishing off Mazatlan. They were also persuaded to sign papers at the Mexican Consulate declaring they were Mexican citizens, despite their lightness of skin.

One of the crewmen was Stuart Thompson, who kept a diary of the feckless voyage.[6] He recorded that the schooner was towed out through the Golden Gate on May 4. A few minutes after raising sail and starting off under her own power, the mainsail and boom tumbled to the deck. When she was in danger of being dashed on the rocky shore, the schooner's eight hunting boats were lowered and the men pulled at lines to hold her against the wind. The chief mate spent an agonizing hour aloft repairing rotted rigging.

The next morning Thompson discovered the vessel was headed north instead of south toward Mexico. He saw a crewman carving "Carmencita" on the reverse side of three *Jennie Thelin* nameplates. The Mexican flag was then hoisted and McLean explained to the crew that England, Japan, and the U.S. had signed a treaty with Russia banning sealing within 60 miles of Copper Island, but Mexico was not a party to the agreement.

The newly-named *Carmencita* took the northerly route to Kamchatka. Soon after making a brief stop at Attu in the Aleutians for water and firewood, the old vessel began to leak. For the rest of the voyage her three pumps were manned around the clock in two-hour shifts. The schooner was intercepted by the cutter *Bear* near Copper Island, but the boarding party found her Mexican papers in good order. The officers did note, however, that the crew looked more Irish than Mexican and marvelled at their command of English. (There was one genuine Mexican aboard, but he was an American citizen.) Pleased with his deception, the cocky McLean handed out cigars to the officers as they returned to the *Bear*.

When the *Carmencita* came within 15 miles of the main Copper Island rookery, the small boats with three men in each were sent ashore. Despite Alex' assurances, the Russians had left guards on the island. As the small boats approached the beach shots rang out. Most of the bullets hit the water around the boats but one crewman, Walter York, was hit in the jaw. McLean managed to escape with the schooner, and made his way to Victoria. En route they met

146

the *Bear* again and York was placed aboard the cutter to get temporary medical treatment. He died later on the operating table in Seattle.

Attempting to hunt seals away from the islands, the *Carmencita* had little success. Thompson recorded that one crew member couldn't hit anything lying still. "He was an expert duck hunter, 90 years old. Rocks were thrown at the seal to get it in motion. Then he never missed."

When the voyage ended in Victoria McLean brazenly paid off each man with a $1 bill because there were no sealskins to sell. The fruitless five-month trip had cost $8,000. He had a pistol beside him in case the men attacked him over the token payment, but nobody tried. That night, however, McLean was assaulted by two crew members in a saloon brawl.

The *Carmencita* stayed in Victoria over the winter, then left in May of 1905 with a clearance for Acapulco to obtain a Mexican charter. After outfitting at Drake's Bay near San Francisco, however, McLean took her sealing again. His crew this time were tough, discharged soldiers from the Philippines. There was plenty of liquor on board and many fights, but few seals. When he went into Clayoquot with only 14 skins, the mate and two crew members deserted. McLean bartered the skins for flour, then headed off for the Bering, where there was no closed season for Mexican vessels. Mexico had ordered its flag removed after the 1904 raid on Copper Island, but McLean operated on this second voyage with a Mexican consular letter. In August he made a raid on a Pribilof rookery while flying a Norwegian flag. The days of the *Carmencita*'s mischief were numbered, however. In June indictments had been issued against McLean and his San Francisco backers. The court action had been instigated by the bitter parents of seaman Walter York.

When the *Carmencita* arrived back in Clayoquot in September with her name changed to *Acapulco*, her skins were seized and the schooner ordered to Victoria. There the crew learned of the arrests in San Francisco and decided to sue for lost wages. The vessel was sold by the Admiralty Court to satisfy the wage claims judgement.

Despite the apparent bravado of these exploits, the *Carmencita-Acapulco* crewmen were scornful of Alex' behaviour. They said he was continually nervous during the 1905 voyage and cut out sections of the newspaper which contained reports of the San Francisco arrests. In the 1904 raid on Copper Island he had remained safely on the schooner, hardly the way of a swashbuckler.

As well as giving evidence presented by the U.S. at Paris, Alex McLean was also called as a witness by the U.S. in compensation hearings in Victoria. The U.S. pictured him as a thorough professional who kept the most detailed records of where his boats caught seals. These were kept as his private property, however, and not entered in the ship's log. "If you have a logbook and you make pretty good catches," McLean once said, "your hunters or crew may get hold of the book and take the positions out of it, and going on board another ship they would give it to them."

That evidence of McLean's shrewdness reinforced the observation of another sealer, Captain Robert McKeil, that "Captain McLean was a rustler, and he was always on the go."

His sealing career ended ingloriously for Alex McLean in 1909 as a crew member aboard the *Pescawha*. An entry in her logbook for May 5 records that he deserted when the schooner called in at Ucluelet. He subsequently worked on a Skeena riverboat, as a halibut fisherman, and captain of a small tug in Vancouver harbour. With his brother Dan he also operated a stern-wheeler on the Yukon River for a time hauling dynamite to mining camps.

Alex died in Vancouver in 1914. His body was found floating in the harbour and, controversial to the end, it was rumoured he had been murdered. The city coroner found, however, that he had accidentally fallen between two moored vessels while clambering to his tugboat and drowned. He was 55 and had been living in the city with his wife and daughter.

With tightened controls in the Bering, rough treatment by the Russians and falling profits, the size of the Victoria fleet began to decline after 1890. There were more than 70 schooners out in 1891, almost all confining their activities to the northern coast or Asia; 65 vessels in 1892; 52 in 1893 and 47 in 1894. In 1891 there had been a total of 42 American schooners sealing — 24 from San Francisco, nine out of Port Townsend, five smaller vessels from Sitka and Kodiak Island, and two each from Astoria and San Diego.

There was one notorious addition to the Victoria fleet during 1893, however. The *Halcyon* had been built as a yacht for San Francisco entre-preneur Harry Tevis at nearby Benicia in 1886. Seventy-four feet in length, she was elegantly fitted out and cost more than $20,000. The *Halcyon* was so swift that she was bought from Tevis to enter the profitable trans-Pacific opium smuggling trade. Opium was passed through Victoria to the U.S. The smugglers wanted the duty raised so that legal importation would decline. An estimated 126,000 pounds were moved through Victoria in 1893 at a price of $6 a pound. The price obtainable in San Francisco was between $11 and $15 a pound.

After she had become too well-known as a smuggler, sealer John Cox of Victoria was able to acquire the *Halcyon* for just $5,200. He renamed her the *Vera* and placed her under the command of Captain William Shields, who had started sealing as a hunter aboard the *Pathfinder*.

Despite the restrictions imposed in 1893 by the Paris Tribunal and the smaller fleet, 1894 was a banner year in the Bering for the pelagic sealers who stuck with the business. Only 15 Victoria schooners went into the Bering but the weather was good in August and their catches were large, totalling 26,341

148

skins. Another 40 schooners on the Asia side took 50,000 off Japan and 7,437 around Copper Island, despite bad weather which took its toll of boats and lives. The *Mascotte, Rosie Sparks* and *Mattie Turner* of San Francisco were lost with all hands off Japan. The *Henry Dennis*, also from San Francisco, went down but her crew was rescued. A number of hunters lost their lives when small boats were caught in a series of storms.

The B.C. coast catch was 11,703, making a total of 94,477 skins caught by Victoria schooners in the year, the highest number ever. The U.S. estimated a pelagic catch of 121,143 seals in 1894 by adding in the skins of 35 American schooners. At the same time, the N.A.C.C. took only 15,000 bachelor skins on the islands. Nevertheless, the U.S. Government filed suit against the company to recover damages for seals unlawfully taken on the islands during the *modus*. It was awarded a judgement of $107,000.

The Victoria schooners tallied 14,636 females and 11,075 males in their Bering catch, an unlikely ratio. The American schooners' report of 16,000 females and 3,000 males was closer to the facts. The bodies of 20,000 pups which had starved to death on the Pribilof rookeries bore mute testimony to the number of nursing mothers killed.

As it became obvious the Paris regulations were ineffective, agitation began in the U.S. to have them stiffened. The spear had proved just as destructive as the shotgun and the 60-mile zone around the Pribilofs was too narrow. The August 1 opening date was too early because the nursing mothers were leaving the islands for food at that time.

Congress became increasingly bitter against the British. Killing off the Pribilof herd to frustrate the pelagic sealers had been mentioned half-heartedly by the frustrated Americans in the past, but now for the first time there was a serious move to bring about that bizarre action. Congressman Nelson Dingley of Maine introduced a bill authorizing a full-scale slaughter on the islands. Dingley carefully added a rider, however, empowering the President to suspend the law if Britain agreed to effective regulations.

While the Dingley bill was pending, a second measure was introduced to set up a joint commission to investigate the fur seal situation and make recommendations for their preservation. Under this bill the President was authorized to sign another *modus vivendi* banning pelagic sealing until the commission reported. If the British did not accept the *modus*, the rookery slaughter would begin. This bill passed the House on February 28, 1895, but was too late to get through the Senate. Secretary of State Gresham was hopeful, however, that the threat contained in the two bills would be enough to bring Britain to the bargaining table. He wrote Pauncefote proposing new regulations to "embrace the whole North Pacific Ocean from the Asiatic side to the American side," with Japan and Russia included.

But Britain was not willing to be coerced into placing new restrictions on the Canadian sealers. The Government contended there was nothing alarming about the size of the 1894 pelagic catch and was not convinced the Paris regulations were a failure. The cause of death of the pups was also inconclusive. There was no need for either a *modus* or a new commission. And there was no point including the Russians and Japanese, because they had no interest in sealing on the North American side of the Pacific. The British had only one patrol vessel in the Bering in 1894 and two, H.M.S. *Nymphe* and H.M.S. *Pheasant*, in 1895. The U.S. kept 12 ships in the area at an annual cost of more than $450,000.

On June 18 Secretary of State Richard Olney, who had been appointed following Gresham's death that spring, complained that British naval officers were not carrying out the terms of the Paris award. Some schooners seized by the U.S. for violations and turned over to the British had been released. British naval officers were assuming too much power in dismissing schooners without a trial, while American patrol vessels acted always "on reasonable grounds of suspicion."

The British had announced May 11 that they did not intend to renew the Paris regulation ordering the "sealing up" of guns and ammunition on vessels travelling in the Bering. The British said this was unnecessary interference, and U.S. boarding parties were "guilty of vexatious and inquisitorial interference." Seizures of British vessels could be made only under British law. The 1894 provision for sealing up arms had been a voluntary arrangement. Besides, the British said, the discovery of skins with bullet holes did not prove the seals had been shot by any particular schooner. They might have been old wounds on animals which had escaped.

Britain protested the seizure of the schooners *Favorite* and *Wanderer* for carrying unsealed arms. Damages were demanded. There was no ban on mere possession of weapons, the British said. It was also alleged that 26 Victoria schooners had been boarded by the Americans a total of 82 times, which was unacceptable harassment. The *Sapphire* alone had been stopped and searched on six separate occasions. The skins of intercepted vessels were often pulled out of their salted layers and scattered about the hold.

The *Beatrice* of Vancouver under Captain Louis Olsen had been seized by the *Rush* because her logbook was not up-to-date. When one skin out of 386 aboard the *E. B. Marvin* was found to have a bullet hole, she too was seized. Some of the sealers, before going to the Bering after the Asian coast season, began to crate up their guns at Yokohama or Hakodate and ship them by steamer to Victoria to avoid harassment by American patrol vessels. Others transferred their guns to a schooner going directly home south of the Aleutians.

When the British flatly rejected a *modus* for 1895, the war of words heated up. Pauncefote complained of "violent invective" by the U.S. press against Britain. The Americans now began to call for a ban on all pelagic sealing north of the 35th parallel.

150

Early in 1896 the British offered a compromise. Rejecting another U.S. bid for a Joint Commission to establish new regulations, Britain agreed only that each country should send its own agents to study the Pribilof situation and determine whether there was any common ground. Congress reluctantly authorized a two-year investigation to be headed by Dr. David Starr Jordan. His associates were naturalists Leonhard Stejneger and Frederic A. Lucas. The British named D'Arcy Wentworth Thompson, professor of zoology at Dundee University, G. E. H. Barrett-Hamilton, a young British naturalist, and James Macoun, a botanist at the Canadian Museum in Ottawa. Canadian Fisheries Department scientist Andrew Halkett also joined the team during the summer of 1896 as an observer on a sealing schooner.

The teams of both countries met in Seattle in June and sailed together on the U.S. research vessel *Albatross* to the Pribilofs. The Canadians were unhappy about this arrangement. They wanted to act independently and the Jordan offer of transport was made to seem a grand gesture by Americans. Ottawa felt that the two sides working together implied agreement that the Paris regulations needed to be revised.

Both sides reported the number of seals on the islands had dropped alarmingly, but could not agree on the reason. Thompson said an unknown number of pups had died from natural causes and not starvation. Jordan said there were only 130,000 breeding females, placing all the blame for the decline on pelagic sealing and the failure of the Paris Arbitration to curb it.

Jordan was one of those bustling, self-important men who seldom have doubts about their own opinions and are critical of others. But on this particular issue, as subsequent events would prove, he was most often on the right side of the argument.

Occasionally, however, Jordan was inclined to go off the track. Such was the case with his scheme to brand the seals as a means of spoiling their fur for the pelagic hunters. Jordan had once claimed that if the Americans had operated the Pribilofs like a cattle ranch the international dispute might not have arisen. It was apparently this conclusion that led him to the misbegotten branding plan and a scheme to fence in the young males. Both were failures. It was found impossible to contain the males in a pen and the branding with an electric iron was abandoned after "several thousand" seals were disfigured. Many were later found with raw wounds inflamed by salt water. The branding had burned through their thick fur and undercoat. There were widespread objections to the practice as being unnecessarily cruel.

When Jordan presented a preliminary report on his group's findings just before Christmas, a second U.S. Commission was appointed by the Department of State to deal with the diplomatic aspects of the case. This body agreed that if the U.S. was to give a strong moral force to its demands for an end to pelagic sealing, it must ban all killing of seals at sea by American citizens and block the import of pelagic skins. Both measures were subsequently enacted by Congress. In some instances travellers arriving in the U.S. with fur coats were required to prove the source of the skins.

Thompson's initial report was submitted to Salisbury in March of 1897. It was an eminently reasonable document, less strident than Jordan's. Thompson conceded that the killing of nursing mothers at sea was responsible for a large number of the pup deaths, but said it was not the sole cause. He found no fault with the killing practices of the lessees on the islands: "The signs of distress were less painful than I have often witnessed in a flock of sheep on a hot and dusty road, and I have seen drovers show less regard for the comfort of their sheep . . . the men employed were clean, skilful and vigorous. A single blow, or two at most, dispatched each seal."

Thompson said the seal population varied from year to year without apparent explanation. But the annual birth-rate of 143,000 was not satisfactory when 20,000 pups were lost for one reason or another on the rookeries, as well as suffering a heavy mortality rate at sea. The margin of safety was narrow, he said. The best that could be expected was a perpetuation of the present numbers. "It is my earnest hope," Thompson concluded, "that a recognition of mutual interests and a regard for the common advantage may suggest measures of prudence which shall keep the pursuit and slaughter of the animal within due and definite bonds."

After studying the Jordan and Thompson reports, Salisbury told Pauncefote they showed there was no reason to fear that the fur seal herd was threatened with extinction. Nevertheless, the British did agree on the need for "some modification" of the Paris regulations when they came up for renewal at the end of the first five-year period in 1898.

One of the regulations set down in Paris required the schooners to keep a record of the sex of the seals that were taken. But as Jordan pointed out, "it was manifestly absurd to suppose that men engaged in a business like pelagic sealing would take the trouble to report accurately facts which must injure their business." So the proportion of females reported rarely exceeded 55 per cent, and this was obviously untrue. The U.S. made a check at its own Customs Houses and found the percentage of females caught on the northwest coast to be about 90 per cent and in the Bering more than 70 per cent. The furriers in London confirmed these figures. American schooners reported a five to one ratio of females, and in one season the catch of the *J. Eppinger* was 1,340 females and 17 males. San Francisco fur dealer Herman Liebes offered bonuses to hunters who brought in the more valuable mature male skins, but few collected.

The British and Canadian authorities must have known they were being misled by the sealers, but they went along with the deception. They insisted it was often difficult to ascertain the sex from the pelt, especially when the hunters were rushed. American inspection of skins aboard the schooners was

152

regarded as "irritating surveillance," in the words of Canadian Fisheries Department official R. N. Venning.

It was Venning who suppressed, perhaps at the bidding of Fisheries Minister John Costigan, the damning report submitted by Andrew Halkett. Assigned to the schooner *Dora Sieward* for the 1896 season, Halkett spent 109 days aboard, from June 21 to October 7. During that time he kept a detailed record of the number of seals caught, their sex and whether the females were nursing.

Soon after leaving Victoria the *Dora Sieward* took 100 seals in one day off Long Beach on Vancouver Island, filling six canoes. Halkett said young seals were frisking in the wake of the schooner and diving under it, but attempts to spear them from the deck usually failed.

He found that in the Bering almost all the seals taken were nursing females. On August 29 all 69 seals taken were in that category. On August 26 there were 78 nursing mothers and five males. Almost all the females were pregnant. The British had claimed that many females were barren, but Halkett disproved this by examining the uterus of each.

When Venning was questioned about Halkett's report, he replied that it would be produced in due course when required. It never was, because it totally contradicted the sealers' records and the position adopted by the Canadian and British governments. Halkett's findings were not included in Thompson's report and remained buried in the internal files of the Department of Marine and Fisheries.[7] While it lay there, the British claimed in 1897 that Jordan's findings were "biased" and there was actually a surplus of females. Pelagic sealing had "helped balance the herd" by harvesting them, it was said. Nothing could have been further from the truth.

Venning claimed the nursing mothers did not go far from shore to feed. He said the pelagic hunt should therefore be allowed in July with only a narrow protective zone around the islands. According to Venning, nursing stopped in August and September. Later research proved this assertion to be false. Even George Barrett-Hamilton, who made some wild and woolly accusations against the Americans in his report to Thompson, conceded in 1896 that the females travelled up to 200 miles from the rookeries in search of food.

Jordan commented bitterly that it was British policy "to permit the Canadian sealers to get out of the fur seal herd everything they can before the failure of the herd forces the alleged industry wholly out of existence." The U.S. estimated that from 1883 through 1897 the loss to the Pribilof herd through pelagic sealing was 536,000 skins secured, in addition to 402,000 unborn pups, based on a 75 per cent pregnancy rate, and 180,000 nursing pups which starved to death. This made a total of 1,118,000, to which was added an indeterminate number of seals shot but unrecovered by the hunters. The total land kill of males during this period was 842,000.

There had been no trouble obtaining a land kill of 100,000 up to 1885, Jordan noted. By 1896 the lessees could take only 30,000 and in 1897 only 20,890. The decline in breeding females was becoming increasingly obvious.

Even the pelagic sealers were beginning to feel the effects of the reduction of the herd. The number of vessels out dropped from 59 in 1895 to 38 in 1897. From a high of 95,000 skins in 1894 the Victoria fleet took 73,614 in 1895 and only 55,678 in 1896. Catches were steady in most areas except the Bering, where the decline was most severe. In 1897 the catch from 41 Victoria-based schooners was down to 30,400.

Britain continued to maintain, unconvincingly, that protection of the herd had become irrelevant, because its depletion had now rendered both land and sea killing unprofitable. But a rise in prices soon made sealing remunerative again and brought new players into the pelagic industry.

New evidence also emerged to show how profitable sealing had been for the original Pribilof lessees. A falling out between two Alaska Commercial Company principals, Louis Sloss and Max Wasserman, led to a lawsuit over ownership of shares. On April 2, 1895, the San Francisco *Examiner* reported that the suit had revealed the "fabulous dividends" earned by A.C.C. share-holders, as much as $80 on every $100 share over one five-year period. The Company had $2,000,000 in its treasury when the lease was taken over by the N.A.C.C. in 1890.

In 1897 Isaac Liebes, president of the N.A.C.C., told John Foster his firm would pay the Canadian sealers any profits they had made in the last three years if the American or British governments would buy out their schooners. Liebes quoted Leopold Boscowitz, the son of Joseph Boscowitz, as telling him that, "if we be compensated for our vessels, the question can be settled in ten minutes." All the Canadians would be glad to be bought out, Boscowitz was alleged to have said. The *Colonist* retorted, however, that the Victoria sealers were insisting on full compensation for their losses. Association President J. G. Cox declared: "We sealers do not want to sell. We have our inherent right to catch seals in the open sea." Foster had the last word, however, when he said the buy-out proposal was pointless because Congress would not vote the money.

CHAPTER ELEVEN

Neah Bay

There is more honour among the Indians than among the average white crew in this business. They don't make an agreement today, and break it tomorrow if they see a chance to make a little more.

—Captain WILLIAM COX

One group of sealers who clearly benefitted from the Paris regulations were the Indians. Few white hunters were able to master the spear — one said it was "like throwing a pitchfork" — and the natives found their skills in demand. Schooners began to compete for the best men.

The more enterprising Indians saw an opportunity to work for themselves by acquiring schooners, now readily available on the market. Taking the lead were the Makahs of Neah Bay on the Olympic Peninsula of Washington. The Makahs were a branch of the Vancouver Island Nuu-chah-nulth and kept in close touch with their kin across the Strait of Juan de Fuca.

The Makahs were among the first Indian tribes to become involved in sealing for furs rather than food, and by 1875 it was their chief source of income.[1] They began operating their own schooners in 1880 when the Neah Bay Fur Sealing Company chartered the pilot boat *Lottie* of Port Townsend, which had been taking seals for some years on her trips to Cape Flattery, just west of Neah Bay. The *Lottie* was subsequently purchased by Chief James Claplanhoo. In the next few years the Makahs purchased three other small schooners before acquiring the old *Discovery* in Victoria. Then, in 1886, Chief Peter Brown bought the schooner *Champion* from Captain E. H. McAlmond of Port Townsend, who had sailed her since she was built there.[2] Most of the Makah schooners had an experienced white sealer as captain.

The Makah schooners were not as large and comfortable, or as well-maintained, as the best vessels of the Victoria sealing fleet. As Captain William Brennan of Victoria once observed: "They (the Indians) always want to ship on a first-class schooner, unless they own it, when any rattletrap will do."

The *Lottie* cleared $8,000 on a sealing voyage to the Bering in 1891 and $7,000 the following year. Encouraged by this success, the Makahs bought more ships, and in December, 1893, a total of 10 Indian-owned sealing schooners were fitting out in Neah Bay for the spring season.

The natives had been prodded by a progressive new government Indian Agent in the village, John P. McGlinn. He urged them to save their money and become independent by abandoning the potlatch and investing in schooners. Chief Brown told an interviewer in 1893: "We have done so, and we now have nine schooners worth about $20,000 in all." He added: "We cannot make a living on the land, this land is not good. I like to have the Government help the Indians work on water — it is all we make our living with. I do not know what the Indians would do if they stopped sealing."[3]

Chief Brown said previous Indian Agents had worked closely with the white sealers and "when the Indians would not work on the traders' schooners the Agent would punish the Indians." They were also compelled to sell their furs at the white man's stores on terms fixed by him — usually 20 percent less than could be obtained elsewhere — and buy trade goods there. Now, however, they began to force out the white storekeepers and open their own trading posts. They sold their furs in Seattle, Port Townsend or Victoria, wherever the price was best.

Under this new system a few entrepreneurs like Claplanhoo became relatively wealthy, but did not spread their riches around as before. The Indians who did not benefit directly from sealing preferred the old potlatch days, but they were outnumbered.

Besides Claplanhoo and Chief Brown, another prosperous Makah was Chestoqua Peterson, who owned the 42-ton *Columbia* and operated a trading post.

The Makahs had a friend in James G. Swan of Port Townsend. Swan was a pioneer on the Olympic Peninsula, arriving in 1850. He was an assistant collector of customs, a collector of artifacts for the Smithsonian Institution, and worked occasionally for the Indian Bureau and the Fisheries Commission. Mildly eccentric, with a fondness for drink, he was known around town affectionately as "Judge Swan."[4]

Swan took a keen interest in the Indians and was a welcome visitor to their villages. For a time he worked as a teacher in Neah Bay, and the Makahs named one of their best schooners after him. Through them he became involved in research into the habits of the fur seal. The U.S. included his evidence in its case at Paris, although his knowledge of the subject did not match his enthusiasm. Swan believed at first that the fur seals caught around Cape Flattery were a different species from the Pribilof herd and that their rookeries were somewhere in Cook Inlet in the northern Gulf of Alaska. He also believed these seals often gave birth on the offshore kelp beds near Cape Flattery. He was led to this misconception by Indians who showed him a fur seal pup in June 1892 which they said had been born near the Cape. The pup, which Swan said was as "large as a black cat and bleats like a young lamb," had been brought to the village by a schooner three weeks before. It was likely taken from the body of its mother and kept alive.

Swan had always been keen about the prospects of the pelagic sealing industry, identifying with the Victoria schooner operators and bitterly opposing the A.C.C. monopoly on the Pribilofs. "It's time that the farce played by the Alaska Commercial Company was ended, and the sorry sight of American Revenue cutters hunting down our own citizens for the benefit of that huge monopoly should cease," he wrote. In 1888 Swan told Senator Joseph Dolph of Oregon that within two years "a colony of several hundred of these fishermen will be here to develop the wealth now dormant and hidden in our waters." He believed that many New England fishermen would come to the area, but only a few ever did.

One was Captain Solomon Jacobs, of Gloucester, Mass., who had his schooner *Mollie Adams* brought round the Horn in 1888. Jacobs took over her command on arrival and used the vessel for fishing cod and halibut when not sealing. He also brought out the *Daniel Webster* from Gloucester.

In January of 1889 Jacobs contracted to sell to fur buyer Henry Baxter of Seattle all the sealskins taken by his two schooners that year. The *Webster* was sunk in a storm, but in April the *Mollie Adams* delivered her coast catch to Baxter. There was a verbal agreement that she would then proceed to the Bering and bring the skins caught there to Baxter. But Jacobs sold his Bering skins instead in Victoria. Baxter sued. Although both men were American citizens and the schooner was registered in the U.S., the case was heard in Victoria, presumably because Jacobs had taken up temporary residence there.

Jacobs' lawyer from Port Townsend came up with a novel defence: the contract between Jacobs and Baxter was not valid because sealing in the Bering violated U.S. law. But in a decision running counter to that of Judge Dawson in Sitka, Judge M. W. T. Drake ruled in effect that the U.S. had no jurisdiction outside the 3-mile limit and the contract was valid. Baxter was awarded $4,191 damages. The case drew wide attention, with the New York *Times* referring to Jacobs as a "shifty defendant." The *Times* added, however, that the U.S. claim to the whole western half of the Bering was "preposterous."

Although the Paris regulations in general had been beneficial to the Makahs, they objected to being included in the ban on sealing during the months of May, June and July. Indians were given special permission to seal from shore in canoes in that period, but the concession did not benefit the Neah Bay natives who hunted from their own schooners. The three months were a prime hunting period for them along the coast, but the cutters were strict in their enforcement of the regulations. On May 1, 1894, the Makah schooners *L. C. Perkins*, 30 tons, owned by James Lighthouse, and the 20-ton *Amateur* were seized off Cape Flattery for sealing one day beyond the legal season.

The Makahs came up with an ingenious solution to the problem. They proposed that they be allowed to use the schooners as a "place of refuge" for the canoe hunters in the event of a storm and for security and protection at night. The Government said it had no objection to their request, but the British must concur. Pauncefote was consulted and London gave its approval, conditional on that of Canada. The Foreign Secretary, the Earl of Kimberley, told Pauncefote: "If the governments of the U.S. and Canada agree not to enforce the Award in the case of the Makah Indians we shall not object. You had better place Sir C. Tupper in communication with the U.S. authorities on the subject."

Fisheries Minister Charles H. Tupper was not sympathetic. He said it would put the Makahs in violation of the treaty. But his real concern, as revealed in departmental papers, was that B.C. Indians might follow suit by getting their own schooners. If that happened they might not then be available to the white schooner operators who needed their skills with the spear. Tupper said Canada was "not prepared to take the responsibility of recommending discrimination in favour of Indians to the detriment of their white competitors."[5] The Victoria sealers got their way again and reconfirmed their attitude toward the Indians.

The tough stance taken by Canada on this relatively small issue might have been influenced by an incident which occurred two months before Tupper gave his negative response. In June of 1894 the 80-foot schooner *C. D. Rand* of Vancouver was sealing on the Portlock Bank off Kodiak Island with 19 Ucluelet hunters and three of their wives when trouble erupted. According to Captain Olaf Westerlund, he had paid off the Indians for skins already taken when the ship stopped at Sitka and they went ashore. He told them to return after visiting the town, but the Indians said they would rejoin the ship only if they were paid more for their skins. He agreed and the sealing voyage resumed.

Westerlund said the Indians then became hostile and he feared for the safety of the five white crewmen. He looked for a warship for help but there were none in the area. Then the Indians, except for two who stayed loyal to the captain, took possession of the schooner. The Indians were said to have acted wildly, terrorizing the crew with knives flashed close to their throats. "We were in the power of demons," Westerlund told a reporter on the arrival of the *Rand* in Vancouver. "Natives of our province they were, but the veneer of civilization was rubbed off as soon as they felt their power." The captain said if the Indians had been able to reach Vancouver Island they would have scuttled the schooner and murdered the whites.

The white crewmen hid below decks, half-starved for five days. Then, when the Indians went below to look for liquor, food or firearms, the six whites and two loyal Indians closed the hatch covers and grabbed hidden rifles, firing over the mutineers' heads. "The mutinous savages were caught like rats in a trap," said Westerlund. The schooner proceeded to Sitka, where the Indians were charged with "piracy and revolt." They were committed for trial at the next assizes, but when Westerlund learned of the delay involved he got permission from the American authorities to secure the prisoners in the hold of the schooner and set sail for Vancouver. They arrived July 17. The rebellious Indians were committed for trial and jailed in New Westminster until the assizes opened November 12.

Headlines in the B.C. press mirrored Westerlund's highly-charged account of the incident: "How the Savages Were Got Below Decks and Made Prisoners." "They Lost All Their Semi-Civilization and Acted Like Incarnate Devils."

But then a different story began to emerge. It came from Indian Agent Frank Devlin, who wrote a report to his superior in Victoria, Superintendent A. W. Vowell. Devlin said he was certain the Indians had no intention of taking over the schooner. They simply wanted to return to their homes and Westerlund refused to turn back.[6]

The Indians had signed on February 23 with no date fixed for their return. The captain told them they would probably be gone for one to three months, although the season closed May 1. They hunted from Barkley Sound north to Sitka, arriving there June 4. The vessel left Sitka at 2 a.m. on June 15, ostensibly for the Bering, although the season did not open there until August 1.

Trouble started when the captain refused to provide food to the Indians because they did not help him raise the anchor. The Indians got together and decided to return in their canoes to Sitka. Faced with this ultimatum, Westerlund promised the natives all the food they wanted and more money. Then he gave them some liquor which he had purchased in Sitka to be used in trading with the Aleuts.

On June 25 the Indians asked Westerlund to show them on the chart where they were and where they were going. The captain said he was proceeding first to Sand Point in the Shumagin Islands, then on to Copper Island on the Asian side. At this the natives balked. Most of the coast Indian hunters were fearful of going to Russian waters, having heard stories of the harsh treatment handed out to poachers. There were 100 Indians hunting off the coast of Japan in 1895, but the majority of hunters there were white because there was no ban on the use of guns. The *Rand* natives demanded to be returned to Sitka. Westerlund refused and an argument ensued. The Indians broke their spears and threw them overboard.

The captain again withheld their food for two days. They offered to pay for a barrel of flour and a barrel of sugar to go off in their canoes to Sitka, but Westerlund stood firm. So they took possession of the schooner on June 27. The Indians insisted there was no violence; they had merely pushed the mate away from the wheel.

Vowell sent Devlin's report to Ottawa and asked B.C. Attorney-General Theodore Davie to hold the trial of the Indians as soon as possible. Their prolonged imprisonment would have a bad effect on other natives, Vowell warned. "Under the new sealing regulations it is very important to the advancement of that valuable industry that the Indians should be available as sealers; but I am afraid from what these Indians say that very few of the west coast Indians will be inclined to engage in that pursuit next year, as the imprisonment of the Indians will not only be resented by themselves as unjust but by all other Indians along the coast."

The jailed Indians were "an orderly, quiet lot," Vowell said, and it was hard to believe they would have behaved as they did unless given liquor by the captain as they claimed.

Ottawa told Vowell to see that the Indians had legal help. On August 16 they were released on $500 bail each. At the Assizes Mr. Justice John Foster McCreight withdrew the charges against the three women and twelve men but sentenced three men to eighteen months and three others to one year in prison. During their imprisonment the men were regularly visited by mothers, wives, children and village elders who made the long journey to New Westminster from Barkley Sound.

Except for the men still in jail, the Ucluelet hunters went out sealing again in June, 1895, and agreed to pay out of the season's earnings some of the costs incurred on their behalf by Agent Devlin.

It was incidents such as this which spurred some of the B.C. Indians, particularly in the San Juan area of southern Vancouver Island, to acquire their own schooners. But only a few vessels were native-owned and despite their greater numbers, the Island Nuu-chah-nulth were never as extensively involved as the Makahs. Some went across the Strait to Neah Bay to sign on the schooners there. One of these was "Charlie," a 55-year-old Nitinaht Indian from Pachena Bay, who sailed as a hunter on the *L. C. Perkins* in 1891.

The Makahs did not fare well with their schooners during the 1890s. In March of 1892 the *James G. Swan*, was ordered confiscated by a Seattle court for sealing in the Bering during the *modus.*

A year later the old pilot boat *Lottie*, owned by James Claplanhoo, was wrecked on Dungeness Spit. Claplanhoo had been trying to pull his little schooner *Deeahks* off the beach at the time. The *Lottie* had been sailing in the area for 25 years.

The Makahs' sealing income came to an abrupt halt in 1897 when the U.S. banned pelagic sealing by its citizens. Suddenly their schooners were worth little or nothing. Since they were smaller and less well maintained than other sealing schooners, the vessels had no resale value for other uses.

Chief Maquinna Jongie Claplanhoo of Neah Bay owned three schooners in 1897. He said a "Navy man" had promised he would receive compensation from the government for the loss of his business. It never came. As late as 1954 the Neah Bay Indians were still appealing to Washington for compensation for the 1897 law.

Vera *Taking in Gaff Topsails*

Sealing canoes on beach at Neah Bay

Halcyon (aka. *Vera*)

The Makahs tried to hire out again as hunters after 1897, but there were no more sealing schooners left in San Francisco, Seattle or Port Townsend. The Victoria schooner owners preferred to stick with the Nuu-chah-nulth of Vancouver Island.

The white schooner owners had differing attitudes toward the Indians. Some favoured them simply because they were cheaper to feed on a long voyage. Victoria outfitters Frederick Carne and William Munsie estimated they could furnish groceries and supplies for an Indian crew for half of what it cost to fit out an equal number of white hunters.

But as the competition for their skills increased, the Indians began to demand better services. As Captain Laughlin McLean (no kin to Alex and Dan) of the schooner *Favorite* said: "Indians are now as expensive as white hunters; they want everything and plenty of it. Five years ago I could feed them on molasses, rice, or anything, and they would be satisfied."

Some sealers thought the Indians were less troublesome than white hunters. Captain William Cox of the *Sapphire* said he preferred Indian hunters to whites because they were easier to get along with. They didn't quarrel and were more trustworthy. "There is more honour among them than among the average white crew in this business," Cox said. "They don't make an agreement today, and break it tomorrow if they see a chance to make a little more."

Others were less positive. Schooner owner Richard Hall of the Victoria business partnership of Hall & Goepel, said: "The great objection to Indians is their superstition. Often some trivial occurrence will be construed by them to presage some disaster, and they will abandon the voyage. Once they make up their minds to this they will go no further."

In a similar vein were the opinions of A. B. Alexander of the U.S. Fisheries Commission, who made an investigative voyage on the *Dora Sieward* of Victoria in 1895. He found the Indians lacking the persistence and judgement of white hunters. They would give up the chase on the slightest pretext, he said, while the whites would stay out as long as there was a chance to get one more. The Indians always came back early. Sometimes when they wanted to go home they would smash their spears and canoes. Alexander added that the Indians were suspicious of any officials seeking information on sealing and were not cooperative with him, which might have influenced his opinion of them.

Another American with a critical view of the Indians was Theodore Williams, city editor of the San Francisco *Examiner* who had been hired by the A.C.C. in 1889 to gather information on the pelagic sealing industry. The company wanted to know about this "illicit" sealing before it made a bid for a renewed lease the following year. It had been feeling the impact on prices of 50,000 to 60,000 pelagic skins placed each year in the London market.

Williams was to work undercover. He went to boat-builders and owners pretending an interest in buying, so was offered boats at their real value rather than the inflated figures given to Victoria Customs Collector A. R. Milne. He also managed to get his hands on the accounts of almost 100 sealing voyages. Williams found the white hunters close-mouthed about the losses of wounded seals, but after spending some time in their haunts gained their trust and learned some facts which the U.S. included in its case at Paris.

Some of the other "facts" contained in Williams' report cast doubt, however, on the reliability of his evidence. He told the A.C.C. there was no money solely invested in sealing because all the Victoria schooners were involved in coastal trading in the off-season, which was not true. He also wrote of the Indians' "skin canoes." Only the Aleuts had skin-covered craft; the coast Indians used nothing but cedar dug-outs.

Williams reported that because the Indian hunters were so much cheaper to keep and therefore more profitable for the operators, "all the schooners would engage Indians were it not for the fact that these Siwash are an extremely troublesome race and require the utmost tact and skill to manage. Only a few captains can handle them to advantage and they are mostly captains who have Siwash blood in their veins." There were few if any schooner skippers with "Siwash blood in their veins," however, and Williams' assertion that the Indians lost one-third of the all the seals they attempted to spear was equally off-base.

Statements made by the U.S. at Paris reflected the views of men like Alexander and Williams. "Mutinous, wilful, and superstitious, an Indian crew demanded experienced men to manage them," the U.S. case said. Several sealing voyages had ended abruptly as the result of some "ignorant fancy of the Indians hunters arising from the sickness of one of their number, the loss of a canoe, a prolonged season of rough weather, the stubborn determination to return home, or some other cause which only the Indians themselves could explain." Another peculiarity of the Indian hunters was said to be their unwillingness to start sealing when it was foggy. Elsewhere in the American presentation, however, it was admitted that fog prevented successful hunting and caused many boats and canoes to be lost.

Eleven Nuu-chah-nulth villages on the west coast of Vancouver Island with a total population of about 3,000 supplied most of the schooner hunters, usually the unmarried men. Their number increased from 80 in 1886 to 495 in 1892.

The missionaries approved of this employment because it kept the men and their families away from what they regarded as the evils of the city and the cannery camps. The Indian Agents generally supported this view, but some pointed out that there were disadvantages to sealing and did their best to alleviate the problems.

One of the most effective was Harry Guillod, who was appointed Indian

Agent at Ucluelet in 1882 and later moved up the inlet to Alberni. A chemist from London who had failed as a gold-hunter in the Cariboo, Guillod was able to use his early training to dispense medicines to his charges. One of his biggest concerns was the practice of paying advance money to the Indians as an inducement to get them to sign on the schooners. This money was often spent on liquor and gambling before they left and their families had no funds for food and clothing. The liquor was often sold to them by the schooner captains.

Guillod reported to Ottawa in 1895 that while many captains and owners wanted to end the practice, "it seems that an arrangement cannot be made which all sealing captains will keep, so that the man who refuses an advance stands a great risk of losing his crew." Some gave advances with a proviso that the hunters agreed to sign on again in the next year. "They are truly a prize commodity and have come to expect advances," Guillod said. In one instance a schooner captain paid an Indian hunter's court fine in Victoria and got him out of jail on to the vessel.

The Agent preferred the schooner captains making out orders on the village stores allowing wives and families anywhere from $2 to $20 a month. This money would be deducted from the hunters' pay when they returned. If the competition was particularly keen for crews the sealers would make a "donation" of food to the hunters' families as an added inducement. Guillod pressed the captains to pay off the Indians at their villages on the way south rather than take them into Victoria. He also urged that crews be hired through the Indian Agents, a practice which was often followed in later years.

Guillod was concerned when the Bering was closed to sealing during the *modus vivendi* of 1892. The Indians did not want to go to the Asian coast and he feared the consequences of a loss of earnings. In the last census the natives had reported receiving $62,000 from sealing, $40,000 of which came from the Bering. In 1891 hunters from Hesquiaht, with a population of 210, had manned two schooners and made $9,000 in the Bering. "And as their families stop quietly at home on the reserve during their absence, it is the best sort of remunerative employment for the men they could procure," Guillod said. Average earnings were about $500 per year and the Indians had built a number of good homes for themselves in Hesquiaht and Alberni.

The schooner captains usually selected an Indian hunter "boss" who got extra pay, perhaps 10 cents a skin, for recruiting hunters and acting as an intermediary during the voyage. Sometimes sums of money were offered to individual hunters who had earned a reputation for skill and hard work. (To keep count of their individual kills, some of the hunters carried a piece of string in their pocket and put in a knot for each seal.)

At least one missionary, Melvin Swartout, was cynical about this wooing of the hunters. The young men were often visited in their houses or invited into the captain's cabin and given liquor in an attempt to exploit their pride. The hunters' friendship was "diligently courted by the aristocratic vessel owner," Swartout wrote, but once on board they became Siwashes again.[7] To some extent this was true, but few of the schooner owners could be described as "aristocrats."

Meanwhile, diplomatic negotiations which would affect Indians and whites alike drifted on into 1897. In the U.S. a new administration under President William McKinley took office in March. The new Secretary of State, John Sherman, expressed the President's concern about the depleted condition and threatened early extinction of the herd. He sent David Starr Jordan's report blaming the decline on pelagic sealing to the British, urging a *modus* with a ban on all killing in the 1897 season. Salisbury insisted Jordan's figures were inconclusive. The matter needed still more study, he said, making no effort to placate American feelings on the issue.

Relations between the two countries deteriorated further in April when the new U.S. Ambassador to Britain, John Hay, was rebuffed when he called at the Foreign Office to discuss sealing. The dyspeptic Sherman called on John W. Foster to write a firm reply to the British stating the American position. Foster went at his task with relish. He said the British had from the beginning persistently failed to respect the real intent and spirit of the Paris Tribunal decision and the obligations it imposed. Patrol duty had been almost totally evaded in the Bering. The British had a "plain duty" to acquiesce in the request by the U.S. for a conference to determine what new measures were needed, Foster wrote.

Hay, a tactful, urbane diplomat who had been private secretary to President Lincoln, had misgivings about giving Foster's acerbic note to Salisbury. He talked first with the influential Colonial Secretary, Joseph Chamberlain, a political rival of Salisbury. Chamberlain raised the possibility of compensating Canadian sealers for abandoning their trade. Hay was intrigued with this idea and asked to have the Foster note delayed. But Foster pushed Sherman, and the Secretary of State ordered it forwarded.

The London *Times*, reflecting the government's point of view, said the letter was an offensively-worded accusation of bad faith against Britain. Hay told McKinley it was the tone of Foster's note which had especially angered the British. "It was an admirable paper in its facts and arguments," Hay said, "but the tone was very unusual." He quoted Chamberlain as warning Foster about U.S. diplomacy, "you will carry it too far some day and get hurt."

But Sherman, brother of the renowned Civil War general, was unmoved. He told the New York *World* cockily that Britain "quarrels oftener than she fights, and it would be exceedingly difficult for her to fight us alone about our seal-catching." He was right, because Salisbury did not want a serious quarrel with the U.S. over the seals. The Prime Minister instead proposed another

164

conference of experts, including Jordan, D'Arcy Thompson et al., but again excluding Russia and Japan.

Dr. Frederick Lucas of the U.S. team discovered that a large number of pups had been killed by a hookworm, confirming Thompson's suspicions that not all had starved to death. It was estimated by Jordan that 12,000 pups were victims of the condition, *uncinaria lucasi*, and another 15,000 from the effects of pelagic sealing.

Jordan, meanwhile, made a crude attempt to co-opt Thompson by offering him the directorship of the U.S. National Museum at $6,000 a year. Thompson immediately advised Salisbury of the overture and told Jordan he would give his answer later. He subsequently declined the post and remained at Dundee.

Foster, now back in his law practice but hired by the government to conduct the sealing negotiations, invited Japanese and Russian officials to Washington in the fall to work out a tripartite agreement. The three nations unanimously agreed the herd would be wiped out under the present regulations and an international agreement was required. On November 6 they signed a convention prohibiting their citizens from killing seals in all waters of the North Pacific outside the three-mile limit for one year. The pact was to take effect only if Britain agreed to sign.

When Salisbury restated his position that the dispute was between the U.S. and Britain alone and rejected the proposal, the Americans were outraged. Jordan said it was evident Britain was "only a nominal agent, always awaiting Canada's initiative in the affair; and Canada herself would do nothing unless and until her joint interest with the United States was recognized." He proposed ceding St. George to Canada or assigning a percentage of the yearly catch to the Canadians to create some form of partnership. But the Americans were not yet willing to make such concessions, which they regarded as a surrender to the British.

John Hay blamed Ottawa for the impasse and told Foster that Canada would do nothing "unless she is bought off." Senator Henry Cabot Lodge said threateningly that Britain should either make Canada behave herself, or "decline responsibility and leave us to settle the matter with Canada."

In fact, Canada was not being quite as obdurate as the Americans claimed. In November of 1896 Prime Minister Sir Wilfrid Laurier had told Foster the two countries should try to settle all their outstanding issues, including sealing. Laurier saw sealing not as a special issue, however, but one to be decided in joint negotiations on such disputes as trade reciprocity, the Atlantic fisheries and the Alaska boundary.

In March of 1898, as the five-year term of the Paris regulations was about to expire, Salisbury finally advised the Americans that Britain was ready to discuss possible revisions. On May 25 Pauncefote and Sir Louis H. Davies, the Canadian Fisheries Minister, met at the State Department with Foster. It was agreed that a Joint High Commission would meet in Quebec to discuss the outstanding issues between the U.S. and Canada, with seals the first item on the agenda.

At Quebec, Britain said it would consider a ban on pelagic sealing if there was "fair and equitable compensation to the owners of sealing vessels and to others engaged in the industry." The British felt they should also be compensated for giving up a national right to fish in the Bering Sea and undertaking to enforce the prohibition. The Americans pointed out that the schooner fleet was shrinking because of the shortage of seals and the doubtful future of the industry, and any compensation should therefore be nominal.

Nevertheless, Senator Charles Fairbanks of the U.S. delegation proposed paying $500,000 for the fleet, one year's profits for the owners and one year's wages for the crews, plus 7½ percent of future U.S. profits. Further negotiations led to an agreement to pay $600,000 for the fleet and 25 percent of gross receipts of all skins taken on the islands in excess of 20,000 annually. The schooners would be left in the hands of the owners to dispose of as they saw fit. Fairbanks noted that 40 percent of the schooners had been idle for some time because of falling profits.

Canadian Justice Minister David Mills told Laurier that Canada "ought not to abandon a sovereign right" to carry on pelagic sealing, but the Prime Minister was not concerned about upholding such principles. A deal on sealing seemed to be at hand. When the Joint High Commission moved on to the Alaska Boundary question, however, a deadlock was soon reached and all the negotiations collapsed. The Commission adjourned February 20, 1899, with nothing accomplished. Said Foster: "We were so near an agreement on the fur seal question, it seems too bad that such a useful herd of animals should be gradually destroyed because of a failure to agree about the ownership of some glaciers."

CHAPTER TWELVE

Victoria

The Indians were talking about their women and little ones starving at home, and all that kind of thing.

—AUGUSTE BJERRE

After leaving Victoria to pursue his business interests in England, Joseph Boscowitz did not return until 1884, having left J. D. Warren in charge of their schooner fleet. Warren had done well for the first few years, but was seized by ambition to acquire wealth as his partner had done. He branched out into other interests and quickly lost $150,000. Warren proceeded to appropriate funds advanced by Boscowitz for the sealing business to pay off his own debts. At the same time he put some of his property in his wife Hannah's name to keep the creditors at bay.

That was the beginning of the end of the partnership, but in the meantime Boscowitz had to work with Warren to avoid losing the schooners. They were assigned, or nominally sold, first to John W. Griffiths, a bookkeeper for Albion Iron Works in Victoria, one of Warren's creditors. Griffiths in turn assigned the vessels to Thomas H. Cooper, a brother-in-law of Warren who lived in San Francisco and was therefore out of reach of the Victoria creditors. Boscowitz took mortgages for the full value of the vessels to secure his interests, which meant he now owned all the schooners and their gear.

Then, to keep them out of reach of Warren's creditors, the schooners were leased back to the partnership, ostensibly by Griffiths. "I was not going to allow his (Warren's) creditors to come and seize my property," Boscowitz later declared.

In 1886 and 1887 it wasn't creditors who grabbed Boscowitz' schooners but rather cutters of the U.S. Revenue Service. He had whole or part ownership of seven vessels at that time and five — *Grace, Dolphin, Anna Beck, W. P. Sayward* and *Thornton* — were apprehended in the Bering. The *Thornton* was seized in 1886, the other four the following year.

The partnership was formally sundered in 1888 and from that time on Boscowitz and Warren did not talk to each other except through lawyers, who thrived on the resulting litigation. Boscowitz sued Warren for misappropriating his funds and the case dragged on for 10 years. Theodore Davie, later to become in turn Attorney-General, Premier and Chief Justice of B.C., was the lawyer acting for Boscowitz. He said he "served an apprenticeship" on the case. "That was one of the heaviest pieces of litigation ever in the province, and the details of it were so confused that one had to make himself thoroughly the master of it."

There were counter-suits by Mrs. Warren and Cooper and it was not until April, 1899, that a settlement was reached. That was after the U.S. had paid $155,000 in compensation claims on losing an argument that Boscowitz was ineligible because he was an American citizen. Of that amount Boscowitz received $90,000, Warren's creditors $55,000 and Warren the remaining $10,000. Both men had to pay their own considerable legal costs, however, leaving little or nothing for Warren. (Earlier in the litigation, in 1890, Warren's lawyers had sued him for their fees.)

Warren was a consistent loser in his dealings with Boscowitz. Newspaperman Theodore Williams, who had investigated the Victoria sealing scene for the A.C.C., said in an 1892 deposition he had been told that Boscowitz charged such high interest on his loans to Warren that all Warren's profits were eaten up. Williams said Boscowitz also got the better of Warren in the purchase of skins.

The compensation hearing which resulted in the $155,000 award was held in Victoria during the litigation. It followed the earlier rejection by Congress of a settlement negotiated in the wake of the Paris Arbitration. On February 8, 1896, the two nations signed a convention establishing a two-man commission to formally consider the claims. The commissioners named were Mr. Justice George Edwin King of the Supreme Court of Canada and Judge William L. Putnam of the U.S. Federal Circuit Court. If they were unable to agree on any particular claim there was a provision to appoint an arbitrator to settle the dispute. If the two sides could not agree on an outside arbitrator, the President of the Swiss Confederation would appoint one.

Counsel for the U.S. were Don M. Dickinson, a former member of the U.S. cabinet and law partner in Detroit of President Cleveland's private secretary, and Robert Lansing of the State Department. Representing Britain and Canada were Frederick Peters, Attorney-General of Prince Edward Island, and lawyer Frederick L. Beique, Q.C., of Montreal. Lawyers Ernest Victor Bodwell and Charles H. Tupper appeared on behalf of a number of schooner owners.

Tupper, the former federal cabinet minister and Canadian representative at Paris, prospered as the focus of the business shifted from hunting seals to seeking compensation. He represented the schooner owners in a number of hearings and at the end of 1897 moved to Victoria to set up a law practice, as did Fred Peters. Both men built handsome architect-designed homes on Oak Bay Road before Tupper moved his practice to Vancouver in 1900.

The Commission held its hearings in the old Legislative Assembly chamber in Victoria, starting November 23, 1896. The two commissioners sat on the Speaker's dais. The *Colonist* noted that at the back of the hall British and U.S. flags hung side by side, "typical of the amicable manner in which the countries are deciding their disputes." It was a somewhat hypocritical observation, since few voices were more strident than that of the *Colonist* in the sealing dispute. And the hearings themselves over the next few weeks were often less than amicable.

The British presented 26 claims to the Commission, totalling $1,289,088 with interest, almost double the amount sought at Paris and three times the figure accepted by Canada after the Tribunal but subsequently rejected by the U.S. Congress. Beginning with the claims drawn up for Ottawa in 1887, it was the third time damage figures had escalated. And five new claims had been added for the Victoria hearing.

Britain wanted to deal with each claim separately, but Dickinson strenuously objected. He said some witnesses were appearing in more than one claim and he did not want to tip his hand in attempting to discredit their testimony. Because it could not compel reluctant witnesses to come to Victoria, the U.S. asked to present its defence in San Francisco after the British case had been completed in Victoria.[1]

Feelings were running high in Victoria and the U.S. complained afterwards that its counsel had been at a disadvantage because the townspeople were hostile. American sealers had to "physically protect themselves and the witnesses among them from the personal violence which was often threatened and from the assaults that were made by sympathizers with the British claimants," it was alleged.

Dickinson said the U.S. did not dispute its liability: "We desire to know which side tells the truth, that is all." He noted that evidence in the British argument came largely from "the same class of men, who are in very intimate association." Both sides agreed to ban depositions, which they said had no value. Witnesses must go on the stand. Conflicting *ex parte* affidavits presented at Paris had raised doubts about the sealers' testimony.

In her case supporting the claims, Britain said the seizures by the U.S. "were equivalent to an unwarranted invasion of a friendly power in time of peace" and constituted an insult to the British flag. "The right asserted was so extraordinary that it could not in the ordinary course of events have been anticipated by any of the persons engaged in pelagic sealing, which it was the avowed intention of the seizures to interrupt and forever destroy." Britain said damages had been aggravated by the U.S. disputing its liability for many years and continually shifting ground.

Somewhat loftily, the Americans responded that "no juridical purpose can be served by imputations upon the good faith of the United States, insinuations against the truthfulness of their ministers, and charges of wantonness and evil motive against the Government. These pervade the argument of Great Britain from its introduction until the close of its general discussion. They are statements of prominent and impressive irrelevance. They are at war with the spirit of arbitration."

The sealers' claims had been given an importance out of all proportion to their significance, a "most incongruous dignity," the U.S. said. Furthermore, the claims were extortionate and padded. The "preposterous" duplication and doubling of claims was said to have been done so that their reduction by a half or more "would still give a result out of all proportion to the truth." Dickinson said the U.S. did not want to compromise on compensation.

The argument that followed revolved largely around the question of ownership of the schooners. The Americans said U.S. citizens were deeply involved in the financing of the fleet and were not entitled to compensation. Britain replied that all the vessels had British registry and flew the Union Jack, which was all that should concern the commissioners. A mortgagee was not an owner, the British counsel said. "The question as to whether foreigners shall be allowed to own registered vessels of another nation and carry its flag is exclusively within the province of that other nation and of its municipal laws."

The flag was merely the apparent sign of nationality of a ship, the U.S. argued. A bill of sale was the proper title "to which the maritime courts of all countries would look. It is the universal instrument of the transfer of ships." If the flag did not truly represent actual ownership, no claim could be made. The Americans also maintained that if a U.S. citizen was even a part owner the whole claim must fail. On these grounds the U.S. sought to rule out claims for 10 schooners, including the five nominally owned by Boscowitz and Warren.

Boscowitz testified at the hearing that he and Warren agreed in 1887 that all the claims should be made in Boscowitz' name, but Warren had changed them to his in the case of the *Thornton*, and Thomas Cooper in the others.

Cooper gave evidence to the commission during a special hearing in San Francisco. He said he was born in England and had lived in the San Francisco area for 33 years, working mostly as a blacksmith, but had never taken out naturalization papers. His sister was married to Warren. Conceding he was the nominal owner of six schooners, Cooper when pressed was unable to name them. "To tell you the truth," he said, "I know very little about them. They were sold at a sheriff's sale up there (in Victoria) and I bought them for one dollar. I was advised to do so by Captain Warren." Cooper said he was so little interested in the transaction that, "I don't know what I signed exactly." Boscowitz and Warren, who had power of attorney for Cooper, had not explained what they were up to. He was in Victoria for only a week or two signing a lot of papers and did not understand mortgages. Cooper never put up any money. He was used simply to cover up the financial manipulations of Boscowitz and Warren.

Warren testified that when his seized vessels had been put up for sale at Port Townsend in 1889, he had not attended even though they had gone cheaply. He had intended to buy them back, Warren said, but had become embroiled in financial problems in Victoria, including the litigation with Boscowitz. Dickinson charged, however, that Warren had made up his mind to "go for the United States and make them pay" rather than reclaim the schooners.

The U.S. condemned "those persons who have suffered their names to be used by American citizens, or have permitted the investments of American citizens, with them jointly, having the object in view to aid such citizens to violate the laws of their country under cover of such arrangements, and have befouled their consciences in the effort to sustain the frauds." It denied the right of Britain to protect Cooper "in his defiance of the sovereignty and violation of the laws of the United States."

Britain argued that international law recognized only states in such a controversy. Injuries to individuals were taken up by the states in which they resided. Individuals claimed the state's protection over their persons and property regardless of citizenship. "By reason of his domicile, an alien acquires the quality of a subject of the country in which he makes his home."

The U.S. insisted Cooper was a resident of the U.S. subject to its laws, turning Britain's argument on domicile against her. Nationality followed ownership in law, the U.S. argued. Citizens of the U.S. were not persons on whose behalf Britain was entitled to claim compensation from the U.S.

There were two classes of persons for which Britain was not entitled to claim compensation, the Americans said. They were British subjects living in U.S., such as Cooper, and U.S. citizens domiciled in Canada or Britain. The U.S. said it had the right to legislate for its own nationals and denied Britain's claim that the showing of the British flag and register was conclusive evidence that the owners of a vessel were British subjects. The claimants were "subjects" of Britain even if not citizens. The U.S. said it was common practice at Victoria for ships wholly or partly owned by U.S. citizens to be registered in the name of British subjects.

As the hearing progressed it became evident that Dickinson was more capable than Peters, who used speculative evidence based on old affidavits and was caught up in more errors. Tupper's questioning was showy but not penetrating. He was blustery and curt with witnesses, often trying to confuse rather than elicit information. As Dickinson grew increasingly impatient, he mocked Tupper's bombastic manner. Tupper frequently belaboured points beyond Putnam's patience and got in a dispute with King at one stage. Sir John A. Macdonald once described Tupper Jr. as "bumptious." He had the argumentative power of his father but lacked his finesse and rough charm. When the commission met in Halifax, however, where both Tuppers were local heroes, the *Herald* reported repeatedly that the young Tupper was the most eloquent and "forcible" of all the counsel.

Putnam was petulant with everyone, making frequent cranky interjections. When he tried to speed up the testimony, Peters protested that it had taken two governments 10 years to get to the commission stage. There was endless wrangling over what evidence should be admitted. King was well-meaning and fair, but bumbling.

Few schooner owners acquitted themselves well on the witness stand. They were often evasive and contradictory in their testimony. William Munsie was particularly uncommunicative. He was neither business-like nor straightforward, talking vaguely about "off-hand transactions." His cash dealings for sealing were separate from Carne & Munsie accounts, Munsie said. No books were kept by him or the firm on sealing activities until after 1891, and there were no records of outfitting costs. For a number of years Munsie had no bank account and used only cash. Carne was Munsie's partner in the grocery business only. By 1896 the Nova Scotia-Born Munsie had bought Carne out and joined forces with Victoria financier Simon Leiser. He went out of the grocery business and became involved in lumbering, mining, real estate, fishing and sealing. Munsie incorporated his six sealing vessels — *Viva, City of San Diego, May Belle, Arietas, Wanderer* and *Otto*— into the Victoria Sealing and Trading Company.

There was money to be made in the sealing business, Munsie conceded. When Dickinson pointed out that 2,300 skins at $7 each would pay $10,000 in wages as well as the $4,000 value of the schooner and leave $3,000 in profit, Munsie replied: "It will pay very handsomely, yes." He admitted entering the sealing business as a "speculation."

Canny in the way he made money, Munsie told the commission that when one of his vessels was being repaired or provisioned in Victoria he put the crew up in the Colonial Hotel. This was cheaper, he said, than keeping a cook on board and having the waterfront loafers scrounging food from the galley. Munsie's credo in the sealing business was "keep the sailor in our debt," which he did through advances and the schooner slop chest. He paid his Indian hunters off only where he could sell them goods from his stores. He was so tight-fisted that in 1899, some 13 years after the event, he sued the estate of James Ogilvie, the *Carolena* skipper who suicided in Sitka, for $500 plus interest. Munsie said the money was given to Ogilvie at the start of the voyage for incidental expenses and advances to the crew and had not been dispensed. He had apparently been spurred to take legal action after the 1896 claims commission awarded $5,000 to Ogilvie's estate.

Munsie was also a bold strategist. In 1899 he wrote to D. O. Mills, president of the N.A.C.C. in San Francisco, proposing an arrangement "whereby a company can be formed to take over all the British schooners and operate jointly with N.A.C.C., thereby regulating the catches and reducing costs of production." He suggested putting all skins in one sale to encourage competition at auctions.[2] Mills was not receptive to the plan.

One of Munsie's cronies in the business was hotel owner J. A. Bechtel. Dickinson said Bechtel was actually a half-owner of the schooner but because he was a U.S. citizen could not register the vessel in his name. In what became a common practice in the industry, the Ohio-born Bechtel switched from American to British citizenship in 1889. Bechtel had put up a small amount with little risk for a big profit, Dickinson said. Munsie admitted Bechtel "had a very good thing," but said it was because Bechtel had given him his start in business. Dickinson was harsh on Bechtel: "He contradicts himself directly by his several oaths, and is shown to be unworthy of credit. His testimony is not to be believed at all." Bechtel, he said, was the owner of the U.S.-registered *City of San Diego* which was later re-registered in Victoria with Munsie listed as "managing owner."

Another slippery witness was Alexander Frank, an American citizen who had been a business partner of Jacob Gutman of Victoria and had investments in the sealing fleet. The U.S. said Frank was guilty of making false affidavits and his testimony before the commission was "entirely unworthy of belief." When Gutman was drowned, Frank made a deal with his brother, Morris, to buy Jacob's property. When Morris left Victoria in 1888 Frank did not want to leave the schooners registered in the name of Jacob's estate and was unable to use his own name because of his American citizenship, so put the name of Morris Moss on the registry.

'Fitz' Moss was one of the more colourful characters in the Victoria sealing business. Born to wealthy Jewish parents in London, he was educated at University College. Over six feet tall, with a cultured accent and manners, he cut an elegant figure in the town. He had learned horsemanship in England, was an excellent shot and expert yachtsman and fitted in well with Victoria society. The city later thought enough of Moss, despite his bizarre ways, to name a street after him.

Moss worked in San Francisco for Liebes and Co. fur dealers for a short time before being sent by the firm to Victoria in 1862 to act as its agent. With some of his family money, Moss bought a boat, stocked it with merchandise, donned bucksin clothing and attempted to trade along the coast. He was not successful in this venture or in a number of others that followed. His epitaph in the Victoria *Times* after his mysterious death read: "Mr. Moss was a most speculative man and invested large sums of money in both mining and sealing, with varied success." The truth was that Moss was a bit of a dandy, erratic and ineffectual.

Against all advice, Moss attempted to open a trading post at Bella Coola, discovering too late that smallpox had killed 90 per cent of his prospective Indian customers. With the help of some Indian guides, however, he reopened the old Alexander Mackenzie trail and ran pack-trains through the mountains to miners at Williams Creek and Barkerville. Moss managed to ingratiate himself with the colony's most powerful man, Sir James Douglas, who appointed him Government Agent for the Northwest Coast and a justice of the peace.

When Alfred Waddington tried to build a road from the head of Bute Inlet to the Interior, the Chilcotin Indians, threatened with the loss of their lands, massacred 17 members of the work party. Moss was summoned by Governor Frederick Seymour to act as an "Indian expert" to advise the cabinet at New Westminster. Waddington subsequently accused Moss of profiteering during the hunt for the killers by bartering privately with the Indians for materials stolen during the uprising.

At the age of 42, Moss was married in 1883 to 22-year-old Hattie Bornstein, daughter of Herman Bornstein, a prominent Victoria fur dealer with interests in San Francisco, where the marriage took place. A son was born the next year named Alexander, after Moss' hero Alexander Mackenzie. Moss soon became restless with domestic life, however, and frequently left home on prospecting junkets.

One morning in June of 1892 he left his wife and son for the Kootenay area and was never seen by them again. He was last spotted leaving the mining town of Rock Creek in the Okanagan with a large amount of gold dust and bank bills. It was feared he had been robbed and murdered and private detectives were hired by his family and friends. His movements were tracked to Spokane and Denver, where in April of 1893 he denied his identity to a Victorian who recognized him on the street. He died in Denver in 1896 at the age of 54.

The U.S. Consul in Victoria, Levi W. Myers, later reported to the State Department that Moss had apparently run out on his debts. A Victoria bank was said to have advanced him $18,000 on the 1891 fur seal catch. Although Moss was listed as the registered owner of the *Lily* and *Black Diamond*, which had claims before the Commission, there was no representative for his estate at the hearing. The probate proceedings had contained no reference to his "ownership" of compensation claims. And there was no bill of sale conveying the schooners to Moss presented in the evidence, just the register.

Not all the men in the sealing business were cast in the mold of Moss, Frank, Bechtel, Warren and Boscowitz. At least one, a schooner captain with the unlikely name of Micajah Pinckney, made a good impression on the stand at the Victoria hearings. Dickinson was impressed with Pinckney's candid honesty and told him he was "a very fair man." When Dickinson asked Pinckney if he had been imprisoned at Sitka after his vessel had been seized the captain replied: "No sir, no more than being up in Sitka. It is almost like being in jail."

Pinckney was master of the *Henrietta* when she was seized in the Bering by the *Yorktown* in September of 1892 while 100 miles from land. She had been involved in the transfer of skins and supplies with the *Coquitlam* earlier in the season and was to be tried under U.S. revenue laws. If that failed she was to be turned over to the British for violating the *modus vivendi* regulations, an apparent case of double jeopardy.

The *Henrietta* was cleared on the revenue charges October 9, 1893, but the schooner and cargo were not returned until November 23. When Pinckney went aboard he found the outfit and provisions had been removed and he was forced to sell 105 skins in Sitka to finance his return to Victoria. He was allowed to pay $50 to get home on the *Coquitlam* after the seizure, but his crewmen were locked up for three hours to prevent their departure on the steamer. They sold fish to soldiers in Sitka and picked up odd jobs, living on the schooner for more than a year until it was released. Pinckney had not been authorized by the *Henrietta*'s owners to go back to retrieve her, and one of them, J. F. Fell, had tried to block him by registering himself as captain. Fell thought there would be more to be made from compensation than by regaining the schooner.

After Pinckney brought her back, the crew launched a suit for their wages. The skins were sold to satisfy a court judgement against the owners and the vessel was sold by the sheriff for $1,000 to satisfy a debt to McQuade's ship chandlery store.

One of the most controversial witnesses was Alex McLean. (Dan McLean never appeared. Alex said he was "somewhere in Central America.") McLean had been called by the U.S. as an expert witness and angered the British by refuting many of their claims. He testified that the *Carolena* was worth about $1,700 when she was seized in 1886, while Warren, Munsie and Charles Spring, McLean's former partner, valued her at $4,000. Counsel Fred Peters subjected McLean to a withering cross-examination but failed to shake his testimony. The British claimed McLean had been paid by the U.S. to assemble his evidence. But he pointed out that he had turned all his material over to the British counsel as soon as he arrived in Victoria for the hearing.

The commission wound up its business in Victoria on February 1, 1897. A one-day hearing was held in Montreal's Windsor Hotel June 16 before oral argument began in Halifax August 25 in the Nova Scotia Legislative Council Chamber, running to September 30. A final week-long session was held in Boston in December.

After the Boston meeting the *Colonist* carried a story claiming the compensation to be awarded by the commission totalled more than $1,000,000. But after a terse listing of the awards by Putnam and King was submitted to their governments, it was announced that the total was $473,151, less than a third of the amount claimed. The actual award was only $294,181, with the balance made up by accrued interest. (The U.S. had realized $83,000 from the sale of confiscated property after the seizures, which reduced their net outlay.) Payment was to be made within six months.

The commissioners ignored the objections raised by the U.S. and compensation was awarded to vessels which were partly owned by American citizens, although Alex McLean and Alexander Frank were specifically excluded from receiving any of the money. The American citizenship of Bechtel and Boscowitz was considered not proven. Payment of legal costs for the *W. P. Sayward* before the U.S. Supreme Court was rejected and there was no payment for prospective lost catches.

The *Colonist* said the award was a "serious disappointment to the sealers" but they must accept it. Ottawa should reimburse the sealers for their legal costs and pay for lost catches resulting from the seizures, the newspaper said. The commission had decided the amount which the U.S. Government could properly be asked to pay, and Canada should make up the difference. The *Colonist* also had a novel suggestion for Ottawa: Introduce fur seals into Hudson's Bay, which it said would be an ideal environment and, more important, a closed sea.

The funds were approved by Congress on June 14 after an appeal by Secretary of State Sherman. After the *Colonist* complained the cheques were being held back by Ottawa, it was announced on September 18, 1898 that 108 cheques had gone out covering all of the award except $30,000 for crew members and hunters who had moved away from British Columbia. Customs Collector Milne was given the job of locating them. He placed advertisements in newspapers as far away as Japan in an effort to track the men down. Lists of the missing men were circulated to consulates around the world. One was found living primitively in the Bonin Islands. His only concession to his old ways was an annual visit to Yokohama for an extended binge. When he made an appearance at the British Consul's office to get the latest news from home he was given the happy word that he had $300 coming.

One result of the commission's award was to put pressure on the American Government to compensate its own citizens affected when U.S.-registered vessels had been seized. A report by a Congressional Committee pointed out that U.S. counsel at Victoria had called upon these same American sealers for expert evidence to refute British claims and reduce the amount of the award. The Russians had previously paid $165,315 to American sealers seized improperly after the U.S. had taken their case to the World

Harry Guillod

Alex McLean

Indian hunters with gear on *Favorite*, 1894

Indian Hunters Returning to Dora Sieward

R. P. Rithet

William Grant

Indian hunters on *Thomas F. Bayard*

Court. That left the American sealers harassed by their own government as the only ones not compensated.

Dickinson told the Committee the American sealers had appeared in Victoria at great cost to themselves. He singled out Captains Alex McLean, E. P. Miner and Charles Raynor. McLean especially had "subjected himself to many unpleasant experiences and personal risk at the hands of British claimants and their friends in Victoria." Dickinson pointed out that McLean had owned a half interest in two schooners — the *Favorite* and the *Onward* — which his co-owner Charles Spring, a British subject, had sworn before the Paris Tribunal he owned by himself. A full award to the two ships would have benefitted McLean to the extent of his equities in them. But "this brave and honest man" admitted part ownership, said Dickinson, "when by silent assent to the perfidy of his partner he would have been benefitted himself."

The U.S. sealers, many now old and penniless, by their "praiseworthy and patriotic conduct" were entitled to compensation, Dickinson told the Committee. "They aided their country at Victoria in exposing the frauds and abating extravagant values in the British claims... their service was invaluable."

Not all Americans agreed these men should be compensated. Henry Wood Elliott told an earlier Congressional Committee looking into the question the U.S. sealers were "pirates." Congressman Richard Wayne Parker said they knew the U.S. considered pelagic sealing unlawful, and freely chose "to run the risk of capture." The Paris Tribunal ruled the U.S. had no jurisdiction in the Bering, Parker said, but "it never decided that we had no jurisdiction over our own vessels." Protesting that the U.S. should not have paid damages to the British, Parker said the U.S. sealers could only be reimbursed for appearing as witnesses at Victoria. In the end, after all the debate, they got nothing.

The other sealers forgotten in the clamour for compensation were the Indians, despite appeals to Ottawa that they be included. Father Brabant had asked Superintendent Vowell at Victoria to see that their interests were represented at the claims hearings. Vowell tried, but the claims were under the control of the Marine and Fisheries Department and it would not say whether the Indians could expect anything.

The U.S. said it would not accept liability for the Indians, presumably on the grounds they worked on contract rather than for wages, even though most of the white hunters also signed on for a "lay" or a share of the catch. The British didn't seem interested in seeking money for the Indians, who were hardly mentioned at the hearing. Only four of the boats making claims did not have Indians aboard.

The case of the 25-ton *Wanderer* was typical. She had set out for the Bering with Indian hunters after sealing along the west coast of Vancouver Island in the spring of 1889. When off Cape Scott at the northern tip of the Island the Indians were reluctant to go on. They had heard from another canoe while out hunting that the Americans were threatening to make seizures. The Indians, from Ahousaht and Clayoquot, asked Captain and part-owner Henry Paxton if he was rich enough to pay them if the schooner was seized. "I told them no," he testified. "They then refused to go. They said they had suffered great hardships and would not go again unless I would guarantee their pay for what skins they might have when the vessel got seized." So Paxton sailed back to Victoria.

Some of the Indians on the *Wanderer* had been on vessels that were seized. "They were talking about their women and little ones starving at home, and all that kind of thing," testified Mate Auguste Bjerre. Paxton said most would not go to the Bering in those days, but because the white hunters demanded and got such big advances the poorer schooners were dependent on the cheap labour of the Indians.

The U.S. took a hard line on the *Wanderer*'s claim for $18,447 for "intimidation" under the presidential proclamation of 1889: "That no damages can be awarded for the interruption of a voyage, the sole reason for which was that some uncivilized Indians aboard the vessel had received from other uncivilized Indians some diaphanous rumor that there were seizures being made in Bering Sea, is beyond question." The U.S. also declared that if Paxton had been wealthy the Indians would have gone to the Bering. (That should have proved they were not as unsophisticated as the Americans maintained.) In any case, the commissioners agreed with the U.S. position and the claim was rejected.

In January of 1896 the *Wanderer* had been caught in a storm off the north end of Vancouver Island, losing her rudder and head sails. She sought shelter in San Josef's Bay but the anchor chain snapped and she was washed ashore, breaking up in the surf. The crew spent eight days on the beach without food or shelter before four men set out in a small salvaged boat for Quatsino Sound, where they met the *Corwin*. The cutter went to the scene and her crew went ashore at great risk to take the marooned men aboard. All were saved. The seven crew members of a second schooner, the *May Belle*, travelling with the *Wanderer* and caught in the same storm, were not so fortunate. She disappeared without a trace while on her way to pick up Indian hunters at Nuchatlaht.

The *W. P. Sayward* was awarded $20,262, but the Indians did not get their share despite the pleas of Indian Agent Harry Guillod, who wrote to Vowell pointing out that the Ohiaht hunters had been cast ashore at Sitka when the schooner was seized in 1887. Guillod suggested $300 per man would be fair compensation. In the end they got $69 each, with nothing for the families of three men who had since died. Indians aboard the other schooners making claims eventually received similar amounts, but only after Ottawa had been pressed by Guillod and others.

Late in 1896, while the claims commission was sitting in Victoria, the sealing owners decided to form a joint company. The object was to handle and market the catch more economically, as well as to enjoy another benefit of a monopoly — keeping a lid on wages, especially those of the Indians.

Since 1889 most of the owners had been members of the Victoria Shipping Owners and Masters Sealers Association, an organization for promotion of the industry and mutual protection in the face of American opposition to pelagic sealing. J. D. Warren was in the chair at the first meeting of the Association and Morris Moss was named secretary. Resolutions passed at Association meetings were forwarded to the Canadian and British governments. Membership cost was nominal: $1 to join and $5 annual dues for each schooner.

The Association had also dealt with the matter of acting jointly on wages. A sliding percentage scale on skin prices was adopted for hunters in the 1891 season so as to lessen competition for experienced men. Wages for crewmen were limited to $30 a month. A proposal to look for hunters in Eastern Canada or California was put off until Victoria hunters had been interviewed to find out how many were willing to accept the owners' terms. A price was also set for the Indians of $3 for adult skins and $1 for pups. There were to be no bonuses for canoes or chiefs or contributions to potlatches except when seeking Indian hunters for the Bering, in which case there could be $10 bounties for the headman or chief and for each canoe.

These last provisions created considerable dissension. A later meeting scrapped the bounty plan in favour of paying a $25 bonus to the hunter with the highest total of skins so as to encourage competition and productivity among the Indians. A week later this plan was dropped and it was agreed that head men or "bosses" could be paid a bounty of $50 for procuring hunting crews.

At a meeting on October 28, 1890, white hunters were said to be unwilling to compromise and it was decided to seek men in the East. In the meantime, on a motion by Morris Moss, the members agreed not to make offers individually to Victoria hunters. A week later the owners decided not to take more than three experienced B.C. white hunters on each vessel; all others had to be greenhorns.

In October of 1891 the Association underwent a transformation of sorts. It took on a new name, The British Columbia Sealing and Fishing Association, and a new president, John G. Cox. Moss was vice-president. A constitution was drawn up declaring the purpose of the Association to be "the mutual benefit and protection of all those interested in or connected with the sealing industry." One of the tasks taken on was the chartering of the steamers *Danube* and *Coquitlam*. The Association also sent a number of protests through Ottawa to Britain, protesting the Imperial Government's willingness to give in to the Americans on such matters as the *modus vivendi*.

In November of 1895 a memorandum was drawn up to regulate the prices paid to Indian hunters and limiting the number of canoes allowed. Schooners of 80 tons and up were permitted 14 canoes, and the others ranged down to four canoes for vessels under 30 tons. It was decided to pay $3 a skin without any bonuses or other remuneration. Warren and H. F. Sieward wanted to pay $5 per canoe to the "boss Indian" for his services but this was voted down. Advances were not to exceed $20 per man and the Indians were to be paid off at Victoria. They would have to make their own way home.

Then in late 1896 came the move to transform the Association into a joint stock company whereby the profits of the fleet would be equally divided among the schooners participating. This would have the effect of securing uniform "lays" and wages and prevent competition in securing crews. The proposal was referred to a committee for study. Boscowitz favoured the pool but Thomas Earle "positively declined" to join such a group. At the same meeting a motion was carried to reduce the payment to Indians to $2 a skin. There was also a heated debate about how much cooks should be paid. Some of the most experienced sealers argued that next to the captain the cook was the most important man aboard and should be paid accordingly. Others scoffed at the idea. The quality of food had never been a high priority on the schooners, and the discussion indicated a new awareness that in order to get and hold good men it must be improved.

The owners of 57 vessels indicated an interest in joining the company, but a number of holdouts blocked its formation. It would take another two years of bad times for the industry before the idea was accepted.

Meanwhile, the Association's continuing efforts to bring the Indian hunters in line resulted in a proposal to import 100 Micmac Indians from Nova Scotia, who were said to have experience spearing hair seal and porpoise. They would bring 14 of their own high-ended birchbark canoes. The supposed industriousness of the Micmacs and their willingness to work for lower wages was intended to give "our Siwashes" an object lesson. The Eastern Indians were to be placed near Clayoquot on Vargas Island, where it was said there were 600 acres of arable land. Egged on by the *Colonist*, seven schooners indicated they would participate. The *Times* scoffed that the whole idea was "a fake, a sell, a scheme to rob the poor wretched Siwash, a lie." Whatever its merits, the proposal was soon quietly forgotten.

The outlook for the 1897 season was not good. The *Colonist* complained there would be a huge U.S. patrol fleet in the Bering: "Altogether there will be a warship for every unfortunate sealer, or very near it." Whether it was the result of this vigilance or not, the catch dropped from 55,677 in 1896 to only 30,410.

There was growing pessimism on the waterfront during the following winter. Harbour "pirates" broke into moored schooners. The U.S. embargo on the import of pelagic skins had a demoralizing effect on the owners. Grocer Thomas Earle switched from seeking the sealers' business to advertising Klondike and miners' outfits. Twelve vessels had gone to Japan in 1897, but only one, the *Director*, under Captain F. W. Gilbert, went in 1898. By January 16 half the 60 schooners remaining in the Victoria fleet were still tied up. Only 34 vessels participated in the coast hunt. E. B. Marvin kept his four schooners moored all spring. The weather was rough and the seals scattered, but the catch was slightly improved over 1897.

In May, John Cox and Richard Hall travelled to Ottawa to meet Fisheries Minister Sir Louis Davies, who was about to participate in the abortive negotiations with Washington over trade, sealing and the Alaska boundary. Hall said on their return that pelagic sealing would be banned after the current season but Victoria's sealers would be looked after and "liberally compensated." Sale of the fleet might bring as much as $600,000, he said. Dreams of gaining money for the aging schooners without taking them back to sea began to dance in the heads of the Victoria owners. Their hopes would not die for many years.

In June Joe Boscowitz tied up his four schooners rather than pay $3 a skin to the Indians, who he said were getting the best of the industry. They were demanding, and being given, large contributions to potlatches, Boscowitz said, and there was not enough profit to warrant such troubles with the "savages".

During the summer Captain Herbert Taylor of Halifax and Captain I. E. Thayer of San Francisco were named to appraise the value of the sealing fleet in the event of a purchase offer by the U.S. The Sealers Association protested Thayer's appointment as well as that of Taylor, who they pointed out was an Easterner unacquainted with the west coast sealing industry. "We also protest against his intention of valuating the sealing fleet without any regard as to the costs of the vessels to their owners or the purpose for which they were purchased."

The Ottawa *Citizen* pointed out that any money paid for the fleet would go to the owners and mortgage-holders and asked what would be done for the seamen who lost their jobs. This was a question that did not seem to concern the Victoria newspapers, which identified with the financial community.

As might be expected, Thayer and Taylor came up with widely divergent appraisal reports, exchanged between the two governments at meetings in Washington. Thayer said the value of the fleet was only $75 a ton or $278,000 for 51 vessels. Taylor gave a valuation of $135 a ton, or a total of $550,000 for 54 vessels. The Association had been claiming a value of $200 a ton or $742,000 for the fleet. Aware this was a highly inflated figure, John Cox advised Ottawa he was authorized to offer the fleet at $125 a ton, or $589,000. He had earlier been rebuked by Fisheries Minister Davies for scorning the $450,000 offered by the U.S. in tentative negotiations.

But the two countries could not agree which vessels should be included in the proposed buy-out. The U.S. said there were just 30 in the business in 1897. Canada insisted there were 54, but Richard Hall later conceded the figure was indeed 30. He blamed the Indians for going salmon fishing instead of accepting the Association's price for sealskins and leaving a number of schooners unmanned. There was also a resurgence of otter along the west coast and some Indians went after those more valuable furs.

In November a number of schooners left port early for the winter season, provisioned for long cruises in case a law was passed banning pelagic sealing. The five-year Paris regulations would expire at the end of the year and they did not want to wait to learn the repercussions.

The Association, meanwhile, sent a petition to the Governor-General to be presented to the Quebec Conference. It said a total of 8,500 persons in British Columbia, including the families of sealers, were dependent upon the schooners, which produced an annual income of $750,000. Where once the fleet earned 100 to 200 percent on its capital investment, it was now "so limited, trammelled and circumscribed by international regulations" as to make it unprofitable. The petition urged Britain and Canada to resist any further restrictions on the industry. It said the Americans, who almost a century before operated the world's greatest pelagic sealing fleet out of Boston, now wanted to halt the business after cleaning out the South Seas themselves. But the main targets of the petition were the Canadian and British governments. The "foreign policy of Empire" and "Imperial reasons" had sacrificed the industry, it said.

In December, 1898, the sealers got together again to transform the Association into a joint stock company. Much of the initiative for this new try came from A. R. Milne, the Victoria Collector of Customs and registrar of shipping. In a report to his superiors in Ottawa Milne wrote: "For the past four or five years I have intimated to owners of sealing vessels that the policy they were pursuing would eventually end in serious losses by each giving more than his neighbour for seal hunters."

The motion to change the status of the Association was made by Boscowitz, seconded by Munsie. A draft agreement was drawn up for the

British Columbia Sealing Company, with capitalization of $600,000. The company later described itself as "simply a consolidation of our interests on a pro rata value."[3]

The draft was adopted June 28, 1899, but not implemented until November of 1900, when directors were named and an official seal and flag selected for the "Victoria Sealing Company." An office was opened December 1 in the Board of Trade Building. Captain William Grant was manager without salary and the company rented Grant's wharf in Victoria harbour. Fred Elworthy was hired as Secretary at $25 a month and A. R. Langley as bookkeeper at $85 a month. Grant persuaded the company to carry its own insurance on the vessels to save $30,000 in premiums.

Grant had arrived in Victoria in 1881 and began sealing in 1887. He bought the schooners *Beatrice, Ainoko* and *Penelope,* all first-class vessels, in Japan, registering them in Shanghai to avoid paying duty in Canada.

The prime movers behind the formation of the new Sealing Company were John Cox, who put in six schooners, and Boscowitz, Grant and Bechtel with three each. Boscowitz kept out one of his vessels, the *Ada.* All the owners who put vessels into the company were given shares evaluated on their tonnage, age, and condition. A basis was fixed at $147.75 a ton, said to have been established independently by Captain Taylor. Owners had to pay to bring their vessels up to that standard or have the value of their shares reduced. There was also a deduction for tonnage exceeding 100, because the Company was not anxious to have large vessels. A total of 33,458 shares were issued, with a value of $418,225.

There was a private agreement made by the owners not to engage in sealing outside the company for 10 years, although the Company's written pledge was for only two years. Victor Jacobson agreed to come in for the minimum period. J. W. Peppett, owner-skipper of the *Umbrina,* said he would abide by the Company rules and regulations and pay whatever prices it decided upon, but declined to become a member.

It was decided to proceed without three schooners held out by their owners, leaving 42 vessels in. A short time later the Company purchased the old schooner *Mermaid* for $2,000. The directors feared someone else might buy her. "We wanted to control all the sealing," Grant said later. The *Mermaid* lay idle for the next decade and never sealed again. She had been built in Portsmouth by the British government in 1853 to hunt down whisky smugglers on the Dogger Banks and was later a revenue cutter in the English Channel. Brought out from London in 1892 by Captain W. H. Whitely in 119 days, she had beams of Italian oak and was finished throughout with teak and mahogany. The *Mermaid* finished her days as a Sandheads lightship at the mouth of the Fraser River, where she was later replaced by the *Thomas F. Bayard,* a former Delaware Bay pilot boat.

Sealing had taken a slight turn for the better in 1898 and 1899 before the company went into operation, mainly because prices were up and fewer boats went out, resulting in higher individual catches. In 1898 only 35 of the 65 vessels remaining in the fleet went out, but they took a total of 27,865 skins, including 17,253 in the Bering and 10,612 on the coast. The total was only 3,000 less than in 1897. Meanwhile, the N.A.C.C. land kill on the Pribilofs, restricted by government quotas, was just 19,000.

On January 1, 1900, the *Colonist* reported a "marked revival" of the industry. Seal fur was back in fashion and since skins were in relatively short supply, prices were high. Of the 34 schooners out, 10 belonged to R. P. Rithet & Sons, the outfitters who had ended up with the largest number of vessels as the result of mortgage defaults and unpaid bills. Five belonged to E. B. Marvin, four to Munsie, and three each to Bechtel and Grant. They took a total of 34,000 skins, an increase over 1898. In 1900 a number of vessels were reactivated on the basis of the 1899 catches and another good year was recorded, with a further increase in prices.

CHAPTER THIRTEEN

Ahousaht

Dear Sir, lately we have found out that you are boss of all the Indians, so we ask you for justice.

— Chief BILLY AUGUST

On August 19, 1898, lawyer Fred Peters placed an advertisement in the *Colonist* asking all claimants for the $473,000 in compensation paid by the U.S. to contact his office. Indian Agent Harry Guillod duly drew up individual claims and told Peters the natives were entitled to between 10 and 20 percent of the award. But Peters complained to Superintendent Vowell that the Indian claims were late and excessive. Vowell told Ottawa that Peters considered it "preposterous" that such large amounts should be given to Indians.[1]

Vowell said the Indians had looked to the captains and owners to ensure they were recompensed for losses and now they saw that group being paid but not themselves. Milne had been sending out cheques to the whites but nothing arrived for the Indians. The natives suspected they were being discriminated against, Vowell said. The Victoria *Times* had reported the natives would receive $73,000 and this had raised their hopes.

Eventually Ottawa announced the Indians would receive about $13,000 of the award money. On May 24, 1899, Guillod wrote Vowell asking where the money was. The Indians were pressing him, he said, but Milne was stalling. Milne in fact had decided the Indians would get nothing until all the white hunters had come forward to claim their money. Since the whites had dispersed, this was taking a long time. It was also reported that any white hunters overlooked would be paid out of funds allocated for the Indians. Some whites were already making claims on the Indian appropriation, while others tried to buy up Indian claims at big discounts.

Meanwhile, the Indian families were in need of money and Guillod said they were threatening to sue. He planned to visit each band to examine the claimants. Their evidence would have to be corroborated by the tribe.

In December of 1899 the Presbyterian missionary at Dodger Cove, Rev. Glendon Swartout, complained the whites had been paid the year before and there was still nothing for the Indians. The natives were saying the government was keeping the money to earn interest on it, Swartout said. Vowell was defensive. He reported to Ottawa that missionaries were "inciting" the Indians to make complaints. (Missionaries were often used as scapegoats by the white authorities when the Indians made a fuss about anything.)

On June 4, 1900, the Department of Marine and Fisheries sent a cheque for $13,333 to the Department of Indian Affairs, requesting the return of any undistributed funds. It said the division should be made on the basis of one white boat with two men being equal to two canoes. Since there were also two men in each canoe, this meant the Indians, on the basis of a purely arbitrary decision, would receive half the amount given white hunters.

The Department also insisted that none but living Indians were to participate in the award. After receiving numerous protests, the Marine and Fisheries Department conceded that the Indian agents should be allowed some flexibility in the distribution of the money. The Department apparently believed the government could get away with ignoring heirs, but Vowell advised Ottawa the B.C. Indians knew their legal rights and would petition if denied them.

The hard line had apparently been adopted by the Department on the advice of Customs Inspector Milne. Milne told Ottawa the deceased Indian hunters had died intestate because they had no will that would be accepted by the courts, and their marriages were not recognized outside the tribe, "unless among the Roman Catholic followers." After being forced to concede on this issue, Milne said there should be half-shares for wives and children, but no others. The Fisheries Department accepted this proposal, ignoring the fact the Indians were well aware of next-of-kin relationships.

Indians Affairs Department law clerk Richard Rimmer in Ottawa said in an internal memo that Milne was unaware of provisions of the Indian Act and wrong about Indian property rights and marriages. Rimmer said 90 per cent of B.C. Indians were Christians and half of those were Catholics. Next-of-kin could be traced to brothers and sisters at least, he said. The Administration Act of B.C. recognized as much, but Milne had quoted solely from the Merchant Shipping Act and Seaman's Act. The only disparity was that a wife without children received a full share under the Indian Act but half under the B.C. Act. Rimmer recommended the Indian Act be applied in these cases and the Fisheries Department withdraw its restrictions. Any share unclaimed after three years should go back to the Marine Department. Rimmer was overruled by his own department, however.

Vowell told his superiors in Ottawa that many Indians in the province were now making out proper wills and Milne, who had close ties to the schooner owners, had been advised by an out-of-date "expert." Milne made his feelings clear in a letter to the Department: "The amounts awarded will be generally much less than anticipated by the Indians—this is due to the exaggeration of white men, who are ever ready to induce the Indians to have a grievance."

Guillod advised that 14 Indians hunters aboard the *Grace* and *Dolphin* were dead, and estimated that one quarter of the claimants had died.

In May, 1901, Vowell sent $2,737.30 via the C.P. steamer to Clayoquot for distribution by Guillod, the first instalment of the $13,333. Some $1,092 went to 17 Ahousaht hunters who had been on the *Black Diamond*, or their heirs. There was disagreement about how many Indians were aboard the schooner when she was seized in 1889. Vowell wrote Guillod a frosty memo saying there were only 15, but according to Captain Owen Thomas' evidence he had taken on 21 at Ahousaht. Whatever the number, the Fisheries Department was anxious to hold on to the money and said that if six of the 21 did not turn up, the money allocated for them should be returned to Ottawa.

The *Black Diamond* recipients included "Topsail Charlie" and "Sailor Jack." These "King George names" had been given to them by the white schooner crewmen, who could not cope with their Indian names. There was $1,056 for four Indian hunters on the *Henrietta*. The surviving two men received $264 each and the widows of the other two got a half share and their children the other half. Another $484, or $30.25 each, went to the 16 hunters of Victor Jacobson's *Minnie*. They were all still alive. The largest amount was $1,881.25 for 14 hunters on the *Juanita*. The awards varied depending on the number of skins taken from each seized schooner. In most cases the allocation was not fully spent.

In April, owner Charles Spring of the *Henrietta* had complained to Guillod that the Indians on his schooner had already collected one half of their claims from him and he wanted that money returned now that they were to be paid. Guillod told Spring sharply that he was late in making such a claim. He said he had tried to meet with Spring on the matter in Victoria as early as 1898 but Spring did not keep their appointment. Spring had apparently "bought" the claims of the Indians at a 50 percent discount and the Indian Affairs Department was not sympathetic. The four Indians on the *Henrietta* had not been paid for their catch as on most of the other schooners. Spring had given them $100 or $200 credits at his store instead.

The conscientious Guillod finished distributing the awards by August 1, 1901, but reported there was "a great deal of dissatisfaction" among the Indians over the arbitrary policy on heirs. The heirs of unmarried men received nothing. The Agent urged that even a nominal amount should be given to these aggrieved claimants. He was forced to send back the unspent $1,394.30 balance to the Fisheries Department, however.

To its credit, the Marine Department later returned $605 to Indian Affairs to distribute to the disappointed claimants. This was ordered by Acting Minister James Sutherland, who succeeded Louis Davies. The $605 was for seven special cases listed by Guillod involving two fathers, a sister, brother and grandchildren of deceased hunters. After receiving more pleas, Guillod sent a further list totalling $802.75 which included more distant relatives such as cousins, nephews and nieces. This sum was also agreed to by Sutherland. There may have been some political pressure from Clifford Sifton, the Minister of the Interior and Superintendent-General of Indian Affairs, who got letters supporting the claims from Nanaimo member of Parliament Ralph Smith. The Indian Department noted Guillod's "care and energy" in his "intricate and arduous task." It was a well-deserved accolade.

A belated claim arrived from Tquiat of Nootka, who told Guillod there were two Indians from his village on the *Thornton* with white hunters when the schooner was seized in 1886. Because the *Thornton* was not on the list of vessels with Indians, nothing could be done. Over the next two years other claims continued to trickle in, and Ottawa grudgingly forwarded further small amounts of compensation. Guillod died in 1903 while still in the process of making his final distribution. His successor, A. W. Neill, tried to complete the job but was not able to locate some of the new claimants. Less than half the $802 sent out by Ottawa was given out and Neill was forced to return $411.

Guillod had been fair with both whites and Indians who appeared before him in his role of Justice of the Peace. In November of 1901 he presided at the trial of Captain Hand of the *Umbrina* after crew member Ole Carlson was accused of selling liquor to some Indians. Guillod said only one bottle was involved and Hand was unaware of the transaction. He convicted the captain but imposed no penalty.

It was not long before Neill, the new Agent at Alberni, was at odds with his Superintendent. Vowell had said it might be a good thing if sealing ended because the men would be able to stay on the reserve with their families and have regular jobs. Neill, a sharp-tongued individualist, did not agree. He pointed out that in 1903 more than $5,000 had gone into one reserve from sealing. Sealing was better work for the natives than the Fraser River canneries or the Washington hop fields where they were more likely to get into trouble. If pelagic sealing was banned, Neill said, the Indians would expect their share of compensation for the loss of livelihood. And they should be allowed to continue hunting from shore, he added.

Neill sat in the B.C. Legislative Assembly from 1898 until he was appointed Agent in 1903, a post he filled for the next decade. He was mayor of Alberni and spent 24 years in Parliament as the Independent member for Comox-Alberni. His work as an MP was widely credited for the institution of the old-age pension in 1921.

Vowell and Neill did agree on one thing: the 270 Ahousahts were their most troublesome clients. Neill said they were the "most impudent and aggressive on the coast." He was annoyed because the band bypassed him and sent their complaints directly to Ottawa. They "boast that they can get anything from the Department direct and nothing through the usual channels," he complained to Vowell. The Superintendent described Chief Billy August as "an agitator and a mischievous man."

What had provoked this particular outburst was a complaint by the Ahousahts that the Sealing Company was slow to pay them after voyages on its vessels. Vowell defended the company, saying the Indians were dropped off at Ahousaht on the way south, but there could be no payout until the schooner reached Victoria and the accounts and records were drawn up. In the meantime the storekeeper at Ahousaht gave out credit.

The matter of trading posts at Ahousaht had been a subject of controversy for some years and perhaps contributed to the frustration of Neill and Vowell with the band. Captain Charles Hackett was operating a store at the adjoining village of Marktosis when the longtime Clayoquot storekeepers, Stockham and Dawley, asked permission from the Indian Affairs Department in 1896 to set up a business not far from Hackett on the site of an old trading post operated by J. D. Warren. Guillod said the Indians approved because they knew that where there was competition, goods were cheaper. Stockham and Dawley were to pay $12 rent a year to the tribe for the use of an old house.

But in June, 1904, Chief Billy wrote to Sifton: "Dear Sir, lately we have found out that you are boss of all the Indians, so we ask you for justice." He said the men had come back from sealing in 1895 to find a new store in the midst of their houses. They had never asked for it, and Hackett's store was only a quarter of a mile away. They claimed that only four Indians had asked for the store. There had been a promise of $6 a month rent for the house and a $20 annual "bribe" for the chief. But the storekeeper for Stockham and Dawley, Fred Thornberg, had married an Ahousaht woman and she pleaded for his job to help raise their children, and the Indians signed a petition of support. Thornberg ran the store for four years, leaving in 1900. He was not replaced and rent had not been paid since that time. The Indians now said they should get about $250 for the old chief. "Please have the whiteman's store removed," said the letter to Sifton.

Ottawa replied that the rent had been paid to the Department up to the present date and the lease could not be broken. Chief Billy was told the Indians did not have to deal at that store. Neill then tried to buy peace by asking permission to distribute the rent money among the people at $1 a head. Later Dawley said if the Indians bought his store building he would remove the goods. The Indians responded that "Dawley pulls out quietly and then complains that he owns the ground."

A similar dispute arose in 1899 at Kyuquot when the Sealing Company abandoned its store without notifying the Department and owing $25 rent. The Company secretary at first refused to answer letters, but paid up later after numerous protests.

The Ahousahts were also the leading agitators for increased payment for skins. In 1901 Charles Hackett advised Fred Elworthy of the Sealing Company the hunters were holding out for $5 a skin, as well as bonuses and boss money. He thought they would give in eventually, however, because many were hard up and in debt to the store. But after a big potlatch attended by 10 tribes, the men decided they wanted $6 a skin. The Indians hoped the schooner captains would fight among themselves over their services. Canoes were scarce and some schooners were forced to buy them outright.

The Presbyterian missionary at Ahousaht, Rev. John W. Russell, supported the Ahousahts in many of their disputes. On one occasion he sent a claim of $10 per man for a group of hunters who had signed on the schooner *Walter L. Rich*. When they had not been paid a promised advance as it came time to sail, they refused to go aboard. After two days they were assured by Captain John T. Walbran of the Government survey ship *Quadra* they would be paid at the increased rate recently negotiated at Clayoquot, and so they set off. On their return, however, they were fined $10 a day for detaining the vessel two days, despite assurances they would not suffer for their action at the start of the voyage. The men refused to sign clearance papers. One hunter said he had signed on for $2.75 a skin and the articles had been tampered with and changed to $2.50.

Russell intervened after the men had waited four months for a settlement and could not sign on with another vessel until they had cleared with the *Walter L. Rich*. Sifton replied: "In such a matter the Indians are in the position of other subjects and have to take the same legal course to obtain redress."

It was not the first time Walbran had been involved with the Indian sealers and their grievances. In June of 1895 Customs Collector Milne had asked Ottawa to assign the *Quadra* to prevent American sealing schooners attempting to lure Indian hunters already signed by Victoria vessels. The schooner owners had urged Milne to have the *Quadra* sent on a two-week patrol along the coast. Her presence was intended to deter U.S. vessels approaching the villages. Ottawa approved the request.[2]

The *Quadra* was used for fisheries patrol and servicing coast lighthouses. She was run like a man-of-war by Walbran, who favoured a gold-braided frock coat with long sword in a scabard. He was a stipendiary magistrate and had a provincial constable aboard and cells below.

The owners complained that Nitinaht hunters had signed articles with the *Penelope* and Clayoquots with the *Triumph* when Captain L. Larsen of the Seattle schooner *Bering Sea* offered $4 a skin instead of $3, and a $30 bounty for canoes, so they had gone off with him. Captain Myers of the *Teresa* was said to have had the same problem in 1894, and Victor Jacobson had lost hunters to a Neah Bay schooner.

But some Indians were aware of their responsibilities. Billy Gibbs of Clooose sent a letter to Captain Grant of the Sealing Company returning a $50 advance: "I do not want to run away from you," he wrote, "but when I can get $4 a skin instead of $3 I must look out for myself. I have no other reason for leaving you." In a similar case a Neah Bay Indian who had jumped ship from the *Annie E. Paint* of Victoria wrote a letter to the captain and returned his advance money.

Milne told Ottawa the signing of Indian crews on B.C. ships had been "haphazard." There was no official supervision, with shipping masters delegating authority to the captains and storekeepers. "Now the Indians quite well understand that such is not binding," Milne wrote. Some were getting as little as $2.50 a skin on the Victoria schooners. The storekeepers who acted as shipping agents for the owners told the Indians they could have anything they wanted from the store if they signed.

The *Quadra* returned on June 29 and Walbran reported that all the schooners had obtained crews and were satisfied. He went into all the ports on the west coast of Vancouver Island up to Nootka and did not see any American vessels. At Nootka he had heard of three men deserting from the *San Jose*, but it turned out they had been sick and provided substitutes. Walbran added that the uniform of the Marine Service had the effect on the Indians of "inducing them to do what is right."

Walbran gathered the Indians together at the various villages and told them they were expected to honour their first agreement with the schooners. The Indians consented, as long as the captains kept their verbal promises to the hunters, which were not always written in the articles. The Indians complained that sometimes their names were put on the articles before they had agreed to go. They were suspicious of the white sealers, who did not always act in good faith. They told of one trip on which an Indian hunter died and his family was not paid for the 34 skins he had taken.

They said they were promised by Captain Clarence Cox of the *Triumph* in 1894 that if they caught more than 4,000 seals they would get a $250 bonus. That was the voyage on which the *Triumph* got 1,320 skins on the coast and 3,240 in five weeks in the Bering for a total of 4,560, the all-time record. Cox said he could have taken more but ran out of salt. The *Triumph* carried 17 canoes on that voyage, manned by 34 Indians. The previous record of 4,262 had been set by Dan McLean, also on the *Triumph*.

Walbran said Cox admitted making the promise. In Victoria the owners had told him the remark was "only made in joke" because it was never anticipated the catch would be so large. "I think it is not advisable to joke with Indians on these matters," Walbran said.

Captain James Gaudin, the head west coast agent for the Federal Marine and Fisheries Department, followed up Walbran's report by telling Ottawa: "The chief trouble appears to be amongst the sealers themselves who in their anxiousness to obtain Indian spearmen for their Bering Sea cruise are outbidding each other in their offers to their hunters, the Indians accepting the highest offer irrespective of any previous agreement." Gaudin added that there were "very slight grounds for the fears entertained by the sealers." The Indians regarded the presence of the *Quadra* as intimidation and were "anxious to carry out their engagements without this show of force."

In June, 1896, the *Quadra* made another voyage up the coast at the start of the sealing season. Walbran said the ship's presence impressed upon the Indians the need to sail on the date specified in the articles, "instead of idling away the days with excuses until it barely left time for the schooners to reach the Bering Sea by the opening of the season." But the captains were to blame for this situation, Walbran said. They gave big advances to the best hunters, who squandered the money gambling. There was then no incentive left for the Indians, who knew they wouldn't get much more by going on the voyage and saw no need to hurry.

The Indian Agents and missionaries condemned the system, which they said resembled the sweat shops of Europe where workers never got out of debt. At the end of the voyage many Indians had no money coming. When they went to the store for food or clothing they had to agree to the storekeepers' demand to sign on for the next season. The missionaries proposed that advances be paid to the families for store goods, with the balance going to the hunters on their return. Most of the captains began to accept the fact they would have to get together on an agreement or some would always give advances.

As early as 1895 Guillod had told Ottawa advances were a difficult problem. "While captains and owners would generally like to put a stop to it, it seems that an arrangement cannot be made which all sealing captains will keep, so that the man who refuses an advance stands a great risk of losing his crew." Some gave advances with the proviso that hunters agree to sign on again next year. Because the Indians had become a "prize commodity," they had come to expect advances. Guillod added that if an Indian "keeps his health and has a canoe and the salt water, he is never in danger of starvation or actual hardship. As a rule when he has money he spends it freely and buys many things he could do without."

A Catholic missionary, Father Meuleman, intervened when Captain Matthison of the *Venture* discharged two Indian hunters at Kyuquot with a promise to send $30 owing to each man later from Victoria. When the money failed to arrive, Meuleman, who was also shipping agent at Kyuquot, asked Milne to take action.

Another incident occurred in 1896 when the *Beatrice* and *Ainoko* were seized and ousted from the Bering and fined for entering the 60-mile protective zone around the Pribilofs. Captain Grant of the *Ainoko* said his hunters had been paid off at Hesquiaht on the way south, but the Indian Affairs Department suggested the Indians should sue the schooner for losses because the seizure was the result of a navigational error by the captain.

Quadra steams out of Victoria harbour

Captain J. T. Walbran

Morris Moss

Mermaid arriving in Victoria from England, 1893

Schooners moored in Victoria harbour

Kyuquot Indian Chief Making Formal Call on Ainoko

James Gaudin

A. W. Vowell

Japanese sealing schooner, Clayoquot Sound.

The *Beatrice* was owned by Arthur Jones of Vancouver, with R. P. Rithet of Victoria acting as agent. There were 16 Alberni Indians aboard — 14 men and two women. Six of the men and the two women were owed $100 each for skins that had been seized. The rest of the hunters were $300 in debt to the schooner for advances and slop chest purchases. Jones was said to be too poor to pay the fine. His schooner was being held with all her gear, including the Indians' spears.

In July of 1898 Father Brabant wrote Walbran from Hesquiaht to complain about the conduct of Joseph Boscowitz. He said Boscowitz had signed hunters for the *Doris, Mary Ellen, Ada* and *C. D. Rand*, then cancelled the voyages and refused to honour the contract. It was not the first time he had taken such action, Brabant said. "The fact is that Mr. Jos. Boscowitz is supposed to be a man of influence, and the Indians are only poor savages! Mr. Boscowitz ought to be called to account and pay his men for breaking contract with them. The Indians cannot go to law about it — it would be of no use for no notice would be taken of them. Since the Dominion Government has seen fit to send you here to remind the Indians that they must stick to their contracts, I sincerely hope that steps will be taken to remind owners of sealing vessels to do their duty also."

Walbran was unable to take action against Boscowitz, but in a report to Ottawa pointed out that it was hard on the Indians financially to be thrown out of work in such a manner.

There were a number of similar incidents over the next few years. On July 1, 1897, Captain H. F. Sieward sent word back to Victoria that Indian hunters at Battle Bay had refused to go to sea for $2 a skin as agreed to in the articles. He asked Walbran to come and enforce the agreement. The *Quadra* was dispatched and after Walbran warned the Indians, who wanted $3 a skin, they reluctantly boarded the *Dora Sieward.* Other schooners, including the *Penelope*, had come into the village and offered $3, but Walbran forced the Indians to stick to their original agreement with Sieward.

About the same time, Captain Patrick Martin of the *Arietas* had warrants issued at Nuchatlaht for seven men who refused to join the ship after accepting advances in Victoria. Walbran settled this dispute amicably by getting $3 a skin placed in the articles of the *Arietas* and the *Zillah May* instead of the listed 25 cents a man per month, which he described as ridiculous.

In his report to Ottawa after this voyage Walbran said the practice of signing Indians on articles at a nominal sum, long before they were needed, should be stopped. He recommended that all signing of crews be done on the *Quadra.*

Gaudin followed up with a report of his own to the federal deputy minister, in which he said there was no doubt the Indians were willing to carry out their agreements if they were dealt with fairly. There was no need for the *Quadra* to be used to help the sealing schooners at the busiest time of the shipping season. But in 1898 the owners petitioned for the *Quadra* again. Gaudin said she was not needed because only half the fleet was going out and no trouble was anticipated. Ottawa ordered the *Quadra* out anyway, indicating the clout of the owners in the capital.

Captains N. Foley of the *Carrie C. W.* and Caleb McDougall of the *Saucy Lass* asked Walbran to arrest and send to Victoria for trial some Clayoquot men refusing to sail. The two skippers were reneging on a promise to pay an extra $1 a skin while others were offering $4. Foley was said to have agreed that he would pay the $4 if any other schooners offered that amount. Chief Joseph of Clayoquot in a letter to "Naval Officer" on the *Quadra*, said the the Indians were being made fools of by Foley.

The Chief also protested the actions of shipping agent John Grice at Clayoquot. He said the Indians wanted police Constable Spain, "a good, honest and reliable man," to be agent. In 1897 Grice had signed the Indians on for $4 a skin but when they returned paid only $3, Chief Joseph said. "Some of the white people are handling us like a blind child," he added. The *Vera* and *Libbie* had offered payment in cash, he said, but Stockham and Dawley had persuaded the captains to give credit orders on their store instead.

The Indians referred to Grice as the "customs man" and told Walbran: "We cannot read, we have to trust to the customs man and he tells us that what we are asking is on the paper and we sign, and then you come and look for justice for us, see the paper and it is not there, what are we to do?" Walbran agreed that no-one involved in trading should be shipping agents. The missionaries would be better. He also concurred that Constable Spain would be a good choice at Clayoquot.

The recruitment of Indian hunters around the turn of the century continued to be a problem for the Sealing Company, or so it claimed. In 1897 a few schooners had been forced to go to the Queen Charlotte Islands to recruit Haida hunters, who were not so skilled as the Nuu-chah-nulth.

In February of 1901 there was a terse telegram from storekeeper David Logan at Clo-oose to Captain George Ferey at San Juan: "Indians don't want to go at $4 without a potlatch." Captain William D. Byers reported to Captain Grant about the same time that the Sheshaht Indians at Village Island in Barkley Sound were getting $10 from the local trader for skins obtained by offshore hunting. The seals were numerous and close to shore that year, and the natives had no desire to go on the schooners when they could make twice as much money staying at home. They said they would go to the Bering later for $4 a skin when the seals had moved on.[3]

In depositions taken for the 1892 Paris Tribunal, a number of coastal Indians described the offshore fishery around that time. There were usually three men on an offshore expedition — two to row and one to steer — so as to be able to get home quickly if caught by a storm. "Charlie," a Nitinaht Indian living at Pachena Bay, said 100 men at Pachena made a living as seal hunters. "We sell the skins, eat the flesh, take the oil out of the blubber and use the paunch for holding it." Chalt-ka-koi of the little village of Toquaht in Barkley Sound said he hunted from five to seven miles offshore and got between five and 10 seals a day. In 1892 the village, with a population of only 22, got 86 seals from four canoes. The seals sometimes followed herring into the Sound but quickly returned to open water. The population of the six main Barkley Sound Indian villages at that time totalled about 1,000, including 260 Ohiahts and 170 Sheshahts. Their numbers were declining, largely as the result of disease, especially tuberculosis among the children.

Ten days after Byers' first message from Village Island, it was reported the seals were still numerous nearby and prices had gone as high as $12 a skin. The Indians were excited about the bonanza they were enjoying. Some of the traders would pay later for their extravagant prices. In May, Liebes and Company advised Captain Grant that several of the largest fur dealers in Europe had gone under in a market slump. Liebes said the Sealing Company's asking price of $10 a skin was too high and his firm could not pay that amount. It was said that too many small skins were bringing down the average price. The Company held back some of its skins for the next year's sales, when prices made a comeback.

Some Indians decided to go to Seattle to dig clams around Puget Sound. Others went salmon fishing at Rivers Inlet and the Fraser River. The skippers asked permission from the Sealing Company to offer the Indians a bonus to lure them away from these pursuits. But when the Indians at Koskino bargained for a $30 advance for signing with Captain John G. Searle of the *C. D. Rand*, the storekeeper attempted to garnishee it, so they dropped their demand. Captain Robert McKeil wrote from Friendly Cove on February 17 that he obtained 12 canoes by paying $4 a skin with a 10-cent bonus as "boss money." Five of his steerers were women, McKeil said.

Captain Grant sent an order to his skippers: "The company especially requests that when two or more vessels are shipping crews in any one port that the Indians be equally divided amongst the schooners according to ability." No Indians were to be boarded or fed on the schooner until the vessel was ready for sea with canoes on board. They must avoid entering California ports and should take skins from schooners leaving the coast for Asia. The captains were told to communicate with the Company office as often as possible. They were warned not to start sealing in the Bering until the season opened August 1, and to "use every precaution not to go within the 60-mile limit or prohibited waters. You will use your best judgement when to leave the sea."

Some Indians sailed on their own schooners. Charlie Chips of Nitinaht, also known as Charlie Gipson, owned the 18-ton *Amateur*, which had been built in Seattle. He paid $1,000, including duty, for her in 1894. She could carry eight canoes and Chips took one of every three skins. He never went to the Bering but was warned by a U.S. cutter 100 miles south of Cape Flattery for sealing out of season. After the *Amateur* was wrecked on Nitinaht Bar, Chips decided to give up and go out on the white men's schooners as a "boss". He said he was tired of being harassed by U.S. patrol ships.

Charlie Chipps lived in San Juan and owned the *Fisher Maid*, which he bought in 1893, also for $1,000. After he died in 1898 the schooner was left to rot on the beach at San Juan. Another San Juan Indian, Jim Nawassum, a brother-in-law of Chief Charlie Quisto, had sailed for a number of years on Neah Bay schooners before buying the *Mountain Chief* from Victor Jacobson. He abandoned her on shore in 1895. Jimmie Nyetom of Nitinaht owned the 18-ton *Pachewallis*, whose hull had been bought by his father for $600 from a Chinese and which was outfitted for another $700.

On February 25 Captain Charles Hackett reported that after a lot of trouble he had succeeded in getting eight canoes and would leave as soon as possible for the sealing ground. Captain Byers got only seven canoes and left short-handed. The available hunters were few and inexperienced. The weather was poor and catches small. A few captains gave up in frustration and returned to Victoria. When the *Ocean Belle* went aground off Clayoquot the crew refused to continue north until they were satisfied the bottom had been properly repaired.

Captain Grant received a number of letters from wives of white crewmen pleading for money for their families. The wives also wrote about their missing husbands. Many men deserted over the years in California ports such as Monterey. One of the captains left while anchored in a bay near his home in Oregon. As well as wives, the operators of boarding houses wrote to the Company attempting to track down men who had skipped out without paying their board.

In December of 1901 the Company advanced $75 train fares to nine white Nova Scotia hunters it had recruited to fill the shortages. Despite such efforts, 14 schooners returned to Victoria in 1902 because the Indians were said to have refused to sign at the offered prices.

As their services became more in demand, the Indians began coming to Victoria to select a schooner rather than wait for the vessels to arrive at their village. They would call in for their canoes on the way north. As well as looking for a particular schooner, they wanted to choose a captain with a reputation for treating his native hunters decently. Grant said the Indians had "superstitions" about some schooners. They also preferred the newer, larger vessels which were safer in bad weather and provided more comfortable accommodation. When they had picked out a schooner, Grant said, "I always made it a point to give it to them."

The Indians' concern about safety was heightened in the fall of 1902 when the schooner *Hatzic* was reported missing with 24 men from Kyuquot and seven whites. One of the crew members was John Daley, who had been skipper of the *Willie McGowan* when she was seized by the Russians in 1892. Since her departure in February there had been no word from the schooner. The anxious villagers wanted a steamer sent to look for her. If the men were lost, they wanted the Department of Indian Affairs to make provision for their widows and children, which it did when the tragedy was confirmed.

Superintendent Vowell was outraged when he read in the *Colonist* about the subsequent destruction of property at Kyuquot over the *Hatzic* loss. He blamed the local missionary, the Rev. E. Sobry, which was a bit irrational since the missionaries did their best to stamp out what were regarded as the Indians' heathenish practices. Sobry, in fact, replied that the newspaper report was exaggerated. The Indians had burned some goods belonging to the dead in their usual custom, he said, and spread over the ground a few yards of calico and about 10 blankets — not 2,000 as reported by the *Colonist*. The newspaper's report was "a most egregious misrepresentation of facts," said Sobry.

There were other tragedies that year. The 21-ton *South Bend* also vanished, with 15 whites aboard. Two Indians were lost when their canoe became separated from the *Penelope*. The *Ocean Belle* had a close call off Monterey when a crazed Chinese cook splashed coal oil around the decks, set the schooner afire, and then committed suicide by jumping overboard. He had also laid down a trail of gunpowder to the powder kegs, but they did not ignite. The crew extinguished the fire after the schooner had suffered considerable damage.

The losses continued in 1903 when the *Triumph* was lost with all hands and the *Penelope* wrecked off Clallam Bay across Juan de Fuca Strait from Sooke. Five white hunters drowned in the *Bering* when their small boats were caught in a storm.

With only 20 vessels out in 1903 and half the Company fleet lying idle, the owners became more anxious than ever to sell out. But the Victoria Board of Trade passed a resolution late in the year protesting the proposal to ban pelagic sealing. It was concerned about compensation to others, such as grocers and outfitters, who would be hurt by the loss of the industry. The Board was reflecting the feeling in the business community that it might be permissible to sell the schooners but not to give up the right to seal for everyone. The vote was 48 to 16, with the opposition coming from Company shareholders and friends. There was a hot debate in which the schooner owners defended their right to sell their property if they desired, indicating they did not care about the Victoria economy as much as they professed to governments and international tribunals. To dampen some of this unrest, the Company decided at its annual meeting in December to pay a 50-cents per share dividend.

In 1904 the London fur price fell from $17.50 to $15.50, causing further dismay in the industry. On January 6, 1905, an advertisement appeared in the Victoria newspapers offering $12.50 Sealing Company shares for $2.50. The only taker was Joe Boscowitz, who acquired 1,560 shares between 1901 and 1910. He also covered his bets, however, by adding to his holdings of N.A.C.C. stock.

Meanwhile, the fleet was rapidly deteriorating. U.S. Consul Abraham E. Smith reported that of the 30 schooners tied up, it was doubtful whether 10 could get out past Cape Flattery. The *Ada* had recently keeled over at her dock "from sheer decrepitude."4 Sealers were complaining more and more about sailing in unsafe vessels.

In the fall of 1905 the *Fawn* went down in a storm with the loss of 25 Indian hunters, 20 of them from the Mowachaht band at Nootka. In March of 1906 the Company sent $1,477 to the Department, the amount owed the *Fawn* Indians for skins landed before she was lost. Agent A. W. Neill was to divide the money among the hunters' heirs. The loss of the *Fawn* prompted a protest from Father Brabant that many schooners were unseaworthy. He said the Indians were constantly complaining to him about the rotting Company vessels. He wanted federal inspectors to go over the schooners before allowing them to sail. Vowell approved the suggestion and passed it on to Ottawa, but nothing was done.

Consul Smith reported to Washington early in 1905 that while Victorians were more resigned to the loss of pelagic sealing now that the salmon and halibut fisheries were expanding, the owners were digging in. On March 27, when Ottawa asked the Company whether it would accept an easing of coast sealing regulations in exchange for a total ban in the Bering, the answer was a firm no. The owners had reached the point where compensation seemed the only way to recoup their losses.

The British and Americans were still anxious to conclude a pact on sealing. In January of 1904 Senator W. P. Dillingham introduced a bill to prevent excessive killing of male seals on the Pribilofs and paved the way for settlement of the dispute through international negotiation. But Ottawa was too annoyed at losing the Alaska Boundary arbitration to consider concessions on any other issue.

The *Colonist* rejected any suggestion that morality was involved in the demands for preservation of the seal herd. "It is purely and simply a matter of business," the newspaper editorialized. "An American concern wants a monopoly of the sealing business, and Canadian sealers propose to compete with them."

Dillingham's bill also revived the idea of killing all the seals on the islands if the British refused to accept amendments to the present regulations. Supporters of this measure persisted in describing it as a "mercy killing." The emotional Henry Elliott declared: "If the Canadian hunter insists upon our supplying him, year after year, with this highly organized life to indecently and cruelly kill at sea . . . then in the name of mercy let us put these animals at once out of pain while we save enough of them to preserve the species."

In April of 1900 Elliott had asked Secretary of State John Hay to send him to the Pribilofs again to investigate the land kill, but the Senate rejected a $15,000 appropriation for this study. The N.A.C.C. still had powerful allies in Congress, but in the summer of 1903 some independent Senators went to the islands on their own and criticized the lessee's rookery practises. Elliott felt vindicated. He said the Senators had found the N.A.C.C. "killing female seals and yearlings in violation of the law: indeed they found that the work of the lessees was more injurious to the life of the fur seal rookeries than was that of the pelagic hunters."

Despite this questionable conclusion, Elliott had private meetings with the British ambassador to the U.S., Sir Mortimer Durand, urging that August and September be closed to pelagic sealing while May and June be opened. Such a move would effectively restrict pelagic sealing to the North Pacific and eliminate the Bering, a step which would protect the nursing mothers but not the pregnant seals on their way to the Islands. Elliott saw this as a first step toward the total elimination of pelagic sealing.

The Dillingham bill was dropped because President Roosevelt thought it unnecessary. Roosevelt instead pushed a measure through the House and Senate in the spring of 1904 calling for new negotiations between Britain and the U.S., to be followed by a four-power pact on seal conservation. But Britain, held back by Canada, delayed. Hay became convinced that only the threat of a mass seal kill would bring them to the bargaining table.

The dispute was stalled again, but new pressure began to be felt from increased activity by Japanese schooners in the Bering. The chauvinistic Roosevelt was angered by the bold poaching of the Japanese and it appeared for a time that war between the two countries was a possibility.

CHAPTER FOURTEEN

Yokohama

There is no question of the legal right of any people to kill seals in the open sea, but the practice is so villainously inhuman that all the world should unite to put an end to it.

—San Francisco *Chronicle*

As the Paris Arbitration hearings drew to a close in 1893, Lord Salisbury asked about the possibility of other maritime nations posing a threat to the Bering Sea fur seal herd. An American spokesman said none would dare in the face of an agreement by the two great powers. Secretary of State James Blaine declared the problem was "remote." Nobody anticipated the role Japan was about to play, a role which would lead eventually to the end of pelagic sealing.

The Paris Accord and the *modus vivendi* preceding it led directly to the Japanese becoming involved. Japan and Russia had been excluded from the arbitration even though they owned fur seal rookeries in the Kuril and Commander Islands respectively. (Russia had ceded the Japanese the two small Kuril rookeries in 1875 in exchange for the northern half of Sakhalin Island. By 1896 the Kuril rookeries had been cleaned out by poachers.) A few American and Canadian schooners, many of them notorious rookery raiders such as Harold Snow, had been sealing along the Japan coast for many years, but the invasion increased dramatically in 1892 and 1893 because of the Bering Sea restrictions. Most of the seals they took off the Japanese coast were bound for the Russian rookeries, but Japan still felt aggrieved. She also awakened to the commercial possibilities for her own national interest.

In 1893 the Japanese Government made a public pronouncement: "England, America and Russia send their ships to the Bering Sea and off Siberia, not only for profit, but to extend the national prestige. So to protect our own prestige we must encourage Japanese in the same enterprise." About this time a Japanese newspaper interviewed Koreyoshi Aikawa, who had fished off the Pacific coast between 1885 and 1890. He declared that Canada was so rich in sea resources, "I hope our people will take the initiative to go there and fish."

Attempting to create a Japanese pelagic fleet, the Government in 1894 banned Japanese citizens from signing on foreign sealing vessels, although two years later Captain Alfred Bissett of the *Annie E. Paint* had a number of Japanese listed as crew. When some of them jumped ship during a stopover in Hakodate, Bissett had no recourse. Four years later Japan introduced a subsidy for fishing vessels, including sealing schooners. Their numbers increased from that time and the Canadians could no longer compete with the Japanese on their own grounds. The number of Victoria-based schooners hunting off Asia dropped from 11 in 1897 to one in 1898. Nine Canadian sealing vessels tried again in 1901 and 1902 but took an average of only 325 skins, hardly enough to cover expenses.

The Japanese schooners began crossing to the North American side in 1901. Five went into the Bering with guns, which were forbidden to the Canadian and American schooners under the Paris regulations. After 1897 American schooners were barred by Congress from hunting seals anywhere in the Pacific north of the 35th latitude, which resulted in a number of American schooners, such as the *Henry Dennis* of San Francisco, being purchased by the Japanese. The Canadians were restricted by seasonal closures and a 60-mile zone around the Pribilofs. These did not apply to the Japanese, who went up to the 3-mile territorial limit and often within it. Their small boats could not be arrested inside the limit unless caught in the act of killing seals.

From 1903 onward the Japanese fleet grew steadily as the Canadians dropped out. This trend was accelerated in 1905 when the Japanese subsidy was increased. The U.S. Consul in Hakodate reported to Washington at that time: "The subsidy as now paid is large enough to pay all expenses for a season... everything that is caught is profit, and, unless the vessel is lost, there can be no loss to the owners."[1]

In 1893 Japan had banned foreign vessels from switching registry to her flag, but the ingenious Canadian and American sealers found ways to get around that restriction. A number of experienced white hunters signed with the Japanese fleet, including three Victorians who stayed on the Asia side after spending 18 months in a Siberian prison for raiding the Commander Islands. At one time an estimated 15 captains and mates from Victoria were employed as "navigators" on Japanese sealing schooners. Japanese law required that only its nationals could serve as masters in order for the schooners to qualify for the subsidy, but on a number of vessels they held that position in name only. As soon as the schooner cleared port the more experienced North American navigator would take over and guide the vessel to the Bering sealing grounds.

One of the best known of these men was Captain John C. Voss, who had won fame by sailing the rebuilt 38-foot cedar dugout canoe *Tilikum* on a rambling three-year, 40,000-mile voyage three-quarters of the way around the world during the years 1901-1903.[2]

Voss was a somewhat mysterious man, taciturn in the manner of a solitary sailor but also wise and humourous. He went to sea in 1877 at the age of 26, serving over the next two decades on a number of large sailing vessels. He came ashore briefly in Victoria as owner of the Queen's Hotel at Store and Johnson Streets, but was off again in 1897 at the helm of the 10-ton sloop *Xora* in search of buried treasure on Cocos Island. All he got for his troubles was a case of tropical fever. (Voss was not the only sealer who hunted for gold on the 4-mile long island off the coast of Costa Rica. Captain Fred Hackett sold 800 shares at $10 each in the Cocos Island Hydraulic and Treasure Co. of Olympia, Wash., and set off in 1906 on the white-hulled schooner *Thomas F. Bayard*. He too returned empty-handed.)

After another stint ashore at his hotel, followed by the voyage of the *Tilikum*, Voss in 1906 bought the little 18-ton schooner *Ella G.* to go seal hunting in the North Pacific. (She had been halibut fishing the previous year under Alex McLean.) The next year Voss took over a bigger, faster vessel, the 75-foot, 104-ton *Jessie*, a former yacht and San Francisco pilot boat. After the *Jessie* had been forced to return to Victoria in July after failing to recruit Indian hunters, Voss took her out with white hunters on December 1 to intercept the herd off California.

In 1908 Voss went to Yokohama and joined the Japanese sealing fleet as master of the 75-foot schooner *Chichijima Maru*. On one voyage a number of his Japanese hunters were shot by Russian guards at an otter rookery on the mainland coast. In 1910 he skippered the *Shino Maru* with four Victoria seal hunters and was top boat with 1,000 skins. Voss sealed until the end of 1911 when pelagic sealing was banned by international agreement. He then hung around the Yokohama Yacht Club spinning yarns, writing a book on his adventures, and waiting for the Japanese Government to pay compensation for the loss of his trade. Eventually he shared in the $566,000 handed out by Japan to sealers who had sailed under her flag.

Another way for displaced North American sealers to participate in the Japanese sealing industry was through covert ownership. Two Americans deeply involved in this manner were J. M. Laffin, who had become a naturalized Japanese citizen living in Yokohama, and his agent, E. J. King, a U.S. citizen living in Hakodate with a Japanese wife. Aside from their direct activities, two schooners were registered in Mrs. King's name. Laffin and King exercised further control by acting as commission merchants on purchases of skins. "In that way," the U.S. Consul reported, "by advancing money to the sealers to their outfits and supplies, they practically controlled the whole sealing business."

Following this report, the U.S. Government in 1901 asked Japan to require its subjects to observe the Paris regulations and end the practice of American citizens "sealing under cover of the Japanese flag." There was no reply. The following year, however, the Japanese advised the U.S. there was no evidence of Japanese vessels being owned by Americans. Japan said it was prepared to sign an international agreement curbing pelagic sealing, but since there was none the country should not be expected to recognize rules which it had played no part in drafting.

Japanese activity in the Bering had placed the U.S. in a difficult position. The Government was under constant pressure from the N.A.C.C. to do something about the declining herd so that it could take more skins on the island, while the Canadians were outraged that the Japanese were getting the seals they were barred from catching. If the Japanese and their Caucasian navigators and hunters had been content to hunt outside the 3-mile limit, the situation might have gone on unchecked for some time. But like their North American counterparts, the Japanese sealers were overcome by greed.

They came into the Bering with guns blazing, caring little for the slaughter and waste left in their wake. On one occasion a Treasury Agent heard incessant shooting just off shore but later found only one dead seal in the boat. The Japanese began by forming a ring of schooners three miles off St. Paul and St. George Islands, cutting off the nursing females going out or returning from the feeding grounds. Then they began assaulting the rookeries directly. Under cover of fog the Japanese schooners would move close to the islands and send their small boats ashore. Two schooners seized off the Seapandi Rookery on St. Paul and later auctioned at Unalaska had been disguised with *papier-mache* yardarms and funnels to resemble, from a distance, the Revenue cutters. On at least one occasion an advance guard of poachers was observed poking out the eyes of the bulls with long poles so that they could not attack the men as they carried out their bloody work on the beach.

It turned to open warfare as Treasury Agents and Aleut guards who tried to protect the herd were fired upon from the decks of the schooners. A report by an Agent to his superiors vividly described the Japanese *modus operandi*: "The watchmen on guard at Northeast Point (on St. Paul) reported on half a dozen occasions that they had observed the small boats from the schooners form a line a mile or so in length and, in that formation, advance abreast on the rookery. When close to shore, the occupants of the boats would begin a fusillade with their shotguns, the noise of which would drive off a number of seals from the rookeries and hauling grounds. The boats would then withdraw a safe distance from shore and there pursue and seek to capture those seals which had just been driven off the land."

The Japanese began using small motorboats about this time to tow the hunting boats around. Then they put motors in the hunting boats themselves, making it easier to escape patrol vessels and rookery guards.

In 1905 two Japanese schooners, with no whites aboard, moved in close to the Northeast Point rookery and sent their small boats ashore. Acting as agents of the N.A.C.C., the Aleutian guards opened fire. Five Japanese raiders were killed and 12 taken prisoner, of whom five were charged with piracy. The offence carried a death sentence, but Washington ordered the charges reduced. The five were sentenced to three months' jail in Sitka. The Japanese Government protested that the men were merely going ashore for water and had been "murdered." A demand for damages was rejected by the U.S.

Some of the Japanese schooners did not stop at seal poaching. Most of the schooners carried large quantities of liquor to trade with the Aleuts. In the summer of 1907 the Aleutian village of Akhiok on Alitak Bay was ransacked by the Japanese while the natives were away. The following year they looted and destroyed Simonoski village after pretending to come ashore to trade. They also killed cattle grazing on Shelikof Island.

In the face of such depredations, the Americans stepped up their Bering patrol. Instructions were issued to the cutter *Bear* in 1904: "Long chases are not advisable. After a vessel is brought within reach of your guns, if she does not bring to, display the national ensign and open fire. Fire one blank and one solid shot as a warning. If the ship still neglects to come to the wind, aim to hit, and use the force at your command to compel her to submit to being boarded and searched."[3]

By 1907 there were five cutters in the area issued with such orders. When a report was received that the Japanese were planning an organized raid on the Pribilofs armed with Gatling machine-guns, a Navy cruiser was rushed to the area. A total of 63 Japanese from two schooners were arrested that summer by the cutter *Manning*. They were taken to Valdez for trial but the Government again acted with restraint. The two crews were deported and one of the schooners confiscated. In all there were 30 schooners from Japan in the Bering that summer and 15 from the Victoria fleet. Bad weather resulted in a poor catch.

Japan's response to the crackdown was joint action by its sealing fleet. In 1908 some 38 schooners worked together as a team around St. Paul, as many as 29 on one day. Four revenue cutters and the warship *Yorktown* were unable to cope with these tactics.

The Japanese invasion also affected research on the Islands. Treasury Agent Walter Lembkey reported that "no attempt was made to count pups on any of the rookeries for the reason that during the latter part of July and early August hardly a day passed that there were not one or more Japanese sealers operating off the rookeries." It was decided that any further disturbance of the herd was undesirable.[4]

Although most of the Japanese schooners went only to the Bering, some also sealed along the coast from northern California to the Aleutians. At one time in the spring of 1908 there were 35 off the Alaska Panhandle. In April,

1909, the *Matsu Maru*, under Captain Thompson, called in at Hesquiaht with nine Victoria hunters aboard. Each was in charge of a small boat with three Japanese crew members. A month later the schooner was caught sealing within the 3-mile limit off Vancouver Island and warned out.

In his report Agent Lembkey noted that "the Canadian fleet is now so small as to be no longer a factor." The few Victoria schooners in the Bering stayed mostly about 75 miles off the Pribilofs, although a few continued to make sneak attacks on the rookeries whenever possible. The Canadians complained the Japanese shotgun barrages kept the seals "on the jump" and difficult to harpoon. The Canadian fleet had been steadily declining since the turn of the century. The Sealing Company blamed its inactivity on a shortage of hunters, a claim that would later be denied. It was indisputable, however, that the voyages were not as profitable as they had once been, and the fleet had fallen into the hands of speculators who saw greater returns in holding out for government compensation.

The Victoria sealers and their supporters were scathing in their condemnation of the Japanese, or "cunning little brown men," as the *Colonist* described them. There was outrage at the Japanese use of guns, but in fact the few Canadian schooners going out at this time were also flaunting the Paris regulations by using firearms and moving within the 60-mile limit under cover of fog. They were better marksmen than the Japanese, however, and only a few engaged in rookery raiding.

The Sealing Company and some of its members acting independently had meanwhile become involved in expeditions below the equator in search of the southern fur seal. William Munsie wrote in 1902 to the Governor of Juan Fernandez Island off the coast of Chile and the British consul at Valparaiso seeking information on fur seals in the area, as well as lobsters.[5] The reports were not encouraging, so Munsie sent his new schooner, the *Florence M. Munsie*, from Halifax under Captain Charles LeBlanc in 1903 to the Falkland Islands, South Shetlands and Cape Horn areas of the South Atlantic. Munsie had told LeBlanc an old seaman had described seals congregated on rookeries west of Elephant Island in the South Shetlands, as well as Staten Island. Two years later the *Florence M. Munsie* under Captain Hans Blakstad was wrecked coming around Cape Horn from Halifax to Victoria. The crew was able to scramble ashore without mishap and were picked up by a ship going the other way. They eventually reached home via Hamburg and Liverpool.

The schooners *Edward Roy* and *Beatrice L. Corkum*, sailing out of Halifax, had done well in that region in 1902. The *Corkum*, under Captain Reuben Balcom and the *Roy*, skippered by Captain L. Gilbert, each took 2,000 skins. The best of them brought a price of $40 in London, but the average was not that high.

In October of 1903 Captain Grant told Ottawa he had been advised by Lampson & Co. that the Falklands government intended to tax skins shipped from the colony by Canadian vessels at a rate of 10 shillings each. Grant said nearby South American ports were unsafe for shipping and the 10 Victoria vessels sealing in the area would be ruined by the tax. His letter to Fisheries Minister Raymond Prefontaine was followed within a few days by one from Premier Richard McBride to Prime Minister Wilfrid Laurier urging that representations be made by Ottawa against the tax. The Victoria Board of Trade had described the tax as "outrageous" and intimated the Americans were somehow behind it. But Laurier advised the Sealing Company that inquiries had revealed the tax was not intended to gather revenue but rather to prevent seals being killed in the closed season, especially gravid females. The British Secretary of State informed the Company that nine shillings of the tax would be remitted when and if it was shown the seals killed were not pregnant. And so another area of the globe was forced to take measures to protect itself against the depredations of the Victoria sealers.

A few months later the *Agnes G. Donahoe*, owned by Sprott Balcom and skippered by Matthew Ryan, was seized in the Rio de la Plata estuary near the Uruguayan rookery on Lobos Island. There were $40,000 worth of sealskins aboard. The crew was released, but Ryan and his mate were held on charges of raiding the rookery. He first used the old excuse of going ashore to get water, but later claimed he was taking the skins to Montevideo for shipment to London in order to avoid the Falklands tax. Ryan was sentenced to three years' imprisonment and the mate to one year, but they were released through the intervention of Britain before their sentences had been served.

In 1908 the *Agnes G. Donahoe*, under Reuben Balcom, landed skins at Durban in South Africa after raiding rookeries on some of the small islands close to Antarctica. J. A. Bechtel's *Beatrice L. Corkum* was also seeking new hunting spots in the same area, which had been almost cleaned out more than a century before by the Boston sealers. The furs brought a good price in London because they were unusually thick.

Meanwhile, pressure was building in a number of quarters for an international treaty on sealing. There was widespread agreement that the existing situation could not be allowed to continue. "It is a dying industry," said the San Francisco *Call*. "The insatiable poacher, whether legally or illegally, will not give the herd a chance."

David Starr Jordan urged President Roosevelt to take the dispute to the World Court at The Hague for arbitration, but after the results at Paris in 1893 the government was not inclined toward that solution. Jordan also recommended that the Pribilof seals be removed from the jurisdiction of the Department of Commerce and placed under the Bureau of Fisheries, with a trained naturalist in charge on the islands. He was critical of the amateur observations of agents such as Walter Lembkey, which he said could be "dangerous" in future negotiations with the British. Lembkey retorted that running the sealing operation was no different than operating a cattle ranch, and fisheries experts were not required.[6]

In the summer of 1906 the Department of Commerce sent Edwin W. Sims to the Pribilofs to report on the condition of the herd. He found it "more seriously threatened than ever before in its history." Sims urged a total ban on pelagic sealing and, noting that Canadian schooners were sealing off Sitka after the May 1 closure, tougher policing in the meantime.

President Roosevelt reprimanded the Revenue Cutter Service for laxity and ordered a detachment of Marines and the *Yorktown* to the area. This tough action was supported by the San Francisco *Chronicle*: "There is no question of the legal right of any people to kill seals in the open sea, but the practice is so villainously inhuman that all the world should unite to put an end to it." The *Chronicle* said even the Japanese were beginning to recognize the need for new protective measures.

The change in attitude in Tokyo had been brought about in part by Japan's acquisition of the Robben Island rookery from the Russians following the 1904-1905 war between the two countries. Robben Island was a bare rock reef, 1,900 feet long and only 30 to 120 feet wide, thick with seals in the breeding season. In 1907 Tokyo took action to curb pelagic sealing around the rookery by adding the gunboat *Musashi* to the patrol fleet. The British cooperated by placing H.M.S. *Shearwater* in the area. Japan's subsidy for sealing schooners was dropped in 1909. The government said it had not intended Japanese vessels to go so far afield, and had wanted only to encourage local industry.

Japan was eager now for friendly relations with other world powers, particularly the U.S. Only the persistent lobbying of the Japanese sealers prevented the government from entering international negotiations. The Russians had made overtures to Tokyo in the summer of 1908 to sign a pact banning pelagic sealing on the Asian coast, but to no avail.

In the fall of 1907 the Victoria Sealing Company's largest shareholder, Joseph Boscowitz, set off on a compensation-seeking mission to Ottawa, Washington and London. In Ottawa he asked Prime Minister Laurier and the British ambassador to Washington, James Bryce, to press for an international agreement, including Japan, to ban pelagic sealing for 10 years.

Lodged at Washington's Grafton Hotel, Boscowitz wrote to Robert Bacon, assistant secretary of the Treasury: "I am certain my company would heartily join in a *modus vivendi* for a term of years to allow the seal herd to increase." The *modus* would have to restrict the land kill to the number of seals needed to feed the Aleuts, he said. "My company would be satisfied with a fair annual subsidy upon the amount of the capital invested."[7] Boscowitz then added a clumsy threat the Americans must have recognized as a bluff: "Some of my co-directors counselled that the Company's vessels should sail under the Japanese flag in order to have the same rights as the Japanese. It looks to me that this is the only remedy to have the same freedom as the Japanese." (Like many self-made men of the period, Boscowitz had difficulty expressing himself on paper. In a subsequent letter to Secretary of State Elihu Root he referred to the "secession" of sealing when he meant "cessation," and his references to "my company" could not have pleased Captain Grant and the other principals of the Sealing Company.)

An internal State Department memo commenting on Boscowitz' letter had this to say: "The Canadian Government has practically declined to consent to any measures for the protection of the seals and the negotiations have come to an end for that reason. Suggest that if he wishes them reopened he should address himself to his own government through whose action they have been lost." Secretary Root replied formally to Boscowitz that unless Canada intimated a new willingness to negotiate, the U.S. did not feel a responsibility to raise the subject again.[8] This 'after you, Alphonse' attitude would be repeated over the next few years. In March of 1908, for example, Laurier was ready once again to talk, but told the Governor-General his government did not want to reopen the issue and the first steps should be taken by the U.S.

Boscowitz also met with President Roosevelt, who told him the U.S. was prepared to kill all the seals if no agreement was reached. Boscowitz reported on his return to Victoria that Washington was anxious to reach an agreement, but Ottawa was dragging its heels and London was waiting on the Canadians.

On January 21, 1909, Root sent a note to the envoys in Washington of Russia, Japan and Britain proposing another conference on the sealing issue. Britain held back, however, because of foot-dragging by Ottawa. The American Ambassador to London, Whitelaw Reid, told Foreign Secretary Sir Edward Grey that Canada's interest in the dispute was "merely that of the ownership by people at Victoria of a fleet of worn out and unprofitable sealers."

Although that fleet was not the thorn in the side of the Americans it had once been, there were still incidents causing tension between the two countries. One occurred in the spring of 1907 when the *Carlotta Cox* was seized on the Fairweather grounds in the Gulf of Alaska after May 1 while on her way to Asia. What galled the Canadians was that five Japanese schooners sealing nearby were unmolested by the American cutters. The schooner was towed to Sitka by the *Rush*, then tied up for eight months awaiting trial while her skins were held in bond. The seizure was protested in Parliament by William Sloan, the MP for Comox-Atlin. Sloan complained that Britain was not pressing for controls on the Japanese and the U.S. was also lax in its dealings

Schooners moored in Victoria's Gorge waterway, 1891

Fred Peters

Markland *Embarking Indian Hunters at Aboushabt*

Thomas F. Bayard leaving
Clayquot Sound, 1911

William Templeman

Captain Hans Blakstad.

White hunters and cook aboard *Thomas F. Bayard*, 1908

with Japan. He urged an immediate ban on oceanic sealing and referral of the dispute to the World Court. Sloan also foreshadowed future disputes between Canada and the U.S. over salmon fishing by drawing a parallel between the two industries. He said American fishermen were taking salmon in their territorial waters which were bound for the Fraser River to spawn.

A second incident was the interception two years later of three Victoria schooners while returning from the Commander Islands. The *Jessie, Pescawha* and *Thomas F. Bayard* were off the north end of Chirikof Island in the Gulf of Alaska June 23, 1909, when approached by the cutter *Bear*. The three captains claimed they were hunting sea otter, but the Americans said their sealed-up firearms were not to be used while they were north of 35 degrees latitude and east of 180 degrees longitude. A U.S. otter hunter nearby was not apprehended, however. A boarding party from the *Bear* ripped up the floor boards of the *Bayard*, pulled out the bunks of crewmen and emptied ditty bags, but no sealskins were found. Nevertheless, guns of the three vessels were sealed and they were warned out of the area.

Later, after claims for damages totalling $143,000 had been submitted on behalf of the three vessels, the U.S. admitted there was no agreement in force in 1909 for the seizing of firearms, but insisted that Captain E. P. Bertholf of the *Bear* had acted in good faith. The seizures were made in an area where sealing was prohibited at the time and it was noted that all three schooners were carrying salt for preserving skins. It had been customary for British sealers to request American officers to seal their firearms before entering the Bering Sea, "and this practice may have tended to mislead the American officers as to their authority in this respect," the government conceded. It was customary, however, to keep guns sealed in the area. The U.S. maintained the schooners' logbooks showed they had left Victoria in the spring on a sealing voyage. Furthermore, the claims were greatly exaggerated through "fraudulent misrepresentation."

There was no law against hunting otter outside the 3-mile limit and they were often found in the area between Chirikof and Tugidak Island in the Trinity Group. It was pointed out, however, that during the 1909 season from May 15 to September 1 there were only four days of weather suitable for hunting.

The schooners had not paid much attention to otter during the fur seal bonanza days, but after 1900 began taking rifles for that purpose. The catches were small. In 1908 the *Jessie* had taken five and the *Bayard* 28. The total otter catch for four vessels in 1909 was only 18. But that didn't stop the owners of the *Bayard, Jessie* and *Pescawha* from claiming for the estimated loss of 275 otter skins. The Americans refused to pay. From 1907 to 1911, the U.S. said, the entire B.C. fleet had taken only 105 otter. Sea otter hunting was "precarious and uncertain" and often used as a cover for illegal sealing, the Americans said.

In Washington the government finally took action on Jordan's advice, placing the Bureau of Fisheries in charge on the Pribilofs and appointing Jordan head of an Advisory Board to report directly to the President. His first recommendation was to end the leasing system. The government should harvest the skins itself, Jordan said, and sell them to the highest bidder. The 20-year N.A.A.C. lease expired at the beginning of 1910, and in April an Act of Congress made the Pribilofs a government reservation. A second bill introduced by Senator Dillingham calling for a 5-year ban on land killing was defeated, however.

The government paid $60,000 to the N.A.C.C. for its plant. The second company to hold a lease on the islands, it had made money, but nothing like the riches of its predecessor. The government was the real loser from the second lease. It received an estimated $3,200,000 revenue from the N.A.C.C. while paying out $5,500,000 for patrol costs over the 20 years from 1890 to 1910.

One of the men who helped bring about the change in U.S. policy was William T. Hornaday of the New York Zoo, a leading member and director of the popular Camp-Fire Clubs of America. (The president of the organization was naturalist and author Ernest Thompson Seton.) In 1907 the tireless campaigner Henry Elliott in despair had sent a letter to Hornaday pleading with him to "do something to save those fur seals." When Hornaday was named chairman of the Club's new Committee on Wild Life Protection in 1909, he launched a two-year campaign to save the seals. His first move was to tell the controversial Elliott he could continue as an adviser but must not write or talk publicly on the issue. That was not easy for a man who so enjoyed the limelight, but Elliott accepted the terms and held his tongue.[9]

Hornaday had told a Senate committee in 1908 that "Mr. Elliott has just one hobby in the world, and that is the preservation of the fur seal." However, during the past five years Elliott had become "almost wild with indignation at the way this valuable industry has been annihilated. At times his language has been violent." Hornaday concluded: "At last he became so wild with anxiety to save his beloved seals from extinction, that his insistence turned savage, and his relations with certain scientists and bureau officers of Washington became a complete wreck."

Hornaday gained the support of Senator Joseph M. Dixon, chairman of the new Senate Committee on the Conservation of National Resources. He appeared February 26, 1910, before the Committee, which almost immediately recommended an end to the leasing system. A bitter battle ensued in Congress, however, after it was learned that the Bureau of Fisheries had taken 13,000 seals that summer. Charges of misconduct against the Bureau were investigated from May 21, 1911 to March 14, 1914, with Elliott again in the centre of battle. During one of the bitter exchanges in the Committee, Elliott

210

admitted he had received $7,000 over a 3-year period as an adviser to the A.C.C., but said he was never an "employee" of the firm.

In 1909 Dr. William O. Stillman, president of the American Humane Association, wrote angrily to President William Howard Taft asking why the U.S. had "refused to consummate a treaty" with Canada to protect the seals. The onus was on the U.S. to take the initiative, Stillman said. "The whole civilized world is beginning to feel horrified and outraged by existing conditions." He was apparently referring to the Pribilof land kill as well as pelagic sealing.

On the diplomatic side there was slow and erratic movement toward an agreement. The principal negotiations were between Canada and the U.S., with Britain acting as intermediary. Canada had felt let down by the British in the Alaska boundary dispute and was determined now to act as independently as her status in the Empire would allow.

The first attempt to reach an agreement after the collapse of the Joint High Commission negotiations in 1898 came in 1905 at the initiative of U.S. Secretary of State John Hay. A joint treaty was drafted in which the U.S., Britain and Canada would end pelagic sealing by mutual agreement and joint control, with a fair division of the profits. The draft was approved March 7 by Hay and two weeks later by Sir Mortimer Durand.

Further negotiations over the specifics of the treaty came to a halt July 1 with the death of John Hay. They resumed in the fall under Hay's successor, Elihu Root, but ended October 5 when Canada rejected the proposed terms. Two weeks later Root offered Canada 20 percent of the land kill in exchange for giving up pelagic sealing, as well as lump sum compensation for the fleet. Talks on this new proposal continued through 1906 until Laurier rejected the plan, offering no counter-proposal.

Laurier said that in addition to compensation for giving up sealing, Canada wanted "some substantial national consideration" from the U.S. He specifically mentioned the Alaska Boundary dispute, which had left a bitter aftertaste in Ottawa. "I confess to a sense of disappointment," Laurier wrote, "that Mr. Root in asking us to surrender this national right offers nothing beyond what I consider hardly adequate pecuniary compensation, leaving the national claim altogether unrecognized."

Root appointed Wall Street lawyer Chandler P. Anderson to make yet another investigation of the fur seal dispute. Anderson's report in 1906 said the Victoria fleet was worth $275,000 at most, well below the $450,000 claimed by Canada.

It was not until 1907, after James Bryce had taken over as British ambassador in Washington, that informal talks resumed, Bryce got on well with both the Americans and his Canadian clients. He kept in close touch with Ottawa and Laurier was moved to remark that "Mr. Bryce has done something new in connection with British diplomacy in Canada—he has visited Canada." Besides getting on well with Laurier, Bryce was an old friend of the Governor-General of the day, Earl Grey.[10]

On March 13, 1908, Laurier advised British Foreign Secretary Sir Edward Grey that he was prepared to accept a 10-year ban on pelagic sealing. The Foreign Secretary replied that the British Government did not want to formally reopen the discussions, that the first steps should be taken by the Americans.

Shortly before leaving office to make way for a new administration, Root formally proposed, on January 21, 1909, a four-nation conference to find ways "to protect and preserve the seals." He proposed a 10-year ban on all sealing, and compensation to Canada "as may be awarded," presumably by arbitration. Taft, who had succeeded Roosevelt in 1909, appointed Philander C. Knox, a Pittsburgh corporation lawyer, as Secretary of State.

Russia and Japan were quick to accept the American overtures and on March 4, shortly after Knox took office, Bryce told him that Canada was also anxious to take steps to preserve the seal herd. But the Canadians insisted on settling the issue of compensation first. As a result, Britain held back from formally agreeing to the talks.

Bryce, a skilled negotiator, then took up the issue with Knox and Taft, who turned out to be more conciliatory than Root and Roosevelt. Also joining in the preliminary talks was Joseph Pope, the Canadian Undersecretary of State for the new Department of External Affairs. Bryce was eager to conclude an agreement on any terms which Canada could be persuaded to accept. He was annoyed when Pope, under instructions from Laurier, pushed for compensation from Japan and Russia as well as the U.S.

In August, Whitelaw Reid, after talks with officials in London, told Knox "the time is ripe" for settlement. After being advised by Washington that Canada's determination to hold out for the best deal was restraining the British negotiators, Reid called on the Foreign Secretary. He told Grey that Britain would be unwise to allow the Canadians to prolong a state of affairs which could only lead to extermination of the herd. Reid pointed out that Britain faced the loss of its large fur dyeing industry. (London's fur monopoly would not last much longer in any case. Part of the U.S. Government decision to take over the Pribilof operation involved the use of American furriers, the Fouke Fur Company of St. Louis.) Reid reported to Washington that Grey seemed too preoccupied with developments in the Balkans to concern himself with the seals. With Lord Salisbury gone, the British Foreign Office was no longer strongly committed to preserving the rights of its subjects in the Bering Sea.

There proved to be other stumbling blocks as the preliminary talks carried on into 1910. On May 16 Governor-General Earl Grey advised Bryce of Canadian objections to a U.S. draft treaty proposing an indefinite rather than a fixed-period ban on pelagic sealing. Canada favoured a 15-year limit on any agreement. Bryce replied that Ottawa should not take a stand in advance but rather let the matter be decided at the four-power conference. Bryce said the U.S. had agreed to let the conference determine how long the ban should last.

Under political pressure from newspaper publisher William Templeman and other Victoria Liberals, Laurier's attitude stiffened. He told Bryce that "public opinion in this country would view with something akin to indignation anything amounting to a surrender of the right of British subjects to hunt seals on the high seas. This opinion is so strong that it cannot be ignored."

It is doubtful whether the rest of the country cared that much about the issue. The Toronto *Globe and Mail* said, "the answer is clear. Pelagic sealing should stop altogether; the killing should be done wholly at the rookeries, in the most merciful way that can be devised." The *Globe* also suggested that a portion of Canadian revenue from a treaty "might well be paid into the exchequer of the province of British Columbia as compensation for the destruction of a profitable business." It was a suggestion that would be consistently ignored by successive federal governments in the face of demands by B.C.

There was also the continuing bitterness of Canada toward Japan. Pope said Japan's "attitude in posing at once as a pelagic sealing power, and as a rookery-owning power, savours of rapacity." And Bryce said Japanese demands for compensation, based on the larger size of her pelagic fleet, were "exorbitant."

On June 2 Templeman told Laurier that Canada should get one-fifth of all skins taken on the Pribilofs and sell them herself. The price could not be fixed at $10 a skin as proposed by the U.S. because it was already $50 to $75 in London and could go to $100 if the supply was kept down. The other alternative was for Canada to receive the market price in London, less transportation costs. Templeman suggested the U.S. put up $200,000 advance compensation and Canada the balance to pay the schooner owners $450,000. Canada would recoup her share of the compensation with a few years' skins, Templeman said. Canada then would repay the U.S. advance from her share of future skins.[11]

As the negotiations ground on toward an inevitable settlement, the Sealing Company was having a difficult time staying in operation. In January of 1908 Boscowitz had written to Templeman and Premier McBride confiding that it was doubtful whether enough schooners could be equipped "to avoid the impression becoming general that the business of sealing has practically been abandoned." Two schooners would go out, however, "in order to keep the question alive." Boscowitz feared the Victoria sealers were in danger of losing compensation after having "fought so strongly to maintain the rights of the nation," not to mention the hope of a little profit.

In 1909 the Company leased only five of its schooners to individual sealers, including Captain George Heater, who went out on the *Vera* with Kyuquot hunters. In December the Company decided that no vessels would be sent out in 1910 because of the impending agreement. That turned out to be a fateful decision — the Company would have been wiser to have made a token effort to get skins in the hope of gaining compensation. The five independently-owned schooners still operating out of Victoria — the *Jessie, Pescawha, Bayard, Umbrina* and *Lady Mine*— sailed once again for the sealing grounds. (The *Umbrina* was sunk later that year off the Oregon coast after colliding with the U.S. steam collier *Saturn.*)

The Japanese were still active in 1910. On July 4 fourteen of their schooners were sighted off St. Paul. There were 25 Japanese schooners in the Bering that year (two were seized), and a total of 40 along the North American coast. Meanwhile, the Quatsino and Clayoquot Indians were making good catches offshore. The hunters were getting $28 a skin and some were earning more than $300 a day.

In April the Sealing Company let it be known it was willing to accept the $450,000 previously offered by the U.S. for its rotting fleet, without interest. But the U.S. was in no mood now to pay anything for the schooners. And Victoria businessmen, especially those of Liberal persuasion, kept the pressure on Ottawa to hold out for a good deal for the sealers. Insurance Agent R. L. Drury complained to Templeman that the government was not taking sufficient interest in their cause and Laurier did not answer their letters. "As you know," Drury wrote, "there are a very large number of influential people concerned in this enterprise and a large amount of capital invested in it. I am anxious that (they) should not have their sympathies alienated from the Liberal party." Like Boscowitz, Drury had no time for subtlety.

Representatives of the four powers gathered in Washington on May 11, 1911, to iron out the final treaty draft. On June 12 Secretary of Commerce Charles Nagel declared the meeting deadlocked over the amount of compensation to be paid Japan. The Japanese had been holding out for 35 percent of the annual U.S. proceeds from the land kill. President Taft appealed directly to the Emperor, who agreed on a compromise.

On July 7 the treaty was signed by all the parties in Washington. The pact was ratified by the U.S. Senate July 24 and signed by the President November 24, a speed unusual for the cumbersome U.S. legislative process. After the treaty had been ratified by Britain August 25, Russia on November 4 and Japan November 6, it was proclaimed December 14, to come into effect the following day. The era of pelagic sealing had ended at last.

Everyone except native Indians, Aleuts and the Ainos of Japan, were banned from hunting seals north of 30 degrees latitude in the Pacific, including the Bering Sea, Kamchatka Sea, Sea of Okhotsk and Sea of Japan. Offenders were to be turned over to their own country for prosecution. Canada and Japan would receive immediate payment of $200,000 each as an advance on future shares of the U.S. harvest. This was to amount to 15 percent of the gross number or value of American skins harvested each year, with a minimum of 1,000 skins in any year, except when the U.S. suspended killing as a protective measure, in which case each country would receive $10,000. The U.S. would recover this amount by deducting sealskins to that value in subsequent years. If the number of seals on the Pribilofs fell below 100,000, the U.S. was not required to pay anything.

Under other terms of the agreement Russia was to give 15 percent of its annual harvest to both Canada and Japan, and Japan agreed to pay 10 percent of its harvest to each of the other three nations. The United States, Japan and Russia, the three rookery owners, each undertook to maintain patrols in waters frequented by the seal herds.

Indians, Aleuts and Ainos were to be allowed to seal in their own canoes, which could not be transported by other vessels or carry more than five men. They could use only sails, oars, or paddles. Guns were forbidden and the natives were not allowed to be employed by, or contracted to deliver to, any outside party.

The treaty also took steps to protect the diminishing number of sea otters. Henceforth no otter were to be hunted beyond the 3-mile limit in the Pacific above latitude 30 degrees.

The length of the treaty was 15 years. At the end of that time it could be terminated by any one of the four nations on 12 months' notice. At any time before the expiry of the treaty one of the four countries could call for a conference to agree on an extension "with such additions and modifications, if any, as may be found desirable."

Shortly after the Treaty was signed in July, a resolution was introduced in the U.S. Congress calling for an unlimited ban on Pribilof land killing. The measure was voted down, however, and a five-year moratorium was agreed upon.

Not all the parties were equally pleased with the agreement. Even though her sealers were late arrivals in the industry, Japan was annoyed that Canada was given an equal share of the U.S. land catch. Russia also resented the benefits reaped by Canada. The two countries believed President Taft had made concessions to the Canadians in a bid to achieve a trade reciprocity treaty. Some complained there was nothing to stop vessels flying the flags of other nations from engaging in pelagic sealing. That would have been difficult, however, since the four nations had agreed to ban the import or transport of pelagic furs within their boundaries.

In general, however, reaction to the Treaty was positive. It was recognized as the first international agreement to preserve a species of marine life. Others would follow, such as the American-Canadian Halibut Treaty of 1923 and the North Pacific salmon agreement. The sealing pact had come just in time: it was estimated that by 1911 the Pribilof herd had dwindled to five percent of its original number.

The Japanese sealed to the end, with 30 schooners in the Bering in the summer of 1911 and a few others along the coast. Their two top vessels were commanded by Victoria skippers. One of them, Alec Ritchie, had previously been imprisoned 18 months at Valdez, Alaska, with the crew of the *Kinsei Maru* after she was seized in 1909 inside the 3-mile-limit at St. Paul. The independent Victoria schooners were also out that summer, unwittingly putting themselves in line for compensation.

There was jubilation over the treaty in Victoria, where the *Colonist* referred to the "great bargain" secured by Canada under the treaty which would bring the country millions of dollars in future years. It was confidently predicted that $500,000 in compensation would be paid by Ottawa to the Sealing Company alone and additional amounts to the independent sealers. The Victorians assumed the $200,000 advance paid by the U.S. was the first instalment of compensation payments for the sealing fleet. But the word compensation did not appear in the text of the treaty and the city was in for a big disappointment.

CHAPTER FIFTEEN

Ottawa

The government never paid any attention to us except to humbug us right through. It is hardly fair to peddle away our means of making a living to another nation, and then throw us out on the beach.

—Captain DAN MACAULEY

J oe Boscowitz was a busy man after the Treaty had been signed. He rushed off to Ottawa to lobby the government for compensation and approval to sell the fleet. The *Colonist* quoted him on May 15, 1912, as saying Prime Minister Robert Borden had given the go-ahead for the sale without prejudice to the claims. Boscowitz said Canada would receive $6,000,000 over the first 15 years of the treaty. He also claimed that because the Sealing Company had turned down a $450,000 offer for the fleet some years before, it deserved credit for preserving the industry and gaining the favourable 1911 pact.

It was a vintage, self-serving Boscowitz performance. He had it all wrong, and not accidentally. In the first place the country would receive considerably less than $6,000,000 — just $316,339 to be exact — between 1911 and 1926; the Sealing Company had desperately wanted to sell the fleet for $450,000, or even less, but never had a firm offer from either Ottawa or Washington. Lastly, Borden had not given "permission" for the sale.

The man Boscowitz saw in Ottawa was Fisheries Minister John D. Hazen, who testified later under oath that Boscowitz' statements were "entirely untrue." Hazen said he told Boscowitz it was not the minister's business whether or not the schooners were sold, and he gave no consent for the sale. Boscowitz pressed hard, but Hazen had remained guarded in his replies. Boscowitz' lawyer, who was present at their meeting, reluctantly confirmed Hazen's version of what took place.

This was not known at the time, however, and so the Sealing Company placed advertisements for the sale in newspapers in Victoria, Vancouver, Seattle and San Francisco. Twelve of the company's schooners had been built in the U.S. and so were eligible for U.S. registry. Despite the *Colonist's* confidence that buyers would "flock here," the June 25 sale conducted by

Maynard's Auctioneers at the company wharf in Victoria harbour was a flop. Many vessels received no bids at all and several schooners were knocked down to $150 and $200.

Boscowitz himself bought the rakish *Vera*, the former *Halcyon* of opium smuggling notoriety, for $2,100 and the *Markland* for $1,900. He sold both vessels the following year to Seattle fishing interests. Another company director, J. A. Bechtel, bought the *Ida Etta* for $500 and the *Mary Taylor* for $400. Bechtel and Boscowitz were vultures at a family funeral.

The *Saucy Lass* went to Victor Jacobson for $275 and the *Casco* was sold for $900 to August Arnet of Clayoquot, who said he planned to put in an engine and send her fishing. He failed to pay up, however, and the company reclaimed the schooner.

Ten vessels in all were sold and 32 chronometers went for an average price of $18. In the fall another three schooners were disposed of when J. Sidney Smith of Vancouver purchased the *Casco, Borealis* and *Carlotta G. Cox* for his halibut-fishing fleet. Smith removed many of the *Casco's* carved mahogany cabin fittings and placed them in a home he maintained at Prince Rupert. The *Casco* was later sold to a U.S. buyer and worked for a time cod-fishing before being wrecked in 1919 near Nome while on a gold-hunting expedition to Siberia — far from Robert Louis Stevenson's sun-kissed haunts.

The ignominious fate of the fleet was underscored a month after the sale when Harbour Master Captain E. E. Clarke laid a charge in police court against the Company for leaving vessels untended for more than three months without permission. Clarke said the public was demanding removal of the rotting schooners.

In June of 1913 the Dominion Government set up a royal commission to investigate claims by the sealers for compensation for loss of their trade resulting from the treaties of 1893 and 1911. Louis Arthur Audette, an assistant judge of the Exchequer Court, was named commissioner.

The Commission published a notice in the *Canada Gazette* June 7, 1913, inviting owners, masters and crews to submit claims. The first hearing was to be held in the Victoria Court House July 15, the second in the Halifax legislative chamber September 2. Sittings would be held daily from 10:30 a.m. to 4:30 p.m. Other hearings would be held later in Sydney, N.S. and Ottawa.

Audette advised the Department of Indian Affairs he anticipated claims by some Indian hunters. William E. Ditchburn, the Superintendent of Indian Agencies based in Victoria, was told June 9 the Indians' claims must be submitted by July 5. He protested the time allowed was "entirely too short" and pressed for an extension. Many natives were away at salmon canneries. Audette said he must proceed on the announced date but the Indians' claims might be considered later. He subsequently announced there would be a second Victoria sitting December 13 to include Indian and white stragglers.

Ditchburn expressed concern to Ottawa about what the Indians could expect in the way of compensation. Rumours were circulating in Victoria, he said, that white hunters would be receiving money, and the Indians had heard these reports. But the schooner owners told Ditchburn the Indians were not entitled to compensation because they could still seal under the Treaty. "I deem it most unfair," he wrote. "It is only from sealing and fishing that Indians have a chance to earn money." It was easier for the white hunters to find other work, Ditchburn said.[1]

Earlier, in 1912, the Indian Agent at Alberni, A. W. Neill, had pressed his superiors in Ottawa to make sure the Indians were included in any compensation for the sealers: "If a large sum is to be paid to the owners of the sealing fleet, the majority of which are rotten old hulks which have been herded up in Victoria harbour for a number of years for the express purpose of claiming compensation when this treaty, which was anticipated, should be enacted — surely an equal claim is held by the Indians who have made a profession of sealing and who are now entirely cut off from it as the offshore catch is very uncertain and only accessible to certain bands favourably situated for the purpose."

At the opening session in Victoria, counsel included Frank J. Curran of Montreal for the government; McGregor Young, K.C., of Toronto for the Department of Indian Affairs and the Indian claimants; and A. E. McPhillips and Arthur J. Patton for individual sealers. But the lawyer who was to emerge as the dominant figure during the hearings was Charles Hibbert Tupper, representing the Sealing Company.

Curran began by outlining the position of the government, which he said did not recognize legal obligation or technical liability in any of the claims, but was prepared to pay compensation. Audette set December 9 as the date for hearing claims of those unable to be present because they were involved in seasonal work. Audette said he was willing to sit over the Christmas holiday to hear the claims. Young said there would likely be only 25 or 30 Indian claims.

Some sealers put in claims even though they had quit sealing or found other work. The only claims ruled out at the start were individual ones by members of the Sealing Company. (J. A. Bechtel had filed an individual suit, which he withdrew.) Audette and Curran also expressed doubts about the validity of claims by those who entered the industry after 1894 when the Paris regulations were in effect.

The first claim considered was that of the owners of the *Thomas F. Bayard*. Audette decided the general evidence in its case would apply to others, as in a class action suit, to save repetition of testimony. The owners, merchants Thomas Stockham, James Maynard and Thomas Lumsden, claimed $164,892 for prospective lost profits for 15 years. Stockham said the 1911 treaty which put an end to their business was "a treaty which might be read as fifteen years, but looks more for all time to come." Captain Hans Blakstad of the *Bayard* put in a personal claim for $14,389 damages from the Paris Regulations and $15,000 from the 1911 Treaty. Blakstad said he stayed in the business after the regulations because he couldn't do any better in another line of work. His pay from 1906 to 1911 was $75 a month and 75 cents a skin.[2]

The case of the *Jessie* was next. She was owned jointly by Richard Hall and J. A. Bechtel but was registered in the name of Herbert Goulding Wilson, coal merchant and insurance agent and a member of the pioneer W. H. Wilson clothing firm. Hall explained it was done that way "for reasons of our own. We were interested in the Victoria Sealing Company, and in order to avoid any ill-will or unpleasantness we put it in the name of Mr. Wilson." Independent owners of schooners could safely defy the regulations but directors of a joint stock company could not, Hall said. Wilson said he got nothing out of the venture except his normal profit from selling groceries and supplies for the *Jessie*. Audette commented drily on the degree to which the people of Victoria apparently trusted one another.

By July 22 some 286 claims had been submitted totalling $3,500,000. They included the Sealing Company, $450,000; R. J. Hall "et al," $107,000; H. G. Wilson, $145,000; Laughlin McLean, $64,000; Berton M. Balcom, $36,300, and Augustus Gerow, a hunter, $49,000.

In the early stages of the hearing Audette appeared muddled, asking bumbling, ill-informed questions. Neither he nor counsel had apparently studied the writings of David Starr Jordan and others on the migratory patterns of the fur seal. Audette said he believed Henry Elliott above all others on the seals.

He undoubtedly raised the hopes of the sealers by being consistently kindly and open with individual claimants. From the beginning, however, he was critical of the Sealing Company. He wondered aloud whether it was an illegal combine which had forced out the small operators. When Tupper claimed that if it had not been for the Company there would be no monetary clauses in the 1911 treaty, Audette was sarcastic: "Do you say that the company took a philanthropic position?"

After a parade of sealers had testified about the rotting condition of the fleet and the unwillingness of the Company to carry on sealing, Tupper charged there was a conspiracy involving malice, lying and perjury to discredit its claim. Sealers with claims were angry at him and the Company for exposing the fact they broke the regulations by using guns, and were now coming in to "stab" the Company. The independents had "foolishly and childishly" combined to damage the Company's claim by undervaluing their vessels. They should have realized, Tupper said, that their claims were dependent on the success of the Company's claim. The Company would fight this "conspiracy born out of revenge. We have our honour at heart, more than the matter of money claims."

Tupper was unsparing on individual claimants, haughty and domineering in cross-examination. He portrayed himself pompously as the expert on sealing and played shamelessly to the galleries.

The first Victoria hearing adjourned August 20 and the Commission moved to Halifax on September 2. Audette repeated there that he was "not hearing claims on strictly legal grounds," and said the claims presented by the Maritimers were tenuous. Typical was that submitted by John Clark.

Clark had built the *Enterprise* in Victoria for $8,500 and owned all 64 shares. He was claiming $141,600. In 1894 the schooner had been seized by the court because the mortgage was in default. Robert Ward & Co. was the creditor. The court ordered Clark to charter the vessel. He got her back in 1900 by paying $6,000, which included heavy interest. "They were swamping me in every shape and form," Clark said. He kept the *Enterprise* out of the Company and in 1904 paid all outstanding bills and brought her back to Halifax. In 1905 she was burned and lost in the South Atlantic.

Meanwhile, preparations went ahead for the hearing of Indian claims starting December 9. All the hunters, including the natives, had to pay to get detailed information from the shipping masters and schooner owners on their length of service and catches. Ditchburn asked his Department to advance the Indians money for preparing their claims. It could be recovered later from their awards, he said. At that time he estimated there would be 300 Indian claims.

About 35 Indians approached Patton, who agreed to take up their claims for 10 percent of the awards. Patton, who was also representing 160 white claimants, advised the Department he would accept a fixed fee of $25 a day if it preferred. Patton also suggested that he and the Agents go to the Indian villages to interview claimants so they would not be put to the expense of travelling to Victoria. Curran, meanwhile, asked Patton to get evidence from the Indians which the government could use to contest the Sealing Company claim.

By this time the total amount of claims submitted at Victoria had reached $6,000,000. Since the advance payment by the U.S. was only $200,000, which it was assumed was for compensation, the Indian Affairs Department estimated that legitimate claims would get only 10 cents on the dollar and the Indians a total of $2,500. It felt that on the basis of those estimates Patton was asking too much—there would be nothing left for the Indians after he had deducted his fees.

Negotiations between Patton and the Department continued. In October he reported that 600 Indians had already filed claims with him. He believed half were of no value, including claims by the heirs of 150 sealers who had died. Patton said he was not willing to risk being paid by the Indians and suggested the Department give him $15 a claim.

Eventually the Department made a deal with Patton and A. R. Langley, the former secretary of the Sealing Company who had offered to make out detailed work records, catches and earnings for the Indians for $4 each, or $2 if they had worked less than two years. Patton had a staff of 12 drawing up the Indian claims. Many of their cases were "more meritorious than those of the white men," he said.

The Department also agreed to pay $5 a day to Charles Spring to act as interpreter at commission hearings. Although many Indians could not speak English, all but one said they were Christians. It was the first question asked when they took the stand, so that they could be sworn. Chief Charlie Quisto of San Juan said he was not a Christian but the court accepted his word that he would tell the truth.

Hunter Darius Barry was the only white man who said he did not believe in a Christian god or future reward or punishment, but said he wanted to tell the truth. Audette was unsympathetic: "You want to come here and perjure yourself without fear of punishment?"

There were others who saw an opportunity to profit from the Indian claims. Real estate agent W. Barrett-Lennard made a deal with 67 Indians from lower Vancouver Island, as well as 16 whites, to handle their claims for half of their awards. He hired a lawyer and an accountant to prepare the documents. Ditchburn said Lennard's terms were "exorbitant." When white hunter John Cotsford attempted to repudiate his agreement with Barrett-Lennard, Audette told him he was unfortunately stuck with it. "It looks bad," the Commissioner added. "I do not like the idea."

The Indians began streaming into Victoria in the expectation of being given money at the hearings. Many were destitute after spending their savings on fares for the whole family on the passenger steamer *Princess Maquinna*. Not all were poor, however. Charles Augustus Cox, Indian Agent for the west coast of Vancouver Island, was asked to give an Indian woman money for her return passage and found she was carrying $450 in cash.

One old Indian told Audette that since sealing ended he had tried to make a living carving 12-inch totems which he sold for 25 cents. He exhibited one and soon made a number of sales among counsel and the commission staff.

Close to 1,000 natives were in the city during December. It was the first trip to the city for some, and the newspapers noted approvingly how well-behaved the visitors were. The hearing of Indian claims took 23 days — from December 9 to January 5, including a sitting on New Year's Day so the natives could catch the steamer that night rather than wait around another 20 days for the next one. Cox herded 180 Indians on the *Maquinna* that evening. One hundred and twelve claims had been rushed through on December 31.

The crowded courtroom had a festive air, with a variety of costumes and weather-beaten faces. Women with colourful bandannas sold baskets on the

222

street outside. Inside, a number of Indian women submitted claims as boat-steerers for their husbands or as cooks, as well as widows of deceased hunters. There was a hierarchy in the courtroom, with the jury boxes designated for owners and masters while the Indians, crewmen, hunters, friends and relatives sat in the spectator's area. At times 100 natives were jammed into the little room.

In all, 861 Indian claims were filed by Patton, including 145 by Clayo-quots. Others included 41 from Alberni, 83 Ahousaht, 16 Cape Mudge, 42 Dodger Cove, 38 Hesquiaht, 44 Kyuquot, 48 Nootka, 22 Nitinaht, 22 Quatsino, 44 Ucluelet, and 50 Ehattesaht. Also represented were Masset, Prince Rupert, Port Simpson and other upcoast villages. Some Masset Indians made claims even though they had gone out only twice on schooners. Ditchburn asked for a special sitting at Alberni to save travel money, but Audette was hearing 50 Indian claims a day and decided to stay in Victoria. When Patton told him 111 claimants were not able to appear because they were ill, Audette said their claims would be considered on the basis of evidence given by the other 750. The Indian claims now totalled $1,000,000, but Patton said only about 400 of the 861 had merit.

Audette was considerate and accommodating to the Indians, expressing concern about the physical condition of those suffering from tuberculosis. He was told there had been a 50 percent decline in the Indian population over the last 20 years, largely as the result of disease. Nevertheless, Audette had the common attitude of the times about the natives: "These people are children. They are not fit to handle money."

His views were echoed by Augustus Cox. He had been a police constable for many years, becoming Agent in 1913. "They are an awful lazy people," Cox told Audette. "Most of them are rather filthy. They lie around and do nothing." Cox, fortunately, was not typical of the Agents.

Some of the Indians expected to be paid by the commissioner as soon as their claims were heard. Audette told them it would take at least a year. They were claiming 15 percent of their annual earnings, which was the amount Patton estimated they had lost as a result of the 1894 regulations. Earnings of Indian hunters had once been between $100 and $500 each season. Patton pointed out that the 1911 Treaty clause permitting them to seal offshore as in the old days was of little value since the seals were scarce. In the springs of 1912 and 1913 they had killed only 125 seals, whereas once they had taken up to 3,000.

The first Indian claimant to take the stand was Jasper Turner of Clayoquot, who had been on the *Bayard* in 1911. His claim for $4,000 was the largest submitted by any of the natives. Some were as small as $16. Turner gave evidence in Chinook, which was translated by Spring.

Chief Joseph of Clayoquot said his men were afraid to go out in recent years because of the age and poor condition of the Sealing Company schooners. "I want to let his Lordship know that I am very hard up," the Chief told Audette, "that I have very little money to live on, and that my people are in the same condition."

Testimony by other Indians confirmed how difficult it was to find work when there was no sealing. There were few jobs for them in the new whaling industry, where most of the boat crews were Norwegians and the shore-workers Chinese and Japanese. The natives were not willing to work for lower wages like the Orientals, but wanted equal pay with whites. They tired quickly of the same job and liked to move on. Employment in the salmon canneries lasted only two months and hop-picking in Washington not more than four weeks. They did not have the money to own fishboats and the cannery operators would not buy fish from them in any case. The Indians lacked the language and job skills to find work in Victoria. There was no work at Alberni except on the roads. In Barkley Sound some cut wood for the cable station at Bamfield.

Billy August, the storekeeper at Ahousaht, claimed to have lost business as a result of the 1911 Treaty. He could not say, however, what his profits had been before. "Not very much," he admitted. "I used to eat up too much myself."

The most unique Indian claim was submitted by Fred S. Carpenter, who had built the 60-foot sealing schooner *Rainbow* in 1906/07 on Campbell Island near Bella Bella. She was constructed with day labour and local lumber at a total cost of $4,000. Audette had difficulty accepting the fact that an Indian could have acquired so much money. But Carpenter was an enterprising native who had earned some from logging, some from a gasboat which he used to carry tourists, and got the balance from his father, a Chief who was also a lighthouse keeper employed by the government. Carpenter did not have receipts for his materials. He said he had simply sent the money to Vancouver and the goods came. Indians were not given credit, so were used to paying in cash. Carpenter was willing to sell his vessel for $4,000 but there were no buyers, he told Audette.

Most of the Indians used their "King George" names in making out claims because that was how they were identified in the schooner records. This created some confusion, since there were 28 Charlies, 28 Toms, 20 Annies, 18 Joes and 13 Billys. There were also more distinguished names such as Mark Twain and Chief Napoleon Maquinna, a descendant of the great Nuu-chah-nulth chief.

The more common names were frequently expanded to "Charlie of Ahousaht," or "Billy from San Juan," to help the Commission keep track of who was who. It was not easy, as shown by this exchange in the transcript for Claim No. 1410, that of "Bob of Ehattesaht":

Audette: "Haven't we had this man before?"

Cox: "I think the Bob heard last fall was Big Bob."

Lady Mine moored in Vancouver

Schooners beached along Gorge. *Carrie C. W.* on right.

Theodore Davie

Captain J. C. Voss

W. A. DRADER

Deck of Japanese sealing schooner, Tofino.

Witness: "There are two Bobs in Ehattesaht. One is Big Bob, and I am Bob."

Audette: "Then we will hear him under the name of Bob."

Patton: "Last fall we heard a man named Bob, and it should have been Big Bob. These papers ought to go in with the last claim, and those papers go in with this claim. The papers got turned around."

Audette: "But there is only one Big Bob, and one Bob. We will hear this man as Bob."

The whites who appeared before the Commission ran the gamut from lowly cook and deckhand to fat-cat schooner owner or mortgage holder. The veteran sealers were the most straightforward in their testimony.

Captain Daniel Macauley came around Cape Horn on the *Araunah* in 1887 from Halifax. Later he served on the *Beatrice* and received compensation from Britain resulting from the 1891 *modus vivendi*. From 1900 on he sealed for the Company. In 1906 he had refused to take out the *Director* because she was leaking and unseaworthy. Macauley said he had told Grant the previous year the schooner was in such bad shape she had to be pumped out for 15 minutes of every hour. No repairs were made, however, and Grant asked him to take her out for one more season in 1906, promising that he would then fix her up.

At that point Tupper jumped to his feet to complain that Macauley was in effect alleging that Captain Grant, the managing director of the Company, was a "murderer." Grant himself cried out: "I am not a murderer."

When Macauley stood up to Tupper's bullying tactics, Tupper accused him of being "impertinent." Macauley concluded his evidence by telling Audette: "The government never paid any attention to us except to humbug us right through. It is hardly fair to peddle away our means of making a living to another nation, and then throw us out on the beach."

Max Lohbrunner sealed from 1904 to 1910. Born in New York, he was 16 when he began sealing in 1904 on the *Diana*. A hunter, he took his own sail for his small boat and spirit compass instead of a cap compass, as well as his own oarlocks, gaff hooks, and knives for skinning. He claimed they helped him get consistently higher catches than the others.

William Clare, a Jamaican cook, said the government was allowing too many Japanese and Chinese into country. They became cooks and so there were no jobs for him ashore.

When a naturalized Japanese, Ugi Otsuka, submitted a claim, Audette was outraged. The Commissioner said "his people" could go into the Bering with impunity. He made no distinction for a naturalized Canadian, and clearly regarded Ugi as a second-class citizen. His claim was "preposterous," Audette declared. Ugi had come to Canada in 1894 and was naturalized in 1899. He was a Methodist.

Laughlin McLean, a schooner owner and captain, was asked by Curran whether he was "any relation to the McLean who wrote a book called *The Sea Wolf* about sealing?" McLean replied: "I never knew he had sense enough to write a book."

Captain Alfred Bissett complained bitterly that "the sealer was always the thief, and he was always considered guilty until he could prove himself innocent."

Charles Spring took time out from his interpreting duties to provide Audette with an outline of the pelagic sealing industry since its beginnings in the 1860s under the direction of his father, William Spring. The decline of the business which he had inherited was one of the few poignant stories among the new breed of sealing speculators whose losses seldom evoked sympathy.

Spring said he and his father had always been able to get Indian hunters because they respected the natives' wishes. They used to get out of the Bering quickly so the Indians would have time to catch their winter fish supply at home. The Springs would then refit their schooners for carrying freight in the off-season.

After William Spring died and Charles took over the business, it was a struggle to keep the creditors and mortgage-holders at bay. In 1892, Spring told Audette, he had lost everything. Without capital he was "thrown down, damaged, crushed." The outfitting firm of Rithet & Sons took over the old *Favorite* as it did so many schooners at that time for unpaid bills, and the *Kate* was lost in a forced sale. Because loans were impossible to obtain, Spring went as a trader to Kyuquot for five years. When his children reached school age he brought them to Victoria and took up farming, which provided little profit for long hours of hard work. He moved then to Seattle, but returned to Victoria in 1911 to go into the motor-boat business.

By far the most colourful and controversial claimant to appear before Audette was the garrulous Victor Jacobson. An individualist, Jacobson had joined the Company reluctantly and got out quickly. He said the Company's vessels used guns in the Bering when they were forbidden by the regulations. The charge was at first denied by Tupper but it was clear from other testimony that Jacobson was telling the truth.

Tupper implied the independents made money by shooting despite the regulations, and Company vessels did not. The independents took chances but there was too much at stake for the Company to condone the use of firearms.

The Company may not have officially condoned the use of guns, but it did look the other way. Tupper admitted as much when he declared there was "not a vessel that went out and made a paying catch in Bering Sea under the regulations which did not violate them." He confirmed the *Carlotta Cox* was using guns when she was seized and attempted to justify it: "There is no moral dishonesty in breaking an unjust regulation."

226

Captain Grant in his testimony later left no doubts about the use of guns by Company vessels. "You could not get a crew after the Japs went into the (Bering) Sea out of Victoria without furnishing them with ammunition and guns," he told Audette. Grant said there were places to hide guns under the floor boards.

Jacobson had been called to the stand by Tupper, but was declared a hostile witness after deriding the worth of Company vessels during cross-examination by Curran. His testimony was often garbled and exaggerated, but his integrity was apparent. He was a fearless, hard-working seaman whose evidence was severely damaging to the Company's case.

Jacobson, who started sealing in 1880 with William Spring, submitted claims totalling $253,500, among the highest by an individual. He said his best year had been 1890 when he cleared $27,000 on his home-built *Minnie*. He paid the Indians $2 a skin and said they cost only 20 cents a day to feed. He took one barrel of beef for them and they ate seal meat and fish caught during the voyage. Jacobson said he never hired white hunters. He went out later in the season because the Indians did not want to waste time at sea. White hunters on the other hand were often destitute and didn't mind loafing for weeks waiting for seals or good weather.

Despite his miserly treatment of the natives, Jacobson had only a few instances of trouble with them. In 1903 they deserted his schooner at Port San Juan. Jacobson said he suspected the Company had told the Indian Agent and missionary there that his vessel was unseaworthy. In any case, he got the same Indians out the following year and they worked out their advances after he had obtained a summons for their arrest. Jacobson paid his white crew members low wages too, but kept them loyal by looking after them ashore.

In 1902 Jacobson had bought an old schooner which he named *Eva Marie* after his daughter. She had been launched in Victoria in 1884 as the steam-powered *Teaser* and later became the *Rainbow* before being abandoned by the C.P.R. Jacobson paid only $250 for the hull and spent $13,000 converting her into a sealer. The only three-masted schooner in the Victoria fleet, she was 110 feet long and could carry 30 canoes.

Jacobson told Audette that there had been no shooting in the Bering after the 1894 Paris regulations until the Company came into being in 1900. "That was the understanding when the Company was formed," he said. "There was no other purpose but to combine to run these risks." The British patrol ships looked the other way. Jacobson became so exasperated in 1905 that, after warning the Company vessels, he alerted the U.S. Revenue cutters to what was going on and they made a search of the *Teresa*. The other schooners then threw all their guns overboard. Jacobson said he started shooting in 1906 because everyone else was doing it. "The whole of the Company's fleet had guns and I had none." After that the Indians would not go without guns. In some instances, Jacobson said, the captains became "slaves" to the Indians because of the guns. If the natives wanted to return home early and the captain refused, they would threaten to report the use of firearms. And it was the captains who had to bear the responsibility, he said, not the company directors.

Jacobson spent May and June waiting for the Bering to open by hunting and hiding in the "corners" of the coast, afraid of being seized and losing his investment. But as a ship's carpenter, Jacobson had a fall-back job. He usually sealed for only five or six months of the year and spent the rest of the time repairing boats.

Hired by Grant to work on the Company fleet, Jacobson said he was not given money or men to do a proper job. In September of 1902 he had been fired by Grant, who told him there were no more funds for repair work. "Captain Grant stayed there till the whole outfit was sold, to pay himself."

The Company vessels were so unseaworthy, Jacobson said, that "only the drunkards and hard-up men would go in any of them, but not a man who thought anything of his life." The *Viva* was rotten in 1901 and not worth $50. The *Walter L. Rich* was also disintegrating, and the mast fell out of the *Teresa* in fine weather.

Jacobson was no doubt bitter toward the Company because he had lost the *Casco* to it. His original $12 shares were worth less than $1 in 1905 and although he got $4.50 a share in 1906 after the dividend payment, Jacobson estimated his loss in the Company at $30,000.

Tupper said Jacobson's testimony should be discounted because he had a grievance against the Company.

"He hit from the shoulder," Audette said.

"He was malicious," said Tupper.

Joe Boscowitz was a cantankerous witness. Jacobson "seems to know everything," he complained. At first Boscowitz claimed he did not know Company schooners were using guns. "I knew less about the vessels than anybody else on the directorate," he told Audette. Later, however, he said that "if the regulations had been carried out as they are on the books no one could go from British Columbia or any other place and make a living at pelagic sealing."

Boscowitz said he had no interest in his own schooners other than as an investment. He would not have put three of his vessels in the Company if he had known about the $9,000 deducted from their value for repairs needed to bring them up to standard. He had found out only on receiving a reduced amount of stock. "I was not a favourite with the company," Boscowitz said, suggesting he was discriminated against in the schooner surveys.

Tupper told Audette the 1893 arbitration decision was "a grave diplomatic blunder" because it did not include all the maritime nations of the world. The U.S had pressured Britain into accepting the regulations. Curran protested that Tupper was imputing ignorance on the part of Britain, an accusation that should be withdrawn "on patriotic grounds." Tupper maintained it was "historically true." In a burst of hyperbole, Tupper declared "there could not be a grosser, meaner or more contemptible plot than has been attempted to be put up by one government upon another."

He did score a debating point, however, by observing that Ottawa had claimed the maximum value of the fleet for the purposes of the Paris arbitration and the 1896 compensation commission but now, faced with claims against itself, was attempting to depreciate its worth.

Frank Adams, a director of the Company, testified that the food on schooners with white hunters was "the best of everything" — including canned chicken, canned and dried fruits, hams and bacon. "There was no stint," Adams said. The Company was not so generous with the Indians, however. "The moment the regulations were adopted," Adams said, "they took advantage of the situation, and what they did not know, the storekeepers put them up to." It was a common refrain.

At the time of the hearing 14 Company schooners were tied up in the harbour, slowly disintegrating beyond repair. Three schooners had recently been burned at the order of the Harbour Master. A second auction was held but there were no serious buyers.

This state of affairs made a mockery of Tupper's statement to Audette that the Company was claiming for compensation resulting from the 1911 treaty and the 1894 regulations because the "fleet was ready to go at any moment." Audette observed that the company "was alive, and that was about all."

Tupper said the company was a "formidable" organization at the beginning. It was made up of "leading men" of the community who had acted "to prevent cutting each other's throats by competition." Backers had the money to go into the business whole-heartedly if it had been feasible. They were stopped not by a lack of means but by "unfair and absurd regulations." Audette was not persuaded, however, that the Company had enough capital. All its assets were tied up in the fleet and operating funds came from bank loans, he said.

"If you had capital," he told Tupper, "your returns would have been very different." Too much was spent paying off high-interest loans. The banks did not regard the aging fleet as a secure investment and set its rates accordingly. Audette suggested the schooner owners would have been better off if they had simply carried on individually as before.

"That might have been so," Tupper conceded.

The men who formed the Company had spent money on "such people as, for instance the Indians, who reaped a rich harvest out of the enterprise of these people," Tupper said. The treaty was a "godsend" to the Indians, he said, and they ought to pay a bounty. "I think they have done pretty well."

Tupper complained that in crippling the industry the regulations were hitting capital. "Private interests were sacrificed for the sake of international peace." The crewmen and hunters could get work elsewhere, he said, despite their evidence to the contrary. Not every man who called himself a sealer or everybody engaged in the business was entitled to compensation. Only those who through their endeavours brought money into Canada deserved "very generous treatment."

"You are not appealing to me that these men (the owners) are more worthy of consideration than anyone else?" Audette asked Tupper. "Of course not, my Lord," he replied. In fact, said Tupper, there was an "understanding between the Company and Ottawa that it would put up a small amount for "any meritorious claims in regard to the men." But Audette got an admission from Tupper that the $450,000, if paid by the U.S. for the fleet, would have gone to owners only.

When Tupper said Japan had paid $600,000 compensation to her fleet soon after the 1911 Treaty, Audette responded: "That was perhaps due also to the fact that the claims were more reasonable." The Japanese settlement was based on a valuation of $70 a ton, half the amount claimed by the Victoria Sealing Company.

The Commission began its last session in Victoria on February 8, 1915, when some late claims were heard and counsel summed up their arguments. Curran said the $200,000 advance paid to Canada by the U.S. should be restricted to sealers put out of business by the 1911 Treaty, and this did not include the Sealing Company. "This Company is not entitled to anything," he said. There was no provision in the 1893 regulations for compensation, Curran said, and the Company was formed long afterwards. It had halted all sealing operations by 1911. Curran pointed out that such men as Lieutenant-Governor T. W. Patterson, C.P.R. Superintendent J. W. Troup, and financier J. A. Mara owned Company shares in 1913 as a speculative investment, not as sealers.

Curran said the Company's argument that it could not find men to take out the schooners was "weak." Many witnesses had come forward to say they tried to get work with the Company but were turned down. The independent schooners had no trouble getting crews, Curran noted. He praised the owner-operators of the *Jessie, Pescawha, Thomas F. Bayard, Umbrina* and *Eva Marie* for taking risks and continuing to seal. "They did more for the sealing industry," he said, "than those who left their vessels idle." The Company's refusal to sell or charter its vessels in the years between 1900 and 1911 was detrimental to both the industry and public policy in general. "They brought upon themselves disaster."

Instead of building up capital, Curran said, the directors had put any profits into their pockets by paying dividends. "Which is like wanting to eat their cake and keep it too," Audette interjected. Curran said $116,000 had been paid in dividends in a three-year period despite the Company's claim that the industry was in a "desperate financial condition." The year after dividends totalling $33,458 had been paid, the Company abandoned all its sealing operations. Tupper later conceded the dividends had not been warranted. There had never been a profitable season if depreciation and other costs were taken into account.

Curran rejected the Company's contention that the Paris regulations were aimed at enhancing the monopoly of the U.S. on the Pribilofs. They were drawn up with the object of preserving the herd, he said. In 1897 the U.S. had shown its good faith by banning its own nationals from pelagic sealing.

Audette concurred with Curran's assessment, even though he conceded that if the Sealing Company had not remained in existence Canada would not have come out so well in the 1911 Treaty. He did not believe, however, that the Company "was doing anything but protecting its own interests." The Company was organized and carried on its business in such a way that it could not succeed. Because the Company failed did not mean it should be compensated, Audette concluded.

The last day of the Commission's hearings — its 120th — was February 20, 1915. The stenographic record of the proceedings comprises 3,300,000 words and 11,000 typewritten pages.

Audette's report was presented to Fisheries Minister Raymond Prefontaine in February, 1916. There was nothing for the Sealing Company and little for anybody else. The awards totalled $60,663, less than a third of the $200,000 advance which the industry had thought would be the minimum distributed. (During the hearings Tupper had expressed the hope that "for no reason will your Lordship endeavour to keep the amount under the amount in hand.") The amount also fell considerably short of the total of the 1,605 claims, which was $9,113,562.59.

Audette gave no reason in his report for rejecting the Company's claim *in toto*, but had made his feelings known in comments during the hearings and in his private notebooks.[3] The directors had formed the Company with their eyes open in the face of the 1893 regulations. It was a combine of mortgage-holders for the purpose of speculating. A notebook entry summed up Audette's attitude toward the Company's policy: "What is the use of having 100 horses if you keep them in your stable and do not allow them to earn anything for you?"

The report was brief, only 62 pages. Audette gave no reasons for rejecting individual claims. Audette defended the 1893 regulations, saying they had kept the herd alive and maintained pelagic sealing up to 1911. "The sealers, in their blindness, actuated by a desire of temporary gain, would have killed the goose that laid the golden eggs but for the regulations."[4]

Britain's role in the Paris proceedings was defended by Audette. Tupper had argued that London was motivated more by a desire to maintain friendly relations with the U.S. than a concern with the merits of the case. But Audette said Britain had been "animated by a high sense of justice and earnest desire of conciliation." A nation can renounce some of its rights in open waters for the general good, he said. As for the Japanese, "who can find fault with (them) coming to our coast when the Canadian sealers had gone over to their country and had exterminated their seals?"

Audette concluded: "One fails to see why the responsible regulation of an industry in the public interest should be regarded as entitling anyone to compensation." None of the sealers had a legal claim, he said, and were simply appealing to the benevolence of the state. "I am unable to find that the sealers were in any manner injured and damaged by the regulations that would entitle them to compensation."

For the few men sealing in 1910 and 1911 who were affected by the Treaty, Audette approved refunding their invested capital and reimbursement for one year's wages or profits. An owner was allowed to recover the value of his vessel and retain her. Masters and hunters recovered the amount of their previous year's returns. Crewmen, boat steerers and pullers on a lay and seamen on wages got 70 percent of their previous year's earnings. Cooks were not compensated because their vocation was not interfered with by the Treaty.

The awards included $9,000 to the owners of the *Pescawba*, the largest single amount; $7,000 to the *Thomas F. Bayard*; $6,000 to the *Jessie*; and $5,000 to the *Lady Mine*. Some 139 individuals received a total of $33,916, including Captain Hans Blakstad, $1,431; Captain Berton M. Balcom, $1,200; hunter Melville Collinson, $1,150; and Captain George Heater, $1,100.

One hundred Indians received a total of $15,240. The largest single award was $230. The money was distributed by Ditchburn on a two-week trip by launch out of Alberni in May of 1917.

"The Indian is (in) an exceedingly happy position," Audette declared, "he is the least hurt of all." Under the Treaty the natives were "especially well treated and protected." The Indian was now able to carry out "his regular and natural avocation to seal off the coast, as he, his father and forefather did before him." Audette noted, however, that after bad experiences in hunting with whites, many Indians shunned sealing and looked elsewhere for work. He did not mention the fact that the seals were far less plentiful offshore than they had been before the schooners entered the trade.

Claims rejected included those of Charles Spring, because he had sought damages sustained before 1894, and Victor Jacobson, who Audette said in his notebook should have switched to another line of work, presumably ship carpentry. Sailmaker Frederick John Jeune was turned down in his claim for $45,000 in lost business. Bella Bella native entrepreneur Fred Carpenter also lost his bid for compensation.

Audette's report was received in Victoria with anger and dismay. The *Times* said it was an "outrage." The Commissioner must have been "instructed" by the Government to confine his award within a fixed, insignificant amount rather than dealing with the merits of the various claims, the newspaper said. It was his duty to distribute at least the $200,000 advance payment from the U.S. The *Times* did concede, however, that many claims had been "extravagant."

While expressing "profound disappointment" in the report, the *Colonist* for a change was more restrained. It said the Liberal *Times* had gone too far in questioning Audette's integrity and was guilty of spreading "venom" because the Commission had been appointed by a Conservative Government. "Political spleen overshadows its judgement," the *Colonist* self-righteously observed. It added, however, that Audette had "misconceived" the question he had been appointed to adjudicate and it was now up to Parliament to set matters right.

Tupper was confident that Parliament would reject Audette's findings. "It certainly will if it is prompted by considerations of justice and fair play," he said in a newspaper interview. Tupper said Audette could have saved a lot of time and money if he had laid down the ground rules at the start of the hearing.

It was apparent, however, that Audette had gone into the hearings with an open mind and had reached his decision on the basis of the testimony he had heard.

In his report the Commissioner noted that some witnesses had claimed the sealers should share in the revenue from the Treaty, but he maintained it was general revenue — a "national fund" — not ear-marked for sealers. He asked why the rest of Canada should pay for the sealers' claims. This attitude, held to by succeeding governments in Ottawa, was a source of bitter resentment in the Victoria sealing community for years to come.

Epilogue

On March 2, 1923, Governor-General Byng wrote to the British ambassador in Washington, Sir Auckland C. Geddes: "I have the honour to inform Your Excellency that the master of the halibut fishing vessel *Thelma I*, registered at the port of Prince Rupert, reported to the Collector of Customs and Excise at that port that he caught a fur seal on one of his halibut trawls while fishing on the banks south of Cape Fairweather, Alaska. The seal was apparently following the herring bait on the trawl as it was hooked in the lower jaw and was dead when it was hauled on board the *Thelma I*. This skin has been confiscated and is being shipped to Fouke Fur Company of St. Louis to be dressed and sold for the credit of the Canadian Government."

This unusual communication, circulated at the highest levels of government as so much of the fur seal dispute correspondence had been in earlier days, points up how complete was the change brought about by the 1911 Treaty. Where once Britain had defended the wanton slaughter of hundreds of thousands of seals by its Canadian subjects, now there was an accounting of the accidental death of a single animal.

Unlike the regulations that followed the Paris Arbitration in 1893, the 1911 pact truly was a victory for the seals. When the treaty was signed it was estimated the Pribilof population had dropped to 123,000. By 1924 this figure had risen to 697,158 and by 1931 to over 1,000,000. By 1946 the herd was estimated to number 3,000,000. When G. Clifford Carl of the British Columbia Provincial Museum visited the Pribilofs in 1946 he praised the fur seal harvest as "an outstanding example of successful wildlife management." The U.S. had proved its contention that rational exploitation of an animal population need not be incompatible with its conservation.

During the years 1916-1931 the U.S. Government was able to take 437,376 skins worth $6,000,000 in sales and a $2,000,000 profit. Canada, under its share of the catch, was paid $1,000,000. By 1941 Canada had been paid a total of $1,700,000 in cash and furs. Prices for skins increased dramatically, reaching a peak of $116 for a prime skin in 1919. The market declined during the 1920s as imitation seal fur made its appearance, and hit bottom during the Depression.

The Indians returned to offshore sealing as the herd increased. In July, 1920, Tofino storekeeper James Sloan bought 428 skins from Clayoquot hunters for $15,000. In 1924 Sloan took in 1,700 skins from the Indians and the following year almost 3,000.

The 15-year Treaty was renewed in 1926, with Canada representing herself for the first time. Starting in 1928 the U.S. Treasury cheques which had been paid to Britain for transfer to Canada began going directly to Ottawa. In 1933 the payments were made in untreated skins at Seattle instead of cash from a share of the St. Louis fur auction. Every fifth barrel of furs was turned over to Canadian representatives at dockside in a random choice system. The skins were sent to London for dyeing until 1937, when a fur treatment plant was established in Montreal.

There was little joy in Victoria over these developments, however. In the face of repeated demands for compensation or a share of the Treaty revenue, Ottawa finally closed the door on B.C. in 1931. Prime Minister R. B. Bennett told the province there was no need for another commission to investigate the sealers' claims. The same stand had been taken earlier by Prime Minister Mackenzie King after he had met with shareholders of the Sealing Company in Victoria.

In 1917, Opposition Leader Sir Wilfrid Laurier told Parliament he had read Audette's report carefully and "it seems to me that he takes a narrow view of the matter. He seems to have approached it more or less from the point of view of narrow justice . . . rather than good conscience and equity." Laurier said he had been in office when the 1911 Treaty was being negotiated "and I thought then that when we received money as compensation, the first men to be paid out of that money ought to be those whose business and livelihood had been destroyed, and whose money had become worthless." He urged the Sealing Company to keep pressing Ottawa because "you have justice on your side." The present Conservative government under Robert Borden should reconsider the matter, Laurier said. His remarks smacked of political expediency. When Laurier had been in office he had done little to assist the sealers.

For the first time, the federal Department of Fisheries conceded in its reports that pelagic sealing had been wasteful and that "by far the greater proportion of kills consisted of females." Commercial fishermen began to complain that the restored fur herd was depleting salmon stocks, but studies in 1935 by Department biologists showed that seals consumed few salmon.

In Victoria, the die-hards kept up their futile campaign for compensation as the Sealing Company collapsed around them. Charles Tupper continued to fuel their anger by telling Company director Frank Adams that Audette's findings were "inexplicable" and "a scandal on the administration of justice." In 1912 the Harbour Master had brought a second action against the Company's anchored schooners, this time for blocking passage up the Gorge waterway at Point Ellice. They were duly towed to Esquimalt. In 1919 there was a falling out of the principals when Joe Boscowitz launched a lawsuit against the Company. The shareholders were called upon to contribute to the Company's defence costs on the basis of three cents a share. They lost the case but paid the $548 legal bill, with R. P. Rithet putting up the largest share, $47. Boscowitz obtained a court order appointing the Colonial Trust Company as receiver, despite the fact that all the other shareholders had asked for liquidation.

The Company dragged on under receivership until April 17, 1925, when the directors named Walter E. Adams Receiver and Manager "with special power to adjust and settle" the outstanding claim for compensation. The agreement was signed by Rithet Consolidated, Sprott and Reuben Balcom, Turpel, Bechtel, and Boscowitz, who now had made peace with the others. The Registrar of Companies wrote Adams in 1931 pointing out that the Company had issued its last annual report in 1925 and was liable to be struck from the register.

D'Arcy B. Plunkett, the M.P. for Victoria, told the House of Commons in 1934: "Daily during the session and at the end of every session when I go home to Victoria I have from one to a dozen requests made to me by private individuals, committees and deputations, to bring before this government the Pelagic Sealing Treaty with a view to having some better arrangements made." Plunkett said the long dispute reminded him of the case of Jarndyce versus Jarndyce in Charles Dickens' *Bleak House*: "They are still hoping something will be done." As late as November 16, 1947, a *Colonist* headline proclaimed: "Descendants of Victoria Sealing Fleet Pioneers Still Hope for Settlement of Due Compensation."

Japanese fishermen had also been agitating about the alleged damage caused by the rejuvenated fur seal herd on their industry, and in 1940 Tokyo announced its intention to abrogate the 1911 Treaty. That action was taken in October, 1941, just two months before launching war on the U.S. The Aleuts were evacuated from the Pribilofs during the war, but in 1943 sealing was resumed under a wartime blackout and 117,184 pelts taken, the largest land kill on the islands since 1868. From 1942 to 1957 the Pribilof herd was protected by a provisional agreement between Canada and the U.S. which gave Canada 20 percent of the harvest.

In the early 1950s biologists noted an increase in pup mortality at sea and decided the Pribilof herd had grown to the limit of available food resources. They therefore started to thin it out by harvesting females, which until then had been taboo. An average of 34,000 females were killed in the eight years between 1955 and 1963. The policy had continued even after a dramatic decline of male seals was observed in 1959. The killing of females is now generally agreed to have been a blunder. From that time there has been a slow decline in the size of the herd, for which a variety of causes have been advanced. One is the increasing use of huge trawl nets which, after breaking loose from their mother ships, drift around in the sea for years as death traps for seals and many other marine creatures.

In February of 1957 a new North Pacific Fur Seal Convention similar to the 1911 Treaty was concluded by the U.S., Canada, Russia and Japan. This pact established a Fur Seal Commission to co-ordinate research and management of the herd. (Japan lost Robben Reef to Russia during the Second World War and the U.S.S.R. now controlled all the Asian coast rookeries.)

In 1973, the island of St. George was set aside as a research reserve, enabling scientists to compare the population dynamics of St. Paul and St. George. Tagging, photographic surveys and other research provided data of a quality not available before. The killing method remained virtually the same as it had been for two centuries. Animal welfare groups such as the National Audubon Society and the National Wildlife Federation approved the system as highly efficient and humane. Only the more extreme organizations objected.

The demand for furs has steadily declined, however, partly the result of synthetic imitations, but largely due to highly-publicized campaigns such as that mounted against the St. Lawrence seal pup harvest. The last recorded pelagic seal catch on the west coast was in 1954. The last Pribilof harvest took place in 1984, after the U.S. Congress, yielding to pressure from conservationist groups, refused to renew the international treaty.

Apart from a few Aleuts and increasing numbers of tourists, the 800,000 remaining fur seals have the Islands to themselves for the first time since Gerassim Pribilof landed 200 years ago.

NOTES

CHAPTER ONE

[1] Alexander, A. B. "Report of Fur Seal Investigations 1896-97." Treasury Department. In Jordan Report.

[2] Jones, Chief Charles, with Stephen Bosustow. *Queesto*. Theytus. 1981.

[3] Spring, Charles. Unpublished Mss. Public Archives of B.C. (PABC).

[4] William Duncan papers. Microfilm. National Archives of Canada. (NAC).

[5] Nicholson, George. *Vancouver Island's West Coast, 1762-1962*. Victoria. 1962.

[6] *Mission to Nootka, 1874-1900*, edited by Charles Lillard. Gray's Publishing. 1977.

[7] Duff, Wilson. "Thoughts on the Nootka Canoe." B.C. Provincial Museum pamphlet. 1965.

[8] Wright, E. D., editor. *Lewis & Dryden's Marine History of the Pacific Northwest*. Superior Publishing Co. reprint. Seattle. 1967.

[9] Logbook of the Cygnet, 1874-1876. Santa Barbara Historical Society Museum.

[10] Snow, Harold J. *In Forbidden Seas*. London. 1910.

CHAPTER TWO

[1] Macy, Suzanne Kay. "Mother-pup Interactions in the Northern Fur Seal." Unpublished Ph.D. thesis. University of Washington. 1982.

[2] Van Nostrand, Jeanne. "The Seals are About Gone..." *American Heritage*. June, 1963. Vol. 14, No. 4.

[3] Gentry, Roger L. "Set In Their Ways: Survival Formula of the Northern Fur Seal." *Oceans*, May-June, 1980.

[4] Burroughs, John. "A Summer Holiday in Bering Sea." *Century Magazine*. August, 1900.

[5] Allis, Watson Colt. *Saturday Evening Post*, March 7, 1936.

[6] Roger Gentry. National Marine Mammal Laboratory. Seattle. Interview with author.

[7] Michael A. Bigg, Pacific Biological Station, Nanaimo, B.C. Interview with author.

[8] "Solid Men of Boston in the Northwest." Bancroft Library Manuscript. Microfilm. PABC.

[9] Scheffer, Victor. *The Year of the Seal*. Scribner's. 1970.

[10] Sloss, Frank H. and Pierce, Richard A. "The Hutchinson, Kohl Story." *Pacific Northwest Quarterly*. January, 1971.

[11] Andrews, Clarence L. *Sitka*. Caxton. 1945.

[12] Rome, David. *The First Two Years: A Record of the Jewish Pioneers on Canada's Pacific Coast 1858-1860*. Caiserman. Montreal. 1942.

[13] Jordan, David Starr. *The Fur Seals and Fur-Seal Islands of the North Pacific Ocean, 1893-1895*. U.S. Treasury Department. Government Printing Office. 1896.

CHAPTER THREE

[1] Townsend, Charles H. *Condition of Seal Life on the Rookeries of the Pribilof Islands, 1893-1895*. U.S. Senate. 1895.

[2] Report of the Committee on Merchant Marine and Fisheries of the House of Representatives. Government Printing Office. Washington. 1889.

[3] Gruening, Ernest. *The State of Alaska*. Random House. 1954.

[4] Martin, Fredericka. *the Hunting of the Silver Fleece*. Greenberg. New York. 1946.

[5] Sherwood, Morgan B. *The Exploration of Alaska, 1865-1900*. Yale University Press. 1965.

[6] Shalkop, Robert, L. Biographical sketch in catalogue for an exhibition of Elliott artworks at the Anchorage Historical and Fine Arts Museum in 1982.

[7] Wishart, Andrew. *The Bering Sea Question and the Award*. Edinburgh. 1893. PABC.

[8] Scheffer, Victor. *The Stopped the Press on His Book*. Pacific Discovery: California Academy of Sciences. Vol. 30. 1977.

9 Nichols, Jeanette Paddock. *Alaska: A History*. Russell, 1963.

10 Sherwood.

11 Scheffer.

12 U.S. Consul Reports. Diplomatic Dispatches. U.S. National Archives Microfilm Reel T-130. PABC.

13 Tansill, Charles C. *The Foreign Policy of Thomas F. Bayard, 1885-1897*. Fordham University Press. New York. 1940.

14 Foster, John, Watson. *Diplomatic Memoirs*. 2 Vols. Houghton Mifflin. 1910.

CHAPTER FOUR

1 Tansill.

2 Sackville-West, V. *Pepita*. Doubleday. 1937.

3 Wishart.

4 Secret Correspondence, Foreign Office and Colonial Office. Microfilm. PABC.

5 Ewart, John Skirving. *The Kingdom Papers*. Ottawa. 1913.

6 Williams, Gerald O. *The Bering Sea Fur Seal Dispute, 1885-1911: A Monograph on the Maritime History of Alaska. 1984.*

7 Tyler, Alice Felt. *The Foreign Policy of James G. Blaine*. Archon. 1965.

8 Rosen, Baron Roman Romanovitch. *Forty Years of Diplomacy*. 2 Vols.

CHAPTER FIVE

1 The largest number of vessels in the fleet, 65, were built in the San Francisco Bay area. Forty-nine schooners were built in Washington and 32 in British Columbia. These statistics were compiled by R. N. D'Armond, city editor of the Daily Alaskan Fishing News of Ketchikan for a series of articles in the magazine Marine Digest.

2 Lewis & Dryden.

3 Letters of Captain R. E. McKeil. PABC.

4 *A Sealer's Journal, Or a Cruise of the Schooner* Umbrina, by Wiliam George. Victoria. 1895. PABC.

5 B. A. McKelvie. "Saga of Sealing." Unpublished manuscript. PABC.

6 J. C. Voss. *The Venturesome Voyages of Captain Voss*, reprint. Sidney: Gray's, 1976.

7 Report of Indian Commissioner Peter O'Reilly to Superintendent-General of Indian Affairs in Ottawa. March 5, 1890. RG10, Vol. 1277, NAC.

8 Secret Correspondence. PABC.

9 Interview with Captain Otto Buckholz. H. L. Cadieux Collection, Vancouver City Archives.

10 Logbook of Schooner *Onward*, 1886. PABC.

11 Diary of Stanley Henderson aboard Schooner *Vancouver Belle* in 1891. PABC.

12 Diary of H. D. Copp on schooner *Vancouver Belle*, 1891. Special Collections, University of British Columbia Library.

CHAPTER SIX

1 Grenville, J. A. S. *Lord Salisbury and Foreign Policy: The Close of the Nineteenth Century*. Athlone Press, 1964.

2 Cecil, Lady Gwendolen. *Life of Robert Marquis of Salisbury*. 4 Vols. Hodder and Stoughton, 1921-32.

3 Mowat, R. B. *The Life of Lord Pauncefote*. Houghton Mifflin, 1929.

4 Cecil.

5 Muzzey, David Saville. *James G. Blaine: A Political Idol of Other Days*. Dodd Mead, 1962.

CHAPTER SEVEN

[1] Copp Diary.

[2] Rome.

CHAPTER EIGHT

[1] Williams, Gerald.

[2] Falk, Edwin A. *Fighting Bob Evans.* Libraries Press reprint. New York, 1969.

[3] Evans, Robley D. *A Sailor's Log: Recollections of 40 Years of Naval Life.* 1901.

[4] U.S. Consul Reports.

[5] Stevenson, Rober L. *In the South Seas: A Footnote to History.* Scribner's. New York, 1918.

CHAPTER NINE

[1] Devine, Michael J. *John W. Foster: Politics and Diplomacy in the Imperial Era 1873-1917.* Ohio University Press, 1981.

[2] Fur Seal Arbitration: Proceedings of the Tribunal of Arbitration convened at Paris, 1893. 16 vols. U.S. Government Printing Office, 1895.

[3] Foster. *Memoirs.*

[4] Mowat, R. B. *The Diplomatic Relations of Great Britain and the United States.* London, 1925.

[5] O'Brien, R. Barry. *The Life of Lord Russell of Killowen.* Green, 1901.

[6] *Ibid.*

[7] Foster.

[8] Williams, William. "Reminiscences of the Bering Sea Arbitration." *The American Journal of International Law.* Vol. 37. October, 1943.

[9] Foster.

[9] Foster.

[10] Tansill, Charles Callan. *Canadian-American Relations, 1875-1911.*

[11] *Williams, William.*

[12] *Ibid.*

[13] Moore, John Bassett. *A Digest of International Law.* Vol. 1, U.S. Government Printing Office, 1906.

[14] Williams, William.

[15] Gresham, Matilda. *The Life of Walter Quintin Gresham, 1832-1895.* Rand McNally, 1919.

[16] Piggot, F. J. Letter to the Times of London. Bound dispatch. University of B.C. Library, Special Collections.

[17] Jordan. *The Days of a Man.* World Book Co. 2 Vols.

[18] Mowat, R. B. *The Diplomatic Relations of Great Britain and the United States.* London, 1925.

CHAPTER TEN

[1] London, Charmian. *The Book of Jack London.* Vol. 1. The Century Co., New York, 1921.

[2] Letter. Huntington Library, San Marino, California. File JL 12561.

[3] Thompson, Stuart. Unpublished Mss. PABC.

[4] Perry, John. *Jack London: An American Myth.* Nelson-Hall. Chicago, 1981.

[5] Ticket. PABC.

[6] Thompson.

[7] Department of Fisheries. Microfilm. T-3990. NAC.

CHAPTER ELEVEN

[1] Whitner, Robert L. "Makah Commercial Sealing, 1860-1897." Unpublished paper prepared for the Fourth North American Fur Trade Conference, 1981.

[2] Lewis and Dryden.

[3] McGlinn, John P. Report. U.S. Bureau of Indian Affairs, 1893.

[4] Doig, Ivan. *Winter Brothers: A Season at the Edge of America.* Harcourt Brace Jovanovich. New York, 1980.

[5] Department of Marine and Fisheries, Ottawa. Microfilm reel No. T-1385. NAC.

[6] Department of Indian Affairs. "Black Series" microfilm. RG 10. PABC.

[7] Swartout, Melvyn. Unpublished Mss. PABC.

CHAPTER TWELVE

[1] Bering Sea Claims Commission, Records, Argument. 4 Vols. PABC.

[2] Munsie, William. Letterbook. PABC.

[3] Sealing Company Records. PABC.

CHAPTER THIRTEEN

[1] Black Series.

[2] Department of Marine and Fisheries. RG 24. Microfilm Reel No. 3218. NAC.

[3] Sealing Company Records. Vol. 3. PABC.

[4] U.S. Consul Reports.

CHAPTER FOURTEEN

[1] Seal Islands of Alaska, 1904-1911. Serial 6113, Doc. 93, 62nd congress. Government papers filed by Charles Nagel, Secretary of Commerce and Labor.

[2] Voss.

[3] Seal Islands.

[4] Scheffer, Victor B., Fiscus, Clifford H., and Todd, Ethel I. "History of Scientific Study and Management of the Alaskan Fur Seal, 1786-1964." National Ocean and Atmospheric Administration Report NMFS SSTF-780. March, 1984.

[5] Munsie Letterbook.

[6] *Seal Islands of Alaska.*

[7] U.S. Department of State Files, 1906-1910. Microfilm No. 33.

[8] *Ibid.*

[9] Hornaday, William T. *Thirty Years War For Wild Life.* 1931.

[10] Fisher, H. A. L. *James Bryce.* Macmillan, 1927.

[11] Laurier Correspondence. Microfilm. PABC.

CHAPTER FIFTEEN

[1] Black Series.

[2] Commission to Investigate Into and Report Upon Claims of Certain Pelagic Sealers, 1913-1915. Transcript of Hearings. 7 Vols. RG 33/107. NAC.

[3] *Ibid.*

[4] Commissioner's Report to House of Commons, February 7, 1916. Sessional Paper No. 79. PABC.

242

Acknowledgements

The number of people who have helped in one way or another to bring this book about cannot all be mentioned here, but my thanks go out to all who have assisted in the gathering of research or photographs. I would like to single out for their special help and encouragement marine biologists Michael Bigg of the Pacific Biological Station at Nanaimo and Roger Gentry of the National Marine Mammal Laboratory in Seattle. Both took time from busy schedules to share some of their expert knowledge of the habits of that fascinating animal, the northern fur seal. Richard Inglis of the Royal British Columbia Museum provided valuable leads on the role in the sealing story of the Nuu-chah-nulth Indians of the west coast of Vancouver Island. Len McCann of the Vancouver Maritime Museum and Brian Clausen of the Maritime Museum of B.C. in Victoria both hunted out useful material. Family photographs were graciously loaned by George Heater of Victoria and Eileen Odowichuk of Campbell River. I am indebted to Charles Lillard once again for invaluable editorial suggestions, and to Joan Goddard for her expertise in checking over the manuscript and catching errors. Most of all I want to thank Maurice Chadwick, not only for his wonderful illustrations of the sealing schooners, but for his unfailing cheerfulness and patience in helping a landlubber cope with the arcane language of seafaring men. Maurice would also like to add his thanks to George Heater for the use of the family album, as well as the staff of the Provincial Archives for help in tracking down photographs of the schooners to provide detail for his paintings. We would both like to thank the owners of some of the original works for their courtesy in connection with the reproductions here.

Sources

Footnotes in the text have been deliberately kept to a minimum. I am in sympathy with British author Duff Cooper, biographer of Talleyrand, who complained that asterisks, numerals, footnotes and so on "tease the eye and disfigure the page." So he dispensed with them, as did many other distinguished British historians of a few decades ago before the blizzard of typographical numerology set in. And so I timidly follow in their path. For the scholar who wishes to delve more deeply into the research materials I have employed, the following bibliography should provide more than enough leads.

Bibliography

BOOKS

Andrews, Clarence L. *Sitka.* Caxton. 1945.

Arima. E. Y. *The West Coast [Nootka] People.* B.C. Provincial Museum. 1983.

Bancroft, Hubert H. *History of Alaska, 1730-1885.* San Francisco. 1886.

Berkh, V. *A Chronological History of the Discovery of the Aleutian Islands.* 1823. Reprinted by The Limestone Press, Kingston, Ont. 1974.

Bevins, Samuel Flagg, ed. *The American Secretaries of State and Their Diplomacy.* Pageant Books. New York. 1958.

Bonner, W. Nigel. *Seals and Man: A Study of Interactions.* University of Washington Press. Seattle. 1982.

Brown, Robert Craig. *Canada's National Policy, 1883-1900.* Princeton University Press. 1964.

Busch, Briton Cooper. *The War Against the Seals: A History of the North American Seal Fishery*. McGill-Queen's University Press. 1985.

Callahan, James Morton. *American Foreign Policy in Canadian Relations*. Macmillan. New York. 1937.

Campbell, Charles S. *Anglo-American Understanding, 1898-1903*. Johns Hopkins Press. Baltimore. 1957.

Cecil, Lady Gwendolen. *Life of Robert, Marquis of Salisbury*. Hodder and Stoughton. 4 Vols. 1921-32.

Devine, Michael J. *John W. Foster: Politics and Diplomacy in the Imperial Era 1873-1917*. Ohio University Press. 1981.

Doig, Ivan. *Winter Brothers: A Season at the Edge of America*. Harcourt Brace Jovanovich. New York. 1980.

Elliott, Henry W. *The Seal-Islands of Alaska*. 1881. Limestone Press reprint. Kingston, Ont. 1976.

Evans, Robley D. *A Sailor's Log: Recollections of 40 Years of Naval Life*. 1901.

Ewart, John Skirving. *The Kingdom Papers*. Ottawa. 1913.

Falk, Edwin A. *Fighting Bob Evans*. New York. Libraries Press reprint. New York. 1969.

Fisher, H. A. L. *James Bryce*. Macmillan. 1927.

Foster, John. W. *Diplomatic Memoirs*. 2 Vols. Houghton Mifflin. 1910.

Gentry, Roger L., and Kooyman, Gerald L. *Fur Seals: Maternal Strategies on Land and at Sea*. Princeton University Press. 1986.

Glanz, Rudolph. *The Jews of California*. New York. 1960.

———. *The Jews in American Alaska, 1867-1880*. 1953.

Grenville, J. A. S. *Lord Salisbury and Foreign Policy: The Close of the Nineteenth Century*. Athlone Press. 1964.

Gresham, Matilda. *The Life of Walter Quintin Gresham 1832-1895*. Rand McNally. 1919.

Gruening, Ernest. *The State of Alaska*. Random House. 1954.

Hornaday, William T. *Thirty Years War for Wild Life*. 1931. Arno reprint. New York. 1970.

Howay, F. W., Sage, W. N., Angus H. F. *British Columbia and the United States: The North Pacific Slope from Fur Trade to Aviation*. Ryerson. 1942.

Hulley, Clarence C. *Alaska, 1741-1953*. Portland. 1953.

Hunt, William R. *Arctic Passage*. Scribner's. 1975.

Hutchison, Isobel Wylie. *The Aleutian Islands*. London. 1937.

Jacobsen, Johan Adrian. Translated from the German text of Adrian Woldt by Erna Gunther. *Alaskan Voyage 1881-1883: An Expedition to the Northwest Coast of America*. The University of Chicago Press. 1977.

Johnston, S. P., ed. *History of the Alaska Commercial Company*. San Francisco. 1940.

Jones, Chief Charles, with Stephen Bosustow. *Queesto: Pacheenaht Chief by Birthright*. Theytus. 1981.

Jordan, David Starr. *The Days of a Man*. World Book Co. 1922.

Jupp, Ursula, ed. *Home Port Victoria.* Victoria. 1967.

Kennedy, A. C. *Salisbury, 1830-1903: Portrait of a Statesman.* London. 1953.

Kitchener, L. D. *Flag Over the North.* Superior Publishing Co. Seattle. 1954.

Lillard, Charles, ed. *Mission to Nootka, 1874-1900.* Gray's Publishing. Sidney, B.C. 1977.

London, Charmian. *The Book of Jack London.* 2 Vols. The Century Company. New York. 1921.

London, Jack. *The Sea Wolf.* Heritage Press reprint. New York. 1961.

MacAskie, Ian. *The Long Beaches: A Voyage in Search of the North Pacific Fur Seal.* Sono Nis Press. Victoria. 1979.

McCurdy, James G. *By Juan de Fuca's Strait.* Reprint. Portland. 1937.

Madsden, Charles. *Arctic Trader.* Dodd, Mead. 1957.

Martin, Fredericka. *The Hunting of the Silver Fleece: Epic of the Fur Seal.* Greenberg. New York. 1946.

Moore, John Bassett. *A Digest of International Law.* Vol. 1. U.S. Government Printing Office. 1906.

Mowat, R. B. *The Diplomatic Relations of Great Britain and the United States.* London. 1925.

———. *The Life of Lord Pauncefote.* Houghton Mifflin. 1929.

Muzzey, David Saville. *James G. Blaine: A Political Idol of Other Days.* Dodd Mead. 1934.

Nicholson, George. *Vancouver Island's West Coast, 1762-1962.* Victoria. 1962.

Nichols, Jeanette Paddock. *Alaska: A History.* Russell, 1963.

O'Brien, R. Barry. *The Life of Lord Russell of Killowen.* Green. 1901.

Perry, John. *Jack London: An American Myth.* Nelson-Hall. Chicago. 1981.

Rogers, Fred. *Shipwrecks of British Columbia.* J. J. Douglas. 1973.

Rome, David. *The First Two Years: A Record of the Jewish Pioneers on Canada's Pacific Coast 1858-1860.* Caiserman. Montreal. 1942.

Rosen, Baron Roman Romanovich. *Forty Years of Diplomacy.* 2 Vols.

Rydell, Carl. *Adventures of Carl Rydell: The Autobiography of a Seafaring Man.* Edward Arnold. London. 1924.

Sackville-West, V. *Pepita.* Doubleday. 1937.

Scheffer, Victor B. *The Year of the Seal.* Scribner's. 1970.

Shepard, Isabel S. *The Cruise of the U.S. Steamer Rush in the Bering Sea, Summer of 1889.* Bancroft Co. San Francisco.

Sherwood, Morgan B. *The Exploration of Alaska, 1865-1900.* Yale University Press. 1965.

———, ed. *Alaska and Its History.* University of Washington Press. 1967.

Shiels, Archie W. *The Purchase of Alaska.* University of Alaska Press. 1967.

Sinclair, Andrew. *Jack: A Biography of Jack London.* Harper & Row. New York. 1977.

Snow, Harold J. *In Forbidden Seas: Recollections of Sea-Otter Hunting in the Kurils.* Edward Arnold. London. 1910.

Stevenson, Robert L. *In The South Seas: A Footnote to History.* Scribner's. New York. 1918.

Swan, James G. *The Indians of Cape Flattery.* Smithsonian. 1869. Shorey Book Store reprint. Seattle. 1964.

Tansill, Charles Callan. *The Foreign Policy of Thomas F. Bayard, 1885-1897.* Fordham University Press. New York. 1940.

———. *Canadian-American Relations, 1875-1911.* Yale University Press. New York. 1943.

Teichmann, Emil. *A Journey to Alaska in the Year 1868.* London. 1925.

Tikhmenev, P. A. *A History of the Russian-American Company.* 1861. University of Washington. 1978.

Tomasaveich, Jozo. *International Agreements on Conservation of Marine Resources.* Stanford University. 1943.

Tyler, Alice Felt. *The Foreign Policy of James G. Blaine.* Archon. 1965.

Van Deusen, Glyndon G. *William Henry Seward.* Oxford. 1957.

Voss, J. C. *The Venturesome Voyages of Captain Voss.* Gray's Publishing. Sidney, B.C. 1976.

Watson, Charles N., Jr. *The Novels of Jack London: A Reappraisal.* University of Wisconsin Press. 1982.

Williams, Gerald O. *The Bering Sea Fur Seal Dispute, 1885-1911.* Alaska Maritime Publications. Eugene, Oregon. 1984.

Wright, E. D., ed. *Lewis & Dryden's Marine History of the Pacific Northwest.* Reprint. Superior Publishing Co. Seattle. 1967.

ARTICLES IN JOURNALS AND MAGAZINES

Allis, Watson Colt. *Saturday Evening Post*, March 7, 1936.

Angell, James B. "American Rights in Bering Sea." *The Forum.* November, 1889.

Bailey, Thomas A. "The North Pacific Sealing Convention of 1911." *Pacific Historical Review.* March, 1935.

Brown, J. Stanley. "Fur Seals and the Bering Sea Arbitration." *Journal of American Geographical Society.* Vol. 26. 1894.

Burroughs, John. "A Summer Holiday in Bering Sea." *Century Magazine.* August, 1900.

Butler, D. J. "A Sealing Voyage on the Pacific." *Canadian Merchant Service Guild Magazine.*

Buzanski, P. M. "Alaska and Nineteenth Century American Diplomacy." *Journal of the West.* Vol. 6, No. 3. 1967.

Campbell Charles S., Jr. "The Anglo-American Crisis in the Bering Sea, 1890-1891." *Mississippi Valley Historical Review.* December, 1961.

————. "The Bering Sea Settlements of 1892." *Pacific Historical Review.* Vol. 32, No. 4. 1963.

Cantwell, J. C. "Review of Fur-Seal Controversy." *The Californian.* 1892.

D'Armond, R. N. "The Sealing Fleet." *Marine Digest.* May 4, 1957 to February 15, 1958.

Doughty, R. W. "The Farallone and the Boston Men." *California Historical Quarterly.* Vol. 53, No. 4. 1974.

Duff, Wilson. *Thoughts on the Nootka Canoe.* Provincial Museum pamphlet. 1965. PABC.

Duncan, Bingham. "A Letter on the Fur Seal in Canadian-American Diplomacy." *Canadian Historical Review.* March, 1962.

Elliott, Henry W. "The Loot and the Ruin of the Fur-Seal Herd of Alaska." *North American Review.* 1907.

————. "The Fur Seal Millions on the Pribilof Islands." *Harper's.* May, 1874.

————. "Ten Years' Acquaintance with Alaska, 1867-1877." *Harper's.* November, 1877.

Emery, W. G. "Hunting the Fur Seal." *Outing.* March, 1898.

Ford, Corey. "Where the Sea Breaks Its Back." *Pacific Historical Review.* 1963.

Foster, John W. "Results of the Bering Sea Arbitration." *North American Review.* December, 1895.

Gay, James T. "Bering Sea Controversy: Harrison, Blaine, and Cronyism." *Alaska Journal.* Winter, 1973.

————. "Henry W. Elliott: Crusading Conservationist." *Alaska Journal.* 1973.

Gentry, Roger L. "Set In Their Ways: Survival Formula of the Northern Fur Seal." *Oceans.* May-June, 1980.

Gluek, Alvin C., Jr. "The North Pacific Fur Seal Convention." *Canadian Historical Review.* June, 1982.

Hinckley, Ted. "Rustlers of the North Pacific." *Journal of the West.* 1963.

James, Mike. *The Fisherman.* 1967.

Kushner, Howard I. "Conflict on the Northwest Coast." *Pacific Historical Review.* 1959.

Lugrin, N. De Bertrand. "Epic of the Seal Hunters." *Canadian Geographical Journal.* Vol. 4, No. 5. 1932.

Mathieson, Captain Matt. "When the Sandheads Lightship was Alive." *Canadian Merchant Service Guild Annual.* 1945.

Mendenhall, T. C. "The Bering Sea Controversy." *Popular Science Monthly.* 1897.

Mills, D. O. "Our Fur Seal Fisheries." *North American Review.* 1890.

Ogden, Adele. "Russian Sea-Otter and Seal-Hunting on the California Coast, 1803-1841." *California Historical Society Quarterly.* 1933.

Patterson, R. M. "The Beaches of Lukannon." *Blackwood's Magazine.* September, 1957.

Pierce. Richard A. "Prince D. P. Maksutov: The Last Governor of Alaska." *Journal of the West.* Vol 6, July, 1967.

———. "New Light on Ivan Petroff, Historian of Alaska." *Pacific Northwest Quarterly.* January, 1968.

Scheffer, Victor B. "They Stopped the Press on His Book." *Pacific Discovery.* Vol. 30. 1972.

———. "The Fur Seal Herd Comes of Age." *National Geographic Society.* 1952.

———. "Use of Fur Seal Carcasses." *Pacific Northwest Quarterly.* 1948.

Sloss, Frank H., and Pierce, Richard A. "The Hutchinson, Kohl Story." *Pacific Northwest Quarterly.* January, 1971.

Stanley-Brown, J. "Fur Seals and the Bering Sea Arbitration." *Journal of American Geographical Society.* 1894.

Taggart, H. F. "Sealing on St. George Island in 1868." *Pacific Historical Review.* Vol. 28, No. 4. 1959.

Tansill, Charles C. "The Fur-Seal Fisheries and the Doctrine of the Freedom of the Seas." *Annual Report of the Canadian Historical Association.* May, 1942.

Townsend, Charles H. "The Fur Seal." *Science.* October, 1911.

Tracy, B. F. "The Bering Sea Question." *North American Review.* May, 1893.

Van Nostrand, Jeanne. "The Seals Are About Gone . . ." *American Heritage.* June, 1963. Vol. 14, No. 4.

Williams, William. "Reminiscences of the Bering Sea Arbitration." *American Journal of International Law.* Vol. 37, October, 1943.

GOVERNMENT DOCUMENTS, THESES, UNPUBLISHED PAPERS, MISCELLANEOUS

Alexander, A. B. Report of Fur Seal Investigations 1896-97. Treasury Department.

———. Observations During a Cruise on the *Dora Sieward,* Aug.-Sept., 1895. U.S. Congress, House Report. 1898.

Audette, Louis Arthur. Report, Papers and Transcript of Commission to Investigate Into and Report Upon Claims of Certain Pelagic Sealers at Victoria and Halifax. 7 Vols. RG 33/107. National Archives of Canada. NAC.

———. Commissioner's Report to House of Commons, Feb. 7, 1916. Sessional Paper No. 79. PABC.

Austin, Oliver L, and Wilke, Ford, eds. Japanese Fur Sealing. U.S. Fish and Wildlife Service Report. 1950.

Bancroft Library microfilm. Solid Men of Boston in the Northwest. Public Archives of B.C. PABC.

————. Alaska Scrapbook. Public Archives of B.C. PABC.

Bering Sea Claims Commission, Records, Argument. 4 Vols. PABC.

Bigg, Michael A. Migration of North Fur Seals in the Eastern North Pacific and Eastern Bering Sea. Pacific Biological Station Report submitted to North Pacific Fur Seal Commission. April, 1982.

Buchanan, Lorna May. History of the Fur Seal Industry of the Pribilof Islands. M.A. Thesis. University of Washington. 1929.

Buckholz, Captain Otto. Interview. H. L. Cadieux Collection manuscript. Vancouver City Archives.

Copp, H. D. Diary of Voyage aboard *Vancouver Belle* to Bering Sea in 1891. University of B.C. Library, Special Collections.

Correspondence Respecting the Seizures of British Sealing Vessels by Russian Cruisers in the North Pacific Ocean. Parliament of Great Britain. 1893.

Department of Indian Affairs. "Black Series" microfilm. RG 10. PABC.

Department of Marine and Fisheries. Microfilm. RG24. Reels T-1385, T-2846, T-3146, T-3155, T-3185, T-3218, T-3990. NAC.

Duncan, William. Papers. Microfilm. *NAC.*

Fur Seal Arbitration: Proceedings of the Tribunal of Arbitration Convened at Paris. 16 vols. U.S. Government Printing Office. 1895.

George, William. A Sealer's Journal, or a Cruise on the Schooner *Umbrina.* Victoria. 1895. PABC.

Henderson, Stanley. Diary of Voyage of *Vancouver Belle* in 1891. PABC.

History of the Wrongs of Alaska. Resolutions of Anti-Monopoly Association of Pacific Coast. Pamphlet. San Francisco. 1875. PABC.

Jacobson, Victor. Papers. PABC.

Jordan, David Starr. The Fur Seals and Fur-Seal Islands of the North Pacific Ocean, 1893-1895. U.S. Treasury Department. Government Printing Office. 1898-99.

Laurier, Sir Wilfrid. Correspondence. Microfilm. PABC.

Leeson, B. W. Voyage of the Rosie Oleson. Unpublished. PABC.

Logbook of the schooner *Cygnet*, 1874-1876. Santa Barbara Historical Society Museum.

Logbook of schooners *Onward*, 1886; *Mary Taylor* 1901; *Thomas Bayard*, 1910; *Annie E. Paint*; *Juanita.* 1887-89. PABC.

Logbooks. Various schooners. Maritime Museum of B.C.

Lohbrunner, Max. Life on a Sealing Schooner. Unpublished. PABC.

McGlinn, John P. Report. U.S. Bureau of Indian Affairs. 1893.

McKeil, Robert Esdale. Letters to Sadie, from Schooner *Maud S.* PABC.

McKelvie, Bruce A. Papers. PABC.

————. Saga of Sealing. Unpublished Mss. PABC.

McMaster, Sir Donald. The Seal Arbitration. Pamphlet. 1893. PABC.

Macy, Suzanne Kay. Mother-Pup Interactions in the Northern Fur Seal. Unpublished PhD. thesis, University of Washington. 1982.

Milne, Alexander R. Correspondence. PABC.

Moser, Rev. Charles. Reminiscences of the West Coast of Vancouver Island. Victoria. 1926.

Munsie, William. Letterbook. PABC.

Murie, Debra Jean. The Migration of the Northern Fur Seal in the Eastern North Pacific Ocean and Eastern Bering Sea: An analysis of Pelagic Sealing Logs of the Years 1886 to 1911. BA thesis. University of Victoria. 1981.

O'Reilly, Peter. Report of Indian Commissioner to Superintendent-General of Indian Affairs in Ottawa. March 5. 1890. RG10, Vol. 1277. NAC.

Piggot, F. J. Letter to the Times of London. Bound dispatch. University of B.C. Library, Special Collections.

Report of the Committee on Merchant Marine and Fisheries of the House of Representatives. Government Printing Office. Washington. 1889.

Riley, Francis. Fur Seal Industry of the Pribilof islands, 1786-1960. U.S. Fish and Wildlife Service pamphlet. 1961.

Scheffer, Victor B. and Roppel, Alton Y. Management of Northern Fur Seals on the Pribilof Islands, 1786-1981. U.S. Department of Commerce. N.O.A.A. Report. 1984.

Scheffer, Victor B., Fiscus, Clifford H., and Todd, Ethel I. History of Scientific Study and Management of the Alaskan Fur Seal, 1786-1964. U.S. Department of Commerce. National Ocean and Atmospheric Administration Report. NMFS SSRF-780. March, 1984.

Seal Islands of Alaska, 1904-1911. Serial 6113, Doc. 93, 62nd congress. Government papers filed by Charles Nagel, Secretary of Commerce and Labor.

Secret Correspondence, Foreign Office and Colonial Office. Microfilm. PABC.

Shalkop, Robert L. Introduction to Henry Wood Elliott, 1846-1930: A Retrospective Exhibition. Anchorage Historical and Fine Arts Museum. 1982.

Smith, J. Gordon. Papers. PABC.

Spring, Charles. Origin of Pelagic Sealing in British Columbia and its Progress. Unpublished MSS. 1927. PABC.

Swartout, Melvyn. On the West Coast of Vancouver Island. Unpublished Mss. PABC.

Thompson, D. W. Report on Mission to Bering Sea in 1896.

Thompson, Stuart. Unpublished Mss. PABC.

Times of London. Bering Sea Arbitration. Pamphlet. 1893. University of B.C. Library, Special Collections.

Townsend, Charles H. Condition of Seal Life on the Rookeries of the Pribilof Islands, 1893-1895. U.S. Senate. 1895.

Tupper, C. H. Papers. University of B.C. Library, Special Collections.

———. Correspondence. PABC.

U.S. Consul Reports. Diplomatic Dispatches. U.S. National Archives Microfilm. Reel T-130. PABC.

U.S. Department of Commerce and Labor. Seal Islands of Alaska, 1904-1911. Series 6113. Doc. 93. 62nd Congress, 1st session.

U.S. Department of State Files, 1906-1910. Microfilm No. 22.

Victoria Sealing Company. Records. PABC.

Whitner, Robert L. Makah Commercial Sealing, 1860-1897: A Study in Acculturation and Conflict. Whitman College. Paper submitted to Fourth North American Fur Trade Conference, October, 1981.

Wishart, Andrew. The Bering Sea Question and the Award. Pamphlet. Edinburgh. 1893. PABC.

INDEX

254

255

256

SCHOONERS

258

PHOTOGRAPHIC CREDITS

Provincial Archives of British Columbia: 3, 5, 6, 7, 9, 10, 11, 16, 17, 18, 21, 22, 23, 24, 28, 30, 31, 35, 37, 43, 44, 47, 49, 50, 51, 52, 53, 54, 55, 58, 60, 65, 66; Royal British Columbia Museum: 4, 41, 59; National Archives of Canada: 12, 27, 38, 39, 57; National Maritime Museum, San Francisco: 15, 25, 34, 36, 40, 42; Maritime Museum of B.C.: 19, 48, 64; Vancouver Maritime Museum: 1, 33, 61, 62; Victoria City Archives: 26, 46; Vancouver City Archives: 32, 63; University of Washington, Northwest Collection: 29, 45; Santa Barbara Historical Society: 14; Jefferson County Historical Society: 20; Sooke Region Museum & Archives: 8; Humphry Davy, Cowichan Bay, B.C.: 2; Elizabeth K. Hansen, Goleta, California: 13; Mrs. Eileen Odowitch, Campbell River, B.C.: 56.

Note: The original Maurice Chadwick painting of "*Favorite...*" is in the collection of Mr. and Mrs. Harold Hosford of Victoria; "*Dora Sieward...*" belongs to Carl I. Jacobson of West Vancouver; "*Mary Ellen...*," Emil Leimanus of Vancouver; "*Pathfinder...*," Ernie E. Peters of West Vancouver; "Indian Hunters...," Mr. and Mrs. Milo F. Coldren, Victoria; "*Penelope* Under Working Sail" (cover), Mr. and Mrs. Peter Murray, Victoria.

260

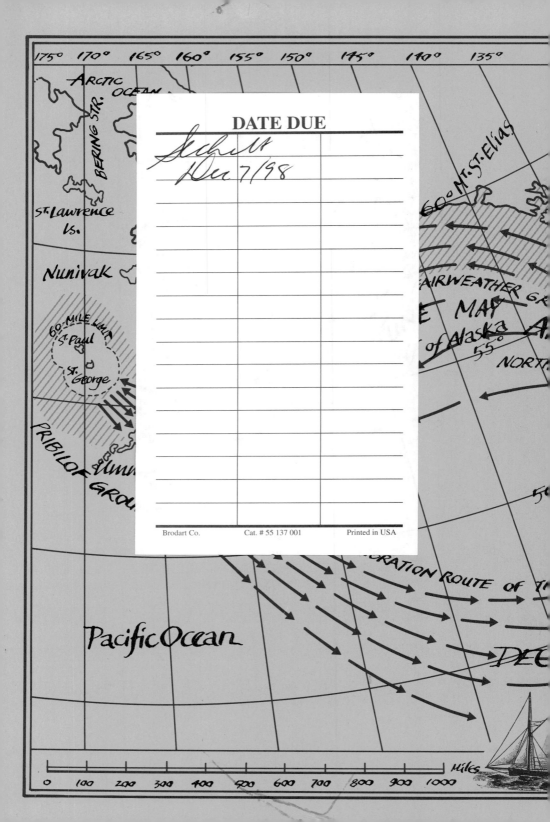

DATE DUE

Schill
Dec 7/98

Brodart Co.   Cat. # 55 137 001   Printed in USA